UPLAND BRITAIN

MARGARET'S SONG

Would now the tall swift mists could lay
Their wet grasp on my hair,
And the great natures of the hills
Round me friendly were.

Lascelles Abercrombie

MARGARET ATHERDEN

Upland Britain
A natural history

Manchester University Press

Manchester and New York

distributed exclusively in the USA and Canada by St. Martin's Press

Published by Manchester University Press
Oxford Road, Manchester M13 9PL, UK
and Room 400, 175 Fifth Avenue, New York, NY 10010, USA

Distribution exclusively in the USA and Canada
by St. Martin's Press, Inc.,
175 Fifth Avenue, New York, NY 10010, USA

British Library Cataloguing-in-Publication Data
A catalogue record for this book is available
from the British Library

Library of Congress Cataloging-in-Publication Data
Atherden, Margaret, 1947–
    Upland Britain: a natural history/Margaret Atherden.
        p.   cm.
    Includes Index.
    ISBN 0-7190-3493-0 (cloth). — ISBN 0-7190-3494-9 (paper)
    1. Natural history — Great Britain.   I. Title.
QH137.A85   1993
508.41—dc20   92-31788

ISBN 0-7190-3493-0 *hardback*
    0-7190-3494-9 *paperback*

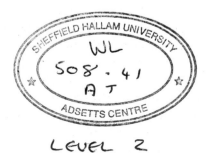
Conversion and pagination in 'Monophoto' Photina
by August Filmsetting, Haydock, St Helens

Printed in Great Britain
by Bell & Bain Limited, Glasgow

FOREWORD

The uplands are the last great refuge of wild nature in Britain. While much of the coast is also unspoiled, the hill country of our north and west is the only really large area of land not completely transformed from its original state by millenia of human occupation. The seeming appearance of naturalness is, nevertheless, largely an illusion. There are few parts even of our remotest mountains where the activity of people has not written its imprint clearly, for those who can read the evidence. In this book, Margaret Atherden carefully examines the record of human impact that has so altered the character of our uplands down the ages. From an understanding of how the underlying variations in climate, geology, topography and soils have affected land use, she traces the evolution of a new and kaleidoscopic pattern of habitat and wildlife no less diverse than the original.

This is a valuable synthesis of information about the regions which cover close on one third of our country, and whose future is now a matter of great concern. While the constraints of their harsh physical environment have always placed a severe limit on human population and development, the uplands are under growing pressure in various ways. Their marginal agriculture is increasingly oppressed by modern economic circumstance, while forestry as an alternative land use has become a focus of bitter controversy. The claims of water supply, energy generation, mineral extraction, defence, field sports and recreation make other and often competing demands on the uplands. Nature conservation sits somewhat uncomfortably against all of these, and struggles to reach an accommodation with their needs.

The author gives a clear and readable account of these interacting interests, set against a framework of the resource itself – the upland habitats, vegetation, flora and fauna. Her description and analysis are an important source of information and insight to all those interested in the uplands, from whatever perspective. The well-chosen photographs help to illuminate the story and reveal the author's personal familiarity with many of the areas and features she discusses. We should be grateful that Margaret Atherden's industry has given us an up-to-date compendium which fills a gap in the literature of the British uplands. Her treatment of conservation achieves a commendable balance that should make the book appeal to both the champions and the critics. It has, indeed, a many-sided relevance, in keeping with her emphasis on multi-purpose land use, and should helpfully inform various aspects of the debate about the future of our uplands.

D A Ratcliffe   16 July 1992

CONTENTS

LIST OF COLOUR PLATES

LIST OF PLATES

FIGURES

TABLES

PREFACE AND ACKNOWLEDGEMENTS

There is another Britain . . . a land of mountains and moorlands and of sun and cloud. . . . It lies now, as always, beyond the margins of our industrial and urban civilisations, fading into the western mists and washed by northern seas, its needs forgotten and its possibilities almost unknown.

W H Pearsall, 1950

Since Professor Pearsall wrote of 'another Britain', more and more people have come to know and love Britain's upland areas. Increasing mobility and leisure time have enabled day visitors and holiday-makers to 'climb every mountain and ford every stream' in search of their own particular dreams. Remote and beautiful areas like the Scottish Highlands and Snowdonia have become suddenly accessible, and their characteristic wildlife has been discovered and enjoyed. Scottish pinewoods, Dartmoor peat bogs, Pennine grasslands and Yorkshire moorlands: all have their own particular communities of plants and animals, which often seem so well adapted to their upland environments that it is easy to believe that they have remained unchanged for thousands of years.

However, nothing could be further from the truth. Over the past 15,000 years, fundamental changes have taken place in all parts of the uplands, which have led to the modification or destruction of some wildlife habitats and the creation of others. Fifteen thousand years ago, upland Britain was in the final throes of the last Ice Age and the landscape resembled the arctic tundra. Since that time, not only has the climate undergone many changes but soils have developed and slopes have been eroded. There have also been dramatic changes in the distribution and abundance of plants and animals. Some species have colonised the uplands, while others have died out or migrated elsewhere. Some species have spread and prospered, while others have been out-competed and have assumed a minor role. Many of these changes have been brought about by human activities. From prehistoric times onwards, people have had an increasing impact on the upland habitats, whether through hunting, farming, building, mining or recreation. Through such impacts, the natural wildlife communities have been converted into the range of semi-natural and artificial ones which we see today.

This book will tell the story of this natural history of the uplands, using detailed case studies, where appropriate, to illustrate the story in greater depth. Individual chapters will focus on mountain tops, woodlands, moorlands, wetlands, grasslands, plantations, highways and boundaries. We shall discover when and how they developed and how people have managed them for their own purposes. As our knowledge of this natural history grows, so also does our awareness of the complexity and vulnerability of wildlife communities. When the full extent of human impact in the past becomes evident, we begin to realise how easy it is to upset the natural balance and break the delicate web of life. At the same time, we appreciate our potential to enhance the ecological interest and sometimes to achieve a new balance. The study of natural history leads inevitably to a consideration of conservation and the priorities for the future, so the book will close with a survey of the efforts being made today to conserve our upland heritage.

As this book is intended to be read by a wide audience, from academics to those with little or no background in ecology, Latin names for plant and animal species have been kept out of the main text. Full lists will be found in the glossary, with each species listed exactly as in the text (for instance, common scoter is listed under 'c' rather than 's'). Plant names follow the *New Flora of the British Isles* by Clive Stace (Cambridge University Press, 1992), which may be unfamiliar to some readers but will form the standard work of reference for several years to come. Literary references and notes in the text have been kept to a minimum and restricted to sources readily available to the general public. The reader who wishes to follow up the general theme of the book might start with *The History of the Countryside* by Oliver Rackham (Dent, London, 1986), *The Flowering of Britain* by Richard Mabey and Tony Evans (Hutchinson, London, 1980), or *Upland Britain* by Roy Millward and Adrian Robinson (David and Charles, Newton Abbot, 1980). Much of the original material on which the book is based was gleaned from research articles in academic journals. The serious student who wishes to read more deeply will find a wealth of information in publications such as the *Journal of Ecology, Journal of Biogeography, New Phytologist, Journal of Quaternary Science, Quaternary Science Reviews*, and *Journal of Archaeological Science*.

A great many people have helped in the production of this book. Particular thanks go to Joy Parry for the illustrations, to Nick Staley for the cartography, to Stephen Ball for the copy editing and to Richard Purslow for his support and encouragement as editor. Richard Smith and Don Spratt read large portions of the text and made useful comments on it. The staff of Manchester University Press were unfailingly helpful and patient.

Representatives of several organisations have given generously of their time, including Ian Findlay, Andrew Brown, David Clayden and Ben Mercer of English Nature; Joanna and James Robertson of the Countryside Council for Wales; Lesley Cranna, William Gray and Terry Keatinge of Scottish Natural Heritage; Peter Burnett, A M Calder, Charles Critchley, R A Farmer, Ian Forshaw, Martin Garnett, E Jones, Gordon Simpson and John Westlake of the Forestry Commission; David Carter of the Ministry of Agriculture, Fisheries and Food; James Rennie of the Department of Agriculture and Fisheries for Scotland; Roger Cadwallader of Fountain Forestry; Charles Couzens of the Royal Society for Nature Conservation, Wildlife Trusts

Partnership; Tim Cleeves of the Royal Society for the Protection of Birds; and Nicholas Alliott of the Woodland Trust.

Amongst the many other individuals who have given information, contributed photographs, commented on the text or provided company in the field, special mention must be made of Jackie Atherden, Pat Clayton, Richard Clough, Peter Cundill, Ian Dunwoodie, Jean Hall, Archibald Heron, Beechy Jarrett, Beatrix Molesworth, Michael Riddick, Ian Robinson, John Rodwell, Ian Simmons, Hilary Smithson, Peter Smithson, Colin Stephenson, Oliver Rackham, Derek Ratcliffe, Graham Swinerd, Nan Sykes, Judith Turner, Sylvia Voisk and Betty West.

I

The physical features
of upland Britain

Amazing scene! Behold! the glooms disclose:
I see the rivers in their infant beds;
Deep, deep I hear them, labouring to get free.
I see the leaning strata, artful ranged;
The gaping fissures to receive the rains,
The melting snows, and ever-dripping fogs.
                    James Thomson, 1730

There have been many definitions of upland Britain or the highland zone. Some
people have used the Tees–Exe line as the boundary; others have taken a specific
contour line, such as the 300 metre contour, above which lies about a third of the
land area of Britain. There is no consensus, and no single criterion seems to satisfy
everyone. However, on the ground the task is much easier. The upland zone feels
quite different from lowland Britain, both in the physical make-up of the land and in
the cultural imprint which people have made upon it. The uplands are characterised
by older, harder, more resistant rocks, which form blocks of higher ground. The
climate tends to be more severe and soils are often less fertile, making the environment less favourable for farming. From prehistoric times onwards, patterns of land
use and settlement developed which were distinct from, and often complementary to,
those of the lowlands. The result is a landscape which looks distinctive and an
environment which offers a characteristic set of habitats for plants and animals, quite
different from those of the lowland zone.

       The areas to be included in upland Britain in this book are shown in Figure 1.
They include regions with significant areas of land above the 300 metre contour,
together with their associated valleys and coastal plains. Towards the north and west
of Britain, the climate, soils and terrain become more challenging for plants and
animals, so that some areas at quite low altitude in northern Scotland or the Western
Isles still feel part of the upland rather than the lowland zone. In this chapter, we shall
explore the geology, topography, climate and soils, which help to create the distinctive upland environment.

FIGURE I Location of the main upland areas

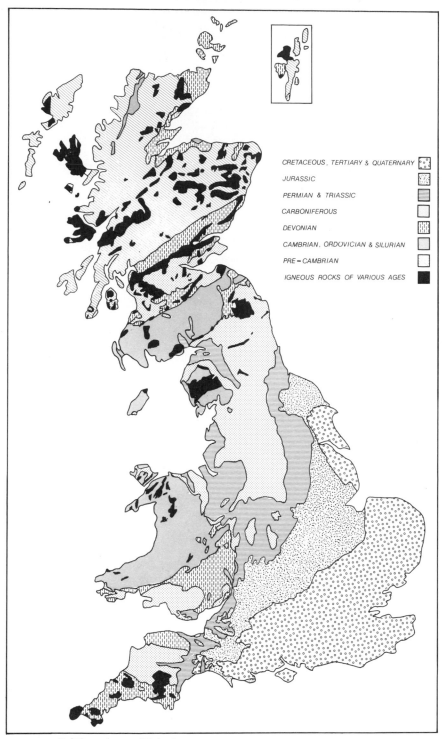

CRETACEOUS, TERTIARY & QUATERNARY

JURASSIC

PERMIAN & TRIASSIC

CARBONIFEROUS

DEVONIAN

CAMBRIAN, ORDOVICIAN & SILURIAN

PRE-CAMBRIAN

IGNEOUS ROCKS OF VARIOUS AGES

FIGURE 2 Solid geology of Britain

Geology and structure

The solid geology is the foundation of upland Britain, the ultimate building block on which everything else depends (Figure 2). The rocks give the land its form and structure and provide the mineral fabric for the upland soils. Their chemical reaction, permeability to water and resistance to weathering and erosion account for many of the contrasts between different regions. They are responsible for the sharp, rugged scenery of the Scottish Highlands and central Lake District; the dark, more rounded topography of Dartmoor and Exmoor; and the gleaming limestone pavements of the Pennines[1].

TABLE 1 Geological table for upland Britain (estimated dates)

Date million years ago	ERA/Period	Main rock types in uplands	Main outcrops in uplands	Climate and major events
	CAENOZOIC			
	Quaternary	Peat, river alluvium	Throughout, valleys	Post-glacial warming of climate and sea level rise
		Glacial till, moraines, outwash sands and gravels	Most uplands except SW England	Pleistocene Ice Age: glacials and inter-glacials
2	Tertiary	Volcanic rocks	W Scotland, Hebrides	Britain reached present latitude, climate cooled from sub-tropical to temperate. Atlantic Ocean continued to open. Alps uplifted ('Alpine Orogeny')
		Igneous dykes and sills	Scotland, N Wales, N England	
65	MESOZOIC			
	Cretaceous	No deposits	Lowland Britain only	Britain 40°N. Climate sub-tropical. Atlantic Ocean begins to open
144	Jurassic	Limestones, sandstones, ironstones, shales	North York Moors	Warm and humid climate
213	Triassic	No deposits	Lowland Britain only	Hot climate with marked wet and dry seasons
248	PALAEOZOIC			
	Permian	No deposits	Lowland Britain only	Hot desert climate, Britain 10–20°N

Date million years ago	ERA/Period	Main rock types in uplands	Main outcrops in uplands	Climate and major events
286				
	Carbon-iferous	Granite, Whin Sill, Coal Measures, Millstone Grit, Yoredales, limestone	SW England, N England, Pennines, S and NE Wales, central Devon, central Scotland.	Uplift of SW England and re-activation of faults on Pennines ('Hercynian Orogeny'). Britain moved from 15°S to 10°N.
		Volcanic rocks	Central Scotland and Southern Uplands	Equatorial climate
360				
	Devonian	Granite	Scottish Highlands, Southern Uplands, Lake District, NW Wales, N Pennines	Hot desert climate. Britain 25°S
		Old Red Sandstone, river-borne and marine deposits	S, central and NE Scotland, Orkneys and Shetlands, S Wales, SW England	
408				
	Silurian	Volcanic rocks, shales	Wales, Lake District, Southern Uplands	Warm climate. Uplift of Scottish Highlands as plates collide ('Caledonian Orogeny')
438				
	Ordovician	Slates, volcanic rocks	Wales, Lake District, Southern Uplands	Warm Climate. Plates begin to approach each other
505				
	Cambrian	Limestones, sandstones, slates	NW Scotland, N Wales, Isle of Man	Former ocean at its widest. Glacial climate at beginning, warm by end
590				
	PRE-CAMBRIAN	Schists, sandstones, limestones, volcanic rocks	Scotland and Hebrides	Scotland and England/Wales on different plates, separated by ocean; in low latitudes south of equator. Several ice ages and periods of uplift
800		oldest rocks in Wales		
2600		oldest rocks in Scotland		
3800		oldest rocks on earth		
4500		formation of solar system		

The rocks cover a total time span of some 2600 million years (Table 1). Our understanding of geological structure has been transformed over recent decades by the revelations of plate tectonics[2,3]. For instance, we now know that Britain was once south of the Equator and that some of the rocks of the uplands were formed when plates collided and former oceans became dry land. The effects of these events of millions of years ago may still be seen, for example in the north-east–south-west trend of many ridges and valleys in the Scottish Highlands.

Very old Pre-Cambrian rocks form the core of the Scottish Highlands and Western Isles[4]. Over the thousands of millions of years since their formation, they have been much altered by heat and pressure (metamorphosed) and affected by major earth movements. The oldest rocks are the grey, banded Lewisian gneisses found in the north-west tip of the mainland and on the Outer Hebrides. Then comes the reddish-brown Torridonian sandstone of other parts of north-western Scotland and the Inner Hebrides. A major fault zone separates these rocks from the Moinian schists, which form the main surface rocks of the Northern Highlands. To the south-east of these are the Dalradian rocks, which include limestones, marine sediments and volcanic rocks and stretch in a broad band from the Grampian Highlands to Kintyre.

The rocks which form the Southern Uplands, the Lake District and the Welsh mountains belong to the next great era of geological time, the Palaeozoic (Table 1). The earliest layers are ancient sedimentary rocks, many of which have been metamorphosed. In Wales, there is a very thick succession of Cambrian sandstones and slates in the Harlech area. The slates were the basis of a thriving industry in the past and may be found on roofs in many parts of Britain. In Scotland, there are important Cambrian deposits in the fault zone between the Torridonian sandstone and the Moinian schists. They include patches of limestone, which can be recognised on the ground by their distinctive flora, as in the rich grasslands of the Elphin–Knockan area and near Durness.

Slates, shales and volcanic deposits are the main rocks of the Ordovician and Silurian periods and the Lake District is an excellent place to see them today. The oldest rocks there are the Skiddaw slates, which form the rounded uplands and gradual slopes of the northern Lake District, including the Skiddaw massif itself. The central Lake District, by contrast, is dominated by volcanic rocks, known as the Borrowdale Volcanic Group, which are much harder and have eroded into the jagged peaks of mountains such as Helvellyn, Scafell and the Langdale Pikes. Further south are the Silurian shales, which form gentler country bordering the mountains. Rocks of similar age cover most of western Wales and form the backbone of the Welsh mountains, and the rocks of the Southern Uplands also date from this period. The earth movements which accompanied the deposition of these rocks buckled, folded and raised up the Pre-Cambrian rocks of the Scottish Highlands, which have remained more or less intact as a major topographic feature throughout the whole of the succeeding 400 million years.

Rocks of Devonian age include sandstones, grits, limestones and slates and are often collectively called the Old Red Sandstone. They occur in central and north-east Scotland, the Orkneys, parts of Shetland, the Brecon Beacons and Black Mountains of southern Wales, and on Exmoor. While these sediments were being deposited above ground, molten magma was being intruded deep under other parts of the uplands to form granite. There are about thirty early Devonian intrusions in the Scottish High-lands and others occur in the Southern Uplands. As granite is a very resistant rock, many of these intrusions now form major mountain tops, such as Cairngorm, Lochnagar and Ben Cruachan, although granites can also be found in low-lying areas, as near Loch Doon. Further south, granites also outcrop in the western Lake District, the Shap area and in north-west Wales. Other granitic masses are known to occur at depth under the northern Pennines.

At the end of the Devonian and beginning of the Carboniferous period, there was considerable volcanic activity in the central lowlands and Southern Uplands of Scotland, with enormous lava flows across the Clyde plateau. Near Edinburgh, thir-teen individual lava flows have been traced, with ash layers between them represent-ing some 100,000 years of volcanic activity. Also in Edinburgh are the remains of two volcanic cones about 350 million years old, which now form the resistant out-crops of Castle Rock and Arthur's Seat.

The rocks of the Pennine chain are mainly of Carboniferous age. Carboniferous limestone is made up of the calcified skeletons of myriads of tiny sea creatures which lived in clear tropical waters. It is a hard rock but has well-developed vertical and horizontal joints. This means that it tends to weather into blocks, and, where there is no overlying soil, it can form limestone pavement. Here large squarish blocks of limestone, known as clints, are separated by deep enlarged joints, called grikes. Another result of the deep jointing is that water tends to disappear down swallow-holes into the grikes to flow as underground streams, often carving out caves as it does so. On other occasions erosion has enlarged joints or under-cut cavern roofs to form spectacular gorges, such as Gordale on the Pennines. Some of the best karst scenery is provided by the Craven and Malham areas of the Pennines, where large areas of more or less horizontal limestone pavement are exposed and large caves and potholes allow us to glimpse the underground world.

Other Carboniferous rocks include fossilised algal reefs, known as reef knolls, and rhythmic successions of limestones, shales and sandstones, called the Yoredales. As the limestones and sandstones are more resistant to erosion than the shale beds, these rocks give the sides of many of the Pennine dales a characteristic stepped topography. Large areas of the Pennines flanking the Carboniferous limestone are covered with coarse deltaic sediments of the Millstone Grit, which often outcrops to form distinctive edges or tors on the valley sides. It also caps some of the higher limestone hills, such as Pen-y-ghent, Whernside and Ingleborough, suggesting that it was once more widespread. Carboniferous limestone and Millstone Grit also outcrop in smaller areas in north and south Wales. In basins on either side of the Pennines, in south Wales and in central Scotland are Upper Carboniferous Coal Measures. The coal seams were formed from peat deposits in tropical swamps at or near sea level and are interspersed with many other sediments, including marine bands, sandstones and clays. They are of great economic importance, although they occur only on the margins of the uplands.

At the end of the Carboniferous period, a large granite mass was emplaced at depth in south-west England. This great mass underlies an enormous area but most of it is covered by later rocks. In a few places, however, erosion has uncovered the tip of it to give us a glimpse of what lies below, as on Dartmoor and Bodmin Moor. Because we are only seeing the tip of it, the granite appears as a fairly smooth-topped dome, although well-developed joints give rise to tors on the upper valley sides, especially on Dartmoor. There are many valuable mineral ores associated with the granite, deposited when water was forced out of it at depth. Cracks or lodes around the granite are rich in tin, tungsten, copper, nickel, silver, cobalt, arsenic, zinc, uranium and lead – all of which have proved of great economic importance in the past. Similar mineral veins are found in the Carboniferous strata of the Pennines, where lead, zinc and copper ores have been worked since Roman times. Associated minerals, such as fluorine and barium, are also of economic importance, as is the Carboniferous limestone itself, which is a valuable source of road metal.

The other important feature from the late Carboniferous period is the Whin Sill, an igneous intrusion which runs through the Carboniferous limestone and covers an area of 2500 km² underground. It outcrops at intervals across Northumbria, Cumbria and the northern Pennines and forms the impressive cliffs of the Farne Islands. Parts of Hadrian's Wall are built on its crags. Perhaps its most spectacular outcrop is in Teesdale, where it forms the magnificent waterfall of High Force (Plate 12). Here it has baked the surrounding limestone to form an unusual metamorphic rock, known as sugar limestone, upon which a distinctive flora has developed (chapter 3).

As we have seen, most of the rocks of upland Britain had been formed by the end of the Palaeozoic era, 280 million years ago. However, one region that has not yet been mentioned is the North York Moors. This is composed of Mesozoic rocks of the Jurassic period. The sediments in the northern and central parts consist of shales, sandstones and ironstones, with occasional marine beds. They include several rocks which have been of great economic importance in the past, including alum shales, ironstone and jet rock (a fossilised driftwood). The southern part consists of rocks of limestones and calcareous grits, which form an impressive north-facing escarpment across the area. Jurassic limestones are less massive and less well jointed than the Carboniferous limestone of the Pennines, so classic karst features are absent from the North York Moors, but much of the drainage is still underground, leaving dry valleys on the surface of the gentle dip-slope.

The youngest rocks of upland Britain date from the Tertiary period. This was the last time volcanoes were active in Britain and their remains are to be found in western Scotland and on the Hebrides. Lava erupted through fissures to form sheet-like dykes, each about 15 metres thick, making the distinctive stepped topography of areas like Mull. Then enormous volcanoes erupted on Skye, Rhum, Mull, Arran and the Ardnamurchan peninsula, whose eroded remnants may still be seen. Slow cooling of lava in columns on the island of Staffa produced beautiful hexagonal columns of basalt. After the volcanoes themselves had died down, tension still existed below ground and basalt dykes travelled outwards, some going as far as north Wales and the North York Moors.

Other areas were also affected by the Tertiary period, even if they lack actual deposits of that age. The plate movements which further south in Europe were responsible for the main uplift of the Alps were felt in Britain in the re-activation of old faults and the uplift of many areas in stages to form a series of erosion surfaces, as seen, for instance, in south Wales and the North York Moors. This was also the period during which the present river systems of many parts of the uplands were established. During the 63 million years of the Tertiary period, the climate gradually cooled from a sub-tropical to a temperate one. This long cooling process culminated in the Ice Age, which was to have a dramatic impact on the scenery of upland Britain.

The Ice Age

During the last two million years (the Quaternary), Britain has experienced the rigours of an ice age, which further modified the physical landscape and had profound effects on plant and animal life, as we shall see in chapter 2. Evidence from deep sea cores has shown at least twenty periods of fluctuating climate within the Quaternary, but only in the most recent three of these is there evidence for ice-sheets spreading over the land[5,6]. Table 2 summarises the main features of the Quaternary in Britain. There were two major expansions of ice, when a great ice-sheet from Scandinavia spread across the North Sea and enveloped most of the British Isles. Apart from south-west England, upland Britain was entirely subsumed, although the higher mountain areas were of sufficient size to direct the flow of ice outwards from their highest points. Such centres of ice flow formed in the Scottish Highlands, the Southern Uplands, the Lake District and the Welsh mountains.

In the most recent ice advance, the Devensian, the ice-sheet did not reach so far south, the boundary lying across East Anglia, South Yorkshire, the West Midlands and south Wales. Some of the higher areas in northern England were not over-ridden by ice this time, so that the North York Moors and parts of the Pennines projected above the ice sheet. These areas would have experienced a very severe climate, making the growth of vegetation almost impossible.

The effect of these glacial advances on the topography of the uplands was dramatic[7]. River valleys and highland glens were gouged out to form great glacial troughs with their sides straightened out and a U-shaped cross profile (Plate 1). Tributary valleys, eroded to a lesser extent by their smaller volume of ice, were left hanging above the main valley floor. Areas of snow accumulation in the mountains from which glaciers had flowed out were eroded into steep-walled circular corries, several of which sometimes cut back from different sides into the same area to leave a sharp ridge or a jagged peak between them. Good examples of such features may be seen in the Cairngorms, the Lake District and north Wales.

Material scraped off the mountain sides by the glaciers and ice sheets was sometimes transported miles away to be left as erratic rocks when the ice eventually

TABLE 2 Main events of the Quaternary period

Years before present (approximate)	Name of period	Climate and characteristics
	HOLOCENE	
	Flandrian	Post-glacial period. Warm climate. Rise in sea level.
10,000		
	UPPER PLEISTOCENE	
	Devensian	Glacial. Ice over most of upland Britain except for SW England and parts of Pennines and North York Moors. Tundra climate. Fall in sea level
115,000		
	Ipswichian	Inter-glacial. Warmest of all inter-glacials. Forest over most of upland Britain. Rise in sea level
165,000		
	Wolstonian	Glacial. Ice over most of upland Britain except for SW England. Tundra climate. Fall in sea level
250,000		
	MIDDLE PLEISTOCENE	
	Hoxnian	Inter-glacial. Longest inter-glacial. Forest over most of upland Britain. Rise in sea level
400,000		
	Anglian	Glacial. Ice over most of upland Britain except for SW England. Tundra climate. Fall in sea level
450,000		
	Cromerian	Inter-glacial. Forest over most of upland Britain.
700,000		
	Beestonian	Cold phase but no ice-sheets on land
	LOWER PLEISTOCENE	
	Alternate warm and cold periods	Mixed deciduous/coniferous forest in warm periods, grassland/tundra in cold periods
2,000,000		
	TERTIARY	

melted. For instance, boulders of Shap Granite, with its distinctive pink crystals, can be found in many areas east of the Pennines. Other material was left as moraines when the glaciers retreated, end-moraines marking the former positions of the ice front in many valleys in north Wales and elsewhere. Water flowing under, through or along the edge of the ice left its own debris load behind and sometimes etched

PLATE I A dramatic glacial trough in the Cairngorms, with blocky scree in the foreground

channels in the rock beneath, as in Glen Roy. Other water was held up as temporary lakes by morainic debris or ice, for example in Eskdale on the North York Moors. Some lakes dating from the Ice Age are still with us today, notably in the Lake District and Scottish Highlands, where ice over-deepened many valleys, forming basins in which water collected.

On the lower ground, vast sheets of glacial material were deposited, plastering many areas with a mantle of drift which obscures the solid geology beneath, as in the Pennine dales and Cumbrian coastal plain. Further out from the ice front, sands and gravels were deposited, partially sorted by the icy waters flowing out from under the ice-sheets. There are also smaller scale features, such as roches moutonnées, which are resistant boulders of rock not moved but scraped by the ice. Some particularly fine examples are preserved in the Spey valley, near Dulnain Bridge. Drumlins are mounds of glacial debris aligned in the direction of ice-flow. Good examples are to be seen in the Lune and Ribble valleys. Crag and tail features occur where a hard rock feature, such as the old volcanic vent of Edinburgh Castle Rock, streamlined the flow of ice around it, protecting a tail of debris in its lee.

The area outside the glacial limit experienced periglacial conditions, where freeze–thaw cycles put great stresses on rocks, and soil masses moved downhill in a semi-frozen state (a process known as solifluction). Some rivers found their previous

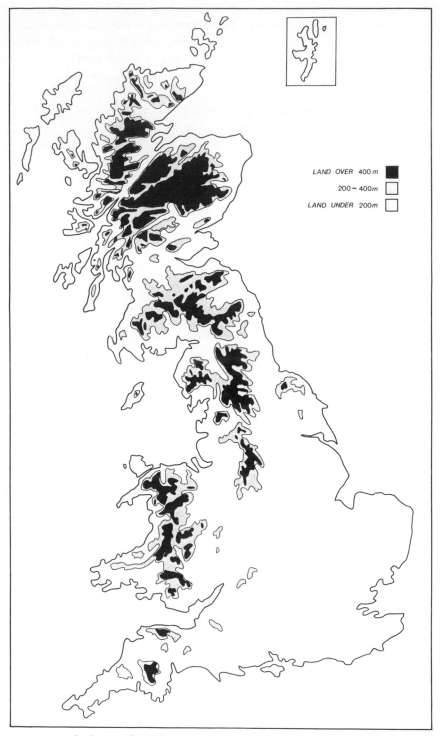

FIGURE 3 Relief map of Britain

courses blocked by glacial debris and were forced to divert, forming steep-sided gorges. In limestone areas, however, the diversion of water was from underground on to the surface, as permafrost prevented the normal seepage of water down through the joints. There are some spectacular valleys and waterfalls in areas which today lack surface drainage, an excellent example being the enormous former waterfall at Malham Cove in North Yorkshire.

During the Ice Age, such large volumes of water were locked up as ice that the sea level was as much as 135 metres lower than today, and Britain was joined to continental Europe. As the ice melted after the Ice Age, the former dry land areas of the English Channel and North Sea basin were gradually flooded again. The lower parts of many of our river valleys were drowned in the process, as can be seen in the fjords of west Scotland. The weight of ice had depressed the uplands, particularly the Scottish Highlands, which have been recovering by rising up ever since. The north and west of Britain is still rising while the south and east are slowly sinking, the hingeline being across the north of England. Around the coast of Scotland are some sequences of raised beaches, representing former sea levels and now elevated above the waves. Those on Mull and Jura are particularly fine examples.

As a result of the geological and glacial history, we are left with a number of upland regions in Britain, differing in their height above sea level and in the degree of erosion of the higher areas and deposition on the lower areas of the landscape. Figure 3 shows the relief of Britain and Table 3 lists the highest peaks in the various upland regions.

TABLE 3 Major peaks in the uplands

Upland area	Major peaks	Height (metres)	Geology
THE GRAMPIAN HIGHLANDS	Ben Nevis	1344	Volcanic, surrounded by granite
	Ben Macdui	1309	Granite
	Braeriach	1296	Granite
	Cairn Toul	1291	Granite
	Cairngorm	1245	Granite
	Aonach Beag	1236	Dalradian schists and granite
	Carn Mor Dearg	1223	Granite
	Aonach Mor	1219	Granite
	Ben Lawers	1217	Dalradian metamorphics
	Ben More	1174	Dalradian metamorphics
	Ben Avon	1171	Granite
	Lochnagar	1155	Granite
	Ben Cruachan	1126	Granite
THE NORTHERN HIGHLANDS	Carn Eighe	1182	Moinian schists
	Mam Sodhail	1180	Moinian schists
	Sgurr na Lapaich	1151	Moinian schists

Upland area	Major peaks	Height (metres)	Geology
	Sgurr nan Ceathream hnan	1151	Moinian schists
	An Riabhachan	1129	Moinian schists
	An Teallach	1062	Torridonian sandstone
	Ben Wyvis	1046	Moinian schists
	Sgurr na Ciche	1040	Moinian schists
	Beinn Fhada	1031	Moinian schists
	Beinn Eighe	1010	Cambrian surrounded by Torridonian sandstone
	Ben More Assynt	998	Cambrian quartzite
	Ben Hope	927	Dalradian and Moinian metamorphics
THE NORTHERN ISLES	Ward hill, Hoy, Orkney	477	Devonian sandstone
	Ronas Hill, Zetland, Shetland	450	Granite
THE WESTERN ISLES	The Cuillins, Skye	1009	Gabbro and volcanics
	Goat Fell, Arran	888	Granite
	Askival, Rhum	812	Ultra-basic intrusion
THE SOUTHERN UPLANDS	Merrick	843	Ordovician and granite
	Broad Law	840	Silurian sediments
	Cairnsmore of Carsphairn	796	Silurian sediments and granite
	Lamachan Hill	716	Ordovician and granite
THE LAKE DISTRICT	Scafell Pikes	979	Ordovician volcanics
	Helvellyn	951	Ordovician volcanics
	Skiddaw	931	Ordovician slates
THE CHEVIOTS	Cheviot	816	Granite
NORTH YORK MOORS	Urra Moor	454	Jurassic sandstone
THE PENNINES	Cross Fell	894	Yoredales over Carboniferous limestone
	Mickle Fell	790	Yoredales over Carboniferous limestone
	Whernside	738	Millstone Grit over Carboniferous limestone
	Ingleborough	724	Millstone Grit over Carboniferous limestone
	Great Whernside	705	Millstone Grit over Carboniferous limestone
	Penyghent	693	Millstone Grit over Carboniferous limestone
	Kinder Scout	637	Millstone Grit
	Bleaklow	628	Millstone grit

Upland area	Major peaks	Height (metres)	Geology
NORTH WALES	Snowdon	1086	Volcanic surrounded by Ordovician and Cambrian
	Carnedd Llywelyn	1062	Volcanic surrounded by Ordovician
	Carnedd Dafydd	1061	Ordovician volcanic
	Glyder Fawr	1016	Ordovician volcanic
	Aran Fawddwy	922	Ordovician volcanic
	Cadair Idris	892	Volcanic surrounded by Ordovician
SOUTH WALES	Brecon Beacons	886	Devonian sandstone
	Black Mountains	811	Devonian sandstone
SOUTH-WEST ENGLAND	Yes Tor, Dartmoor	619	Granite
	Brown Willy, Bodmin Moor	572	Granite
	Dunkery Beacon, Exmoor	520	Devonian sandstone

Climate

The topography plays a major part in determining the climate of upland Britain. However, other important factors are the latitude of Britain and its position as a set of off-shore islands to the west of a major land mass. On a more local scale, factors such as aspect, slope and exposure can produce changes in climate over distances of a few kilometres or even a few metres[8]. The weather experienced in any part of Britain can vary enormously from year to year, producing some dramatic events, such as the rainstorm and floods in Exmoor in 1952 or the drought experienced over much of Britain from 1989 to 1992. However, we are concerned here mainly with the long-term typical climate of the uplands rather than with the short-term vagaries of the weather.

   Table 4 gives climatic figures for some stations in upland Britain. There is a general decrease in temperatures northwards, caused by the ten degree span of latitude from Cornwall to the Shetlands. This is well illustrated by the average daily maximum temperatures for July and the contrast in annual sunshine hours between Penzance and Lerwick [9]. However, there is also a decrease in temperature with altitude of about 1°C for every 150 metres gained, which means that the mountainous areas are several degrees colder than their equivalent areas at sea level. For example, the top of Ben Nevis (1344 metres) is on average about 8.6°C colder than Fort William (near sea level), although there is only 7 km distance between them. British lapse rates for temperature are some of the steepest in the world and the decrease in temperatures with altitude is one of the most obvious features of the

TABLE 4 Climatic figures for selected upland stations in Britain

Station	Altitude (metres)	Average annual rainfall (millimetres)	Average daily temperature (°C) January		July		Average annual bright sunshine hours
			max	min	max	min	
Ambleside (Cumbria)	46	1865	5.9	0.2	19.1	10.8	1185
Braemar (Grampian)	339	859	3.7	−2.5	17.2	8.2	1137
Buxton (Derbyshire)	307	1289	4.3	−0.3	17.4	10.3	1149
Edinburgh (Royal Botanic Garden)	26	626	6.2	0.4	18.4	10.9	1351
Eskdalemuir (Dumfries and Galloway)	242	1456	4.3	−1.5	17.4	8.7	1198
Lerwick (Shetland)	82	1177	5.1	1.0	13.7	9.0	1056
Llandrindod Wells (Powys)	235	1003	5.5	0.1	19.5	10.3	1244
Penzance (Cornwall)	19	1131	9.4	4.4	19.4	12.7	1738
Stornoway (Western Isles)	3	1094	6.4	1.3	15.7	10.1	1244
Valley (Gwynedd)	10	871	7.5	2.5	18.1	12.0	1612
Wick (Highland)	36	783	5.6	0.8	15.4	9.3	1240

Source: Figures are averages for the period 1951 to 1980, from the Meteorological Office, 1989.

upland climate[10]. There is another factor which affects temperature, the North Atlantic Drift, which brings warm water across the Atlantic Ocean to the western coasts. It is particularly marked in winter, when sea temperatures off western coasts are 1 or 2°C warmer than those off eastern coasts. Because of the North Atlantic Drift, the main contrasts in temperature in winter are between west and east, rather than north and south, as shown by the mean daily minimum temperatures in January for Stornoway (58°N) and Edinburgh (56°N).

Temperature is one of the critical factors for plants in upland Britain, as it largely determines the length of the growing season (Figure 4B). Growth of grass is only possible when temperatures are above 6°C. In sheltered parts of Devon and Cornwall, mean temperatures rarely drop below this, so some growth takes place in nearly every month of the year. Other favourable areas are the coast of south Wales and coastal parts of Cumbria and Galloway. However, the growing season is reduced rapidly with altitude, decreasing by about 13 days for every 100 metres[8]. The rate at which crops mature and the yields they give also decrease, and the greater the altitude, the more significant small changes in temperature become for plant growth.

Rainfall is closely linked with topography in Britain, as most of the rain falls as a result of the cooling of air as it rises over higher ground (Figure 4A). As the main rain-bearing winds are south-westerlies, there is greater rainfall in the west of the country, with many eastern areas lying in the rain shadow of the hills. For instance, the mountains of the Northern Highlands receive more rainfall than the Cairngorms, and the high central Lake District receives more than the eastern Pennines. The driest of the British uplands is the North York Moors, only the very highest parts of which receive over 1000 mm a year, owing to its easterly position. The highest rainfall amounts are recorded where valleys converge and rain-bearing winds are funnelled towards higher ground, as in the central Lake District and near Glen Garry in the Northern Highlands, which is probably the wettest place in Britain[11].

Snowfall is more characteristic of the north and east of Britain, as it usually comes as a result of cold north-easterly winds in winter (Plate 2). The areas to receive most are the Northern Isles, north-east Scotland and the Cheviots, where sleet or snow falls on average between 35 and 40 days a year. The Grampian Highlands, the

PLATE 2 Winter in Farndale. North York Moors. The rigours of the upland climate pose a challenge for both wildlife and farmers

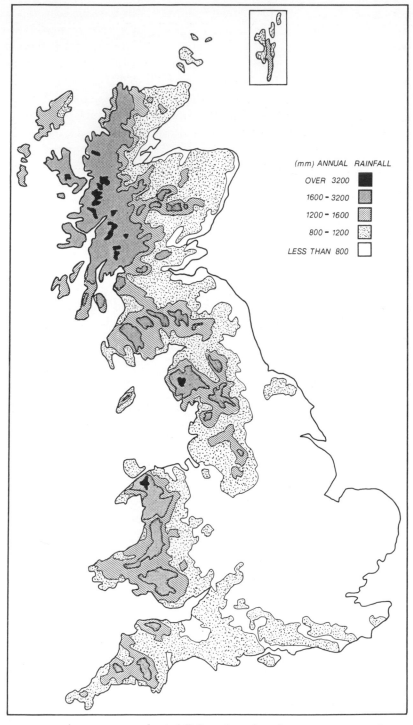

FIGURE 4A Average annual rainfall (based on data for 1941 to 1970, from the
Meteorological Office)

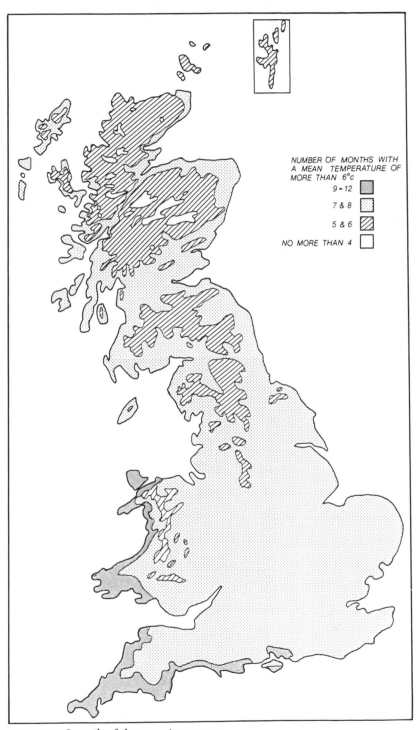

NUMBER OF MONTHS WITH
A MEAN TEMPERATURE OF
MORE THAN 6°c

9 – 12

7 & 8

5 & 6

NO MORE THAN 4

FIGURE 4B Length of the growing season

eastern part of the Southern Uplands and the North York Moors also receive significant amounts of snow and sleet, whereas in southern Wales and south-west
England, it is unusual to have sleet or snow falling on more than 10 days a year[12].
Snow may lie for several days after it has fallen, especially on higher ground, so that
the highest parts of the Grampian Highlands have snow lying for over 100 days a
year and a few snow-beds are semi-permanent.

Another major component of the upland climate is wind. The combination of
strong winds and very low temperatures is responsible for the extreme wind chill
factor experienced on the highest summits. Exposure increases with altitude, so wind
speeds on Cairngorm summit are on average three times those of the Spey valley[10].
The average wind speed on Ben Nevis is 77 kph. However, winds speeds are also
greater in coastal areas than inland, because the sea offers less resistance than the
land. One way of measuring windiness, used by the Meteorological Office, is to note
the number of days with gales recorded (that is, a wind speed of 34 knots (62 kph)
maintained for at least 10 minutes). For example, the Cumbrian coast has 20 gale
days a year whereas inland areas in the Lake District only experience 5. Most gale
force winds blow from the west, so the western coasts receive more wind than the
eastern ones, and the windiest places in Britain are the Northern Isles and north-west
coast of Scotland, Lerwick in Shetland having 47 days of gale a year. Exposure may
be limiting to plant growth in mountainous or coastal areas, especially if it brings
with it salt spray.

Topography causes smaller-scale effects on climate, such as the funnelling of
winds up valleys. Topographic obstacles may lead to turbulence, a good example
being the northern Pennines, where winds from the east produce a very strong local
wind on the western side of the hills, known as the helm wind. The turbulence also
causes a local stationary cloud to form a few kilometres west of the summits, known
as the helm bar[10]. The alignment of the valleys can be important, too, as south-facing
slopes receive more sunshine than those with northerly aspects, raising temperatures
significantly. In areas of marked relief, cold air drainage may occur, where air cooled
rapidly over the uplands after sunset sinks down into the valleys, lowering temperatures in the valley bottoms. The phenomenon is often seen in Snowdonia, where
cold air from Carneddau drains down into the Ogwen valley[11]. Some areas which
receive cold air drainage are well known as frost hollows, such as Braemar in the
Grampians and Corwen in Clwyd. The lowest temperature ever recorded at a standard British observing station was − 27.2°C at Braemar in 1982[9].

Fog is another feature of our climate. Two types are particularly prevalent on
the uplands, one being hill fog. Sometimes the base of the clouds is so low that the hill
tops are literally in the clouds and visibility on the summits is reduced to a few metres.
This is very common over higher ground, for example in the Scottish Highlands. On
other occasions, fog is formed when the air cools at night. The warmer air over the
surrounding valleys may be clear, although sometimes the cool air will drain down
into them after a while, leaving the tops clear of fog. Another type of fog occurs
particularly frequently along the coast of north-eastern England and Scotland. This is

sea fog, sometimes known as haar, which results from moisture-laden air passing over very cold land. This can last for many hours, the fog preventing the sun's heat from warming the land, and its effects are often felt several miles inland.

Thus, there is a great range of climate found in upland Britain, from the relatively mild climate of south-west England to the wet, windy climate of the Hebrides and the cold, snowy climate of north-east Scotland. Everywhere, altitude tends to decrease temperatures, increase rainfall and cloudiness and shorten the growing season, but there are great contrasts also between north and south, east and west, coastal and inland areas. The combined effects of geology, topography and climate produce a range of soil and vegetation types, adding further diversity to the landscape.

Soils

The soils of the uplands are the product of chemical and biological processes breaking down and re-arranging mineral material and organic matter. They vary enormously in their characteristics, according to the underlying parent material, climate, steepness of slope and surface vegetation. A change in any one of these factors may bring about a modification in the soil. Human activities have often resulted in soil changes also, as we shall see in later chapters. In reality, no two soils are identical and no soil is unchanging for any length of time, but, for convenience, soils can be described and mapped in a number of general categories[13].

The best agricultural soils in the uplands are the brown earths. They are widespread on gentle to moderate slopes in well-drained positions and they may be calcareous or acid, according to the nature of the parent material. They are often found under grassland or deciduous woodland and have fairly uniform brown profiles, with no sharp changes from top-soil to sub-soil. Usually the top-soil will be slightly darker in colour, as it receives organic matter from the vegetation above, whereas the sub-soil may be a brighter, more orangey colour, due to the movement of iron and other compounds down the profile in the drainage water – a process known as leaching. In some acid brown earths, clay particles are also washed down the profile to give the sub-soil a heavier texture. Similar soils are often found under cultivated land, but here there is usually a more obvious boundary between the ploughed top-soil and the unploughed sub-soil.

Brown earths are the commonest type of soil in Wales and south-west England, where they occupy most of the valleys and lower slopes. They are also found on the flanks of the Pennines, in the southern Lake District and in the southern part of the North York Moors. In Scotland, many valleys and coastal plains have acid brown earths. Agricultural practices, such as ploughing, draining and fertilising, have often transformed other soil types into brown earths. In some other areas, soils have changed in the opposite direction. Most of Britain south of the Scottish Highlands was once covered with deciduous woodland and this almost certainly overlay brown earth soils. When this woodland was cleared and replaced with vegetation such as moorland, soils became acidified and the process known as podzolisation started.

Podzolic soils are produced when the surface horizons become very acid and weathered. The top-soil becomes depleted of most of the nutrients needed for plant growth and ends up as a very pale, ash-like layer. The nutrients are washed down the soil profile and accumulate in the sub-soil to form a series of horizons with very sharp boundaries between them. First there may be a dark brown layer of organic matter, then sometimes a thin, hard iron pan and below this a bright orange layer, stained with iron and other minerals. In order for podzolisation to occur, there must be free drainage and a supply of acid litter at the surface, as a build-up of acids is essential to mobilise the iron, organic matter and other constituents which move down the profile. This acid litter often accumulates to form a thick layer of raw humus on the surface of the soil, known as a 'mor'.

Podzolic soils are found wherever moorland or coniferous forests overlie freely draining parent materials. They are very common in the Highlands, Islands and Southern Uplands of Scotland. They occupy much of the higher ground in the Cheviots, the central Lake District and the Welsh mountains and also occur in parts of south-west England, such as central Dartmoor and Bodmin Moor. Smaller areas of podzolic soils can be found on steep slopes in the Pennines and the North York Moors. As with brown earths, there is much variation within these soils, some podzols having more iron and some having more organic matter in the sub-soil, some lacking a definite iron pan and some developing a peaty surface layer.

Some parent materials, such as shales, are impermeable or let water through very slowly. This can lead to waterlogging in the lower layers of the soil. More commonly, there is some impedance to drainage within the soil profile itself, such as an iron pan or a clay layer, and the soil horizons above this layer then become waterlogged. Such soils are described as gleys and the waterlogged layers are easy to identify by their pale blue or grey colours, caused by the chemical reduction of iron compounds. If these layers sometimes dry out, some of the iron compounds become oxidised again and rusty mottles are seen in the soil. Gleyed soils are very characteristic of the lower ground in areas such as central Scotland, but they are also widespread on higher areas which are flat or gently sloping. The processes of leaching and podzolisation often lead to gleying. The formation of an iron pan, for instance, may prevent water from draining freely through it. This makes the top-soil waterlogged and a peaty layer may eventually form at the surface. These soils, with a wet top-soil and a dry sub-soil, are common in the North York Moors, south Wales, the Pennines, the northern Lake District and central Exmoor. Gleyed soils also occur in the valley bottoms in many parts of Scotland. The commonest land use over gleyed soils is pasture but, in some areas, gleys have been drained or ploughed (to break up an iron pan) and used for arable cultivation or forestry.

If drainage deteriorates even further, the peaty surface layer may deepen until it dominates the soil profile. The soil is then classified as a peat or organic soil and is more or less permanently waterlogged. In these conditions, plant remains are very slow to break down and may be preserved for hundreds or thousands of years, building up in horizontal layers and preserving within them tree trunks, pollen grains and other organic remains. Blanket peat now covers those parts of the uplands where rainfall is high and flat plateau surfaces encourage waterlogging. Many parts of the Northern Highlands and Islands of Scotland have extensive tracts of blanket bog, such as Benbecula, North and South Uist, Rannoch Moor and the Flow Country of northern Scotland. Peats are also found on high plateau areas in Snowdonia, the Cheviots, the Pennines, the North York Moors, south Wales and the granite massifs of south-west England. In some of these areas, they have been dug for fuel and, in others, drainage has been carried out for forestry. Most remain, however, as waterlogged areas, supporting characteristic wetland plant and animal life.

In some regions, soils are dominated by the underlying rock. The Carboniferous limestone areas of the Pennines and southern Lake District have very thin soils, associated with the karst scenery described above. The limestone itself is so soluble that the slightly acid rainfall can dissolve and carry away most of the weathered mineral material. Only a small insoluble residue of particles, such as quartz, is left behind to form a soil. On limestone pavement areas, much of what does form is washed down the grikes. Where a vegetation cover has become established, organic litter forms a thin, dark top-soil directly overlying the limestone rock to form a rendzina soil. However, many of these areas were originally covered with glacial drift or wind-blown deposits. The soils developed on these superficial deposits were deeper and more acidic than those over the bare limestone. Sometimes even blanket peat formed, as can be seen on Ingleborough today. It is likely that most karst areas had much deeper soils in the past, developed over drift. There are some parts of the Pennines where over-grazing has led to destruction of the vegetation cover and erosion of the soils. Here, fresh areas of limestone pavement can be seen emerging from under their drift cover (Colour plate 14). In other places, where grazing has been prevented by fencing, vegetation can be seen colonising the limestone pavements, starting with lichens encrusting the limestone clints, followed by mosses, grasses and other plants, until a layer of organic material covers the bare rock to form a rendzina again.

On steep slopes, where it is difficult for any depth of soil to build up because of the constant erosion of material downslope, soils are very thin and dominated by rock. Most of them develop over acidic rocks and are known as rankers. There are some good examples of rankers on the steep upper slopes of the central Lake District, over rocks of the Borrowdale Volcanic Group. It is difficult for vegetation to get a foot-hold in these unstable areas, so the soils are low in organic matter. They grade into areas of rock scree, with no real soil development at all. Rock-dominated soils can also be found on steep slopes in Snowdonia, over vertically bedded shales in mid-Wales and in the Scottish Highlands.

The summits of the Cairngorms and Grampians are high enough to experience a sub-arctic climate. Here, soil development is limited by such processes as frost-heaving and solifluction. Mineral particles tend to get arranged according to size, as a result of these movements, to form a range of features known collectively as patterned ground. Stone polygons, 10 to 30 cm in diameter, may form on more or less flat ground above 1000 metres. As water expands into ice in the soil, it pushes up a small mound of earth above it, dislodging the soil particles, which roll downslope away from the centre of the mound. On slightly steeper slopes, the stones arrange themselves in stripes rather than polygons, each stripe at right angles to the contours. Because of the constant disturbance of the ground by frost in these areas, soils are never stable for long enough to develop marked horizons, except for an organic layer at the surface. This may be peaty, as the cool mountain climate leads to very slow breakdown of plant litter.

The physical features described in this chapter interact to produce an amazing variety of scenery and habitats for wildlife. Constrasts in the geology, topography, climate and soils of different parts of the uplands have led to a corresponding diversity of plant and animal communities, and changes in the physical features are constantly causing alterations to the flora and fauna. Human impact has superimposed various patterns of land use and has brought about other modifications to the landscape and its wildlife. Woodlands have been felled or planted, wetlands have been drained, grasslands and moorlands have been grazed or burned. Not even the highest mountain tops or the remotest Scottish islands have escaped human influence. This ever-changing pattern of scenery and wildlife is what makes the uplands so fascinating to study.

References

1   Full accounts of the geology of the different parts of the uplands may be found in the British Regional Geologies published by the Geological Survey.
2   Owen, T R, *The geological evolution of the British Isles*. Pergamon Press, Oxford, 1976.
3   Wood, R M, *On the rocks*. BBC, London, 1978.
4   Price, R, *Highland landforms*. Aberdeen University Press, Aberdeen, 1991.
5   Sparks, B W and West, R G, *The Ice Age in Britain*. Methuen, London, 1972.
6   Gray, M, *Update: The Quaternary Ice Age*. Cambridge University Press, Cambridge, 1985.
7   Sugden, D E and John, B S, *Glaciers and landscape*. Edward Arnold, London, 1976.
8   Chandler, T J and Gregory, S, *The climate of the British Isles*. Longman, London, 1976.
9   Meteorological Office, Climatological memoranda for various parts of Britain, 1988 *et seq.*
10   Langmuir, E, *Mountaincraft and leadership*. Scottish Sports Council, Edinburgh, 1984.
11   Millward, R and Robinson, A, *Upland Britain*. David and Charles, Newton Abbot, 1980.
12   *Climatological Atlas of Great Britain*. HMSO, London, 1952.
13   Soil Survey and Land Research Centre. Maps and memoirs for various parts of the uplands.

2

Fifteen thousand years of change

Though nothing can bring back the hour
Of splendour in the grass, of glory in the flower;
We will grieve not, rather find
Strength in what remains behind.

William Wordsworth

In this chapter, we shall consider the various types of evidence which allow ecologists to study past environments and their wildlife. By examining old documents, archaeological artefacts and the remains of plants and animals preserved in peat bogs or lake sediments, it has been possible to reconstruct the major changes in the uplands over the past 15,000 years.

Documentary and archaeological evidence

One of the earliest types of written evidence is that of place-names. The English Place-name Society has published county volumes for some parts of the uplands but less work has been done in Wales and Scotland. There are many limitations to place-name evidence and it is often hard to be certain when a name was first used and precisely what it meant[1]. However, some place-name elements do give us general information about past landscapes, such as 'ley', an Anglo-Saxon element meaning a clearing in a wood, or 'hege', meaning a hedge. The Old Norse 'saetr' (often corrupted to 'side' in modern names) meant a summer pasture or shieling, so gives us information on land use.

For the more recent periods, there are written documents, which give us information about some of the upland habitats[2]. County record offices hold many old manuscripts, including Anglo-Saxon charters, leases of land, accounts, wills, records of court cases and other legal documents. Some of them give information about vegetation or land use, but specific references to wildlife are usually few and far between and are often incidental to the main purpose of the document. For instance, a record of a fine imposed on someone for stealing wood may mention the species of tree involved but does not tell us if that tree was common or rare. More general surveys give a better coverage, an early example being the Book of Llandaff, a record for Wales in the Dark Ages. The Domesday Book of 1086 contains a wealth of useful information for southern England but is less comprehensive further north and does not include Wales, Scotland or the English counties north of the Tees[3]. The information in it includes population, woodland areas, farming and 'waste' land, but the units of measurement tend to vary from county to county, so that it is not always possible to estimate the true areas or precise locations of habitats such as woodlands or meadows. The emphasis was on the value of land, as the document was compiled for taxation purposes, so the less valuable and wilder parts of the uplands received scant attention from the Domesday surveyors. For the medieval period, some information may be gleaned from the records of monastic houses, such as Rievaulx Abbey, which owned large areas of the uplands.

Other areas were the subject of later surveys, such as those of Crown properties. An example is the Parliamentary Survey of Exmoor, carried out in 1651, but its inaccuracies have been revealed by later research. An attempt was made in the eighteenth and nineteenth centuries to gather information on Scotland, by asking the Church of Scotland ministers to complete returns for their areas. The results were published as the *Statistical accounts of Scotland* in 1791–9 and 1845–58, but they vary considerably in their accuracy and detail. Smaller-scale surveys include county agricultural surveys carried out for the Board of Agriculture between 1790 and 1820, such as Arthur Young's survey of Derbyshire, and records of individual estates.

Some sources give more specific information on animals and plants. The records of the former Royal Forests sometimes provide detailed information on the trees, deer and other wildlife and the uses of the forest by local inhabitants. A good example is the excellent set of records which exists for the Royal Forest of Pickering, which covered a large part of the eastern North York Moors[4]. County floras occasionally yield interesting snippets on habitats, although they are often disappointingly vague about locations. Even the records of game birds bagged on nineteenth century shoots or bounties paid for skins of certain animals can yield some useful information.

Other sources are the accounts written by early travellers, such as James Plumptree[5], John Byng[6] or Thomas Pennant[7]. These often display considerable bias, as the more remote, wild uplands were generally regarded as barren, fearful places until the middle of the nineteenth century, as shown by Daniel Defoe's description of the Pennines as

> a country all mountainous and full of innumerable high hills. . . . . Nor were these hills high and formidable only, but they had a kind of an unhospitable terror in them. . . . all barren and wild, of no use or advantage either to man or beast.[8]

Illustrations are useful for the last few centuries. J M W Turner toured northern England in 1797 and sketched and described places such as Malham, Semer Water and many of the Yorkshire dales[9]. Surveying techniques were not developed until the sixteenth century, so the very few earlier maps still extant tend to be highly inaccurate in both scale and the relative position of features. Nineteenth century tithe maps and enclosure maps are reasonably accurate but only cover the agricultural areas, thus excluding much of the uplands. It was not until the mid-nineteenth century that the Ordnance Survey set about the systematic mapping of the whole of Britain, and, even then, habitat information other than for woodlands is shown on relatively few maps, such the Land Utilization Surveys of the 1930s.

Archaeological evidence sometimes complements the documentary record but it is particularly useful for the earlier periods, for which there are no written records. For instance, from bone and antler tools, we learn about some of the animals hunted by early prehistoric people. For later periods, clues about land use are provided by quern stones for grinding corn or spindle whorls for spinning wool. The remains of iron forges imply the existence of woodland which could be exploited for charcoal. However, the value of archaeological evidence is limited by the chance of preservation and the luck of discovery, so it gives us a very incomplete picture of the former distribution of habitats. Clearly, if we had to rely only on written or archaeological evidence, our knowledge of past habitats would be patchy, inaccurate and biased. Luckily, there are other, more scientific lines of evidence, which can help redress the balance.

Biological evidence

The remains of past plants and animals provide the most important source of information[10]. Some material, such as bone or shell, is relatively resistant to decay but very special environmental conditions are needed for other remains to be preserved. The commonest preserving environment for plant material is a waterlogged one, such as a peat bog or a lake. Almost any part of the plant can be preserved but some parts are more resistant to decay than others, especially wood, charcoal, seeds and fruits. These are usually found close to where the plants grew, so the remains most frequently found are those of wetland plants. Those which grew on dry limestone grassslands or on burned heather moorlands are unlikely to be preserved.

However, smaller plant remains offer greater scope, being more easily blown into waterlogged environments from a greater distance. Most important are the microscopic pollen grains of flowering plants and spores of ferns and mosses. They are produced in great abundance, are very resistant to decay and are easily transported by wind or water. They are incorporated in large numbers into the sediments accumulating on the bottom of lakes and the layers building up in peat bogs (Colour plate 1). With the use of various chemical procedures, they can be recovered from the sediment or peat, identified under a microscope and counted to give us an idea of the relative proportions of the different types of plant. Figure 5 shows an example of a pollen diagram from the North York Moors (Colour plate 1), in which each type of pollen or spore recognised has been shown as a separate graph. The vertical scale represents the depth of peat (the oldest being at the base) and the horizontal scale represents the percentage of the total pollen.

Lakes and peat bogs are plentifully distributed in the uplands, so there are many sites from which pollen diagrams have been constructed, giving us an idea of

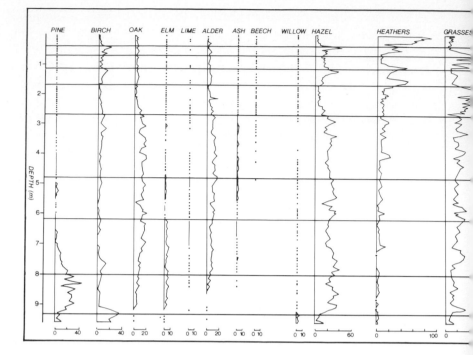

what the vegetation cover was like at various periods in the past. It is not a completely accurate picture, however, as the pollen grains which are most frequent are those from wind-pollinated rather than insect-pollinated plants. Most of our forest trees are wind-pollinated, so we have a good idea of what the woodlands were like, but many herbaceous plants are insect-pollinated, so we know less about the habitats in which they grew. Pollen analysis is also a rather imprecise tool, as we can never be sure exactly how far the pollen grains have blown; but, by comparing pollen diagrams from many different sites, a surprisingly detailed picture emerges. For lakes and marshes, the microscopic remains of diatoms (algae) are a useful additional source of information, especially about water temperature and acidity.

Lakes may also contain animal remains, such as the bones and teeth of mammals and birds. Large animals may drown, fall through an ice cover or get stuck in the mud. Predatory animals may accumulate remains of their prey in caves; for instance, pellets from roosting owls often contain bones of small mammals. Such sites are relatively uncommon, though, and the information they yield is localised and very selective. Of greater use are the remains of insects, some of the most resistant being the wing-cases of beetles. These are a useful form of evidence to compare with pollen and spores, as insects are able to colonise new areas and respond to changes in climate much faster than plants. Snail shells are also resistant to decay and are often best preserved in habitats such as calcareous soils, where pollen and other remains are scarce. Even if the shells have been broken into fragments, it may be possible to identify the species from which they came, which will usually give a clue to the

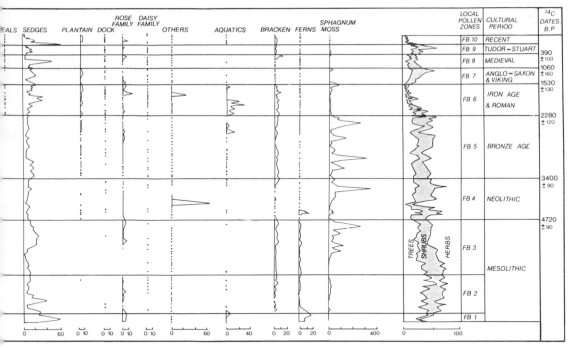

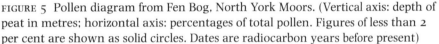

FIGURE 5 Pollen diagram from Fen Bog, North York Moors. (Vertical axis: depth of peat in metres; horizontal axis: percentages of total pollen. Figures of less than 2 per cent are shown as solid circles. Dates are radiocarbon years before present)

habitat, such as woodland or marsh. Other shells are of marine origin and these are important lines of evidence, particularly about climatic change over the last two million years.

Dating methods

In order to make full use of the techniques outlined above, it is necessary to be able to date the deposits accurately. The most important dating method for the Post-glacial period is radiocarbon dating. A tiny fraction of the carbon in all living plants and animals is the radioactive isotope, carbon-14 (^{14}C). When the organisms die, the radioactive carbon starts to decay, emitting beta radiation. By measuring the amount of ^{14}C left, it is possible to work out how much time has elapsed since an organism died. The procedure is an involved and costly one, but it has enabled many organic remains to be dated with a fair degree of accuracy, including wood, peat and shells.

Another method of dating is by counting the annual growth rings of trees. The width of the rings varies according to the weather conditions, so it is possible to learn a great deal about the past climate by studying the pattern of rings. We can also assess the age of tree trunks buried in peat bogs or timbers from archaeological sites, by seeing where their tree-ring patterns overlap with those of trees of known age. In this way, it is possible to extend the tree-ring dating technique back for several thousand years. A tree-ring chronology is being constructed for Britain, based on oak trunks preserved in peat bogs.

Pollen analysis can also be used as a very rough method of dating. Pollen diagrams from many different sites in Britain have been compared and some generalised patterns have emerged[11]. This has enabled a general set of zones to be delineated, as shown on Table 5. The zone boundaries have been dated at several sites by radiocarbon dating, thus providing an approximate time-scale for sites where no radiocarbon dates are available.

The Late-glacial period

Using the types of evidence and dating techniques described above, it is possible to piece together the history of the upland environment during the past 15,000 years. Our story starts at the end of the Ice Age, when Britain was still in the grip of sub-arctic conditions – a period known as the Late-glacial. This was a period of transition between real glacial conditions and the present temperate conditions. It began about 15,000 years ago, when ice-sheets still covered much of Scotland and

TABLE 5 Pollen zoning schemes for Great Britain

Date (BP)	Godwin's zoning scheme	West's zoning scheme	Traditional climatic periods
	VIII Alder–Birch–oak –(beech) zone	Late Flandrian (period when man becomes dominant ecological factor)	Sub-atlantic (cool and wet)
2500	– – – – – – – – – – –		– – – – – – – – – – –
5000	VIIb Alder–oak–lime zone – – – – – – – – – – – – – –	ELM DECLINE	Sub-boreal (warm and dry) – – – – – – – – – – –
7000	VIIa Alder–oak–elm–lime zone – – – – – – – – – – –	Middle Flandrian (period of maximum forest cover)	Atlantic (warm and wet) – – – – – – – – – – –
8800	VI Pine–hazel–(mixed oak forest zone) – – – – – – – – – –	Early Flandrian (period of colonisation	Boreal (warm and dry)
9500	V Hazel–birch–pine zone – – – – – – – – – –		– – – – – – – – – – –
10,000	IV Birch–(pine) zone – – – – – – – – – – –		Pre-boreal (becoming warmer) – – – – – – – – – – –
	I, II & III Tundra	Late-Devensian	Sub-arctic

Dates are approximate years before present. Late-Devensian = Late-glacial; Flandrian = Post-glacial.

the higher areas of Wales and northern England. Elsewhere the vegetation was similar to that of the tundra regions today, dominated by grasses, sedges and other herbaceous species. There were extensive heaths of dwarf shrubs such as crowberry; the only other woody plants were dwarf species of birch, willow and juniper. One plant which seems to have been particularly common was mountain avens (Plate 3), but there were many other arctic-alpine species, including club-mosses, mountain sorrel and purple saxifrage (Colour plate 3). The permanently frozen sub-soil prevented the downward drainage of water, so myriads of small lakes formed in summer, as in the tundra today. Evaporation from these lakes drew salts up from below and deposited them on the surface, creating habitats for salt-tolerant plants. Animal life included some extinct species as well as those found in tundra areas today. Large herds of elk, reindeer, wild horse and bison (Plate 4) were preyed upon by arctic wolves, foxes and lynx. Insects and birds could migrate quite easily, many of them colonising the tundra plains in summer but moving to warmer areas further south in winter. No doubt the many lakes and marshy sites attracted large numbers of ducks, geese and wading birds and also swarms of mosquitoes and midges.

Gradually the great ice-sheets began to melt, creating many wetland habitats as they did so. Most of Britain was probably free of ice by 13,000 years ago[12]. Temperatures by then were at least as warm as they are today, the average annual temperature being around 11°C in northern Scotland and as high as 17°C in southwest England. We know from the beetle species found that the peak of warmth was reached about 12,500 years ago, but it took another 1500 years for the vegetation to reach its maximum development. Tree birches gradually spread to form a light woodland canopy over much of the uplands, giving way to scrub and open herbaceous vegetation on the highest ground and in northern Scotland. This warm period is known as the interstadial and was a sort of false start to the Post-glacial period.

By 11,000 years ago the climate had deteriorated again. Ice-sheets formed to a thickness of 400 metres over the Northern Highlands, with smaller ice caps on the Grampian Highlands, Skye and Mull. There were also hundreds of valley glaciers, not only in Scotland and the islands but also in Snowdonia, the Brecon Beacons and the highest parts of the Lake District. This period is known as the Loch Lomond stadial. The climate was unlike any known today, the nearest modern equivalent being that of Siberia or Greenland. In winter, a vast anticyclone over Europe sent biting easterly winds towards Britain, while in summer it was replaced by a deep low pressure system, which drew in rain- and snow-bearing winds from the Atlantic. Winter temperatures were about 10°C lower and summer ones about 5°C lower than those of the interstadial, and the range of temperature increased by 50 per cent. Vegetation development suffered a major setback during the Loch Lomond stadial, and most parts of the uplands reverted to a tundra-like landscape. Soils became unstable again and pioneering vegetation types were re-established, similar to those at the start of the Late-glacial period. For about 1000 years Britain was again in the grip of glaciation but this was to be the final phase of the Ice Age. About 10,000 years ago the ice-sheets melted for the last time and plant and animal colonisation recommenced.

PLATE 3 Mountain avens, a common plant in many parts of Britain during the
Late-glacial period

PLATE 4 The European bison, a member of the Late-glacial fauna, which died out
during the Post-glacial period

The early Post-glacial period

Temperatures increased rapidly about 10,000 years ago, as the ice-sheets finally retreated from northern Britain. However, it took some time for plants to respond to the change and colonise the newly available habitats. This is because most plants spread fairly slowly by seed, compared with animals, which can move into a new area without waiting for a new generation to be born. During the Ice Age, a large volume of water was locked up as ice, causing a drop in sea level of about 100 metres. Much of the southern North Sea basin was dry land, so it was possible for plants to colonise Britain from mainland Europe as the temperature started to rise. Most species spread from the south and east, reaching the lowlands first and then gradually colonising the uplands over a period of several centuries.

There is much more evidence about plants than animals for the Post-glacial period, but to a large extent we can infer animal communities, as they are dependent on plants for food and/or shelter. One of the first changes on the pollen diagrams (the main source of evidence) is an increase in juniper pollen. Juniper is a native shrub which was certainly present during the closing stages of the Ice Age, but which flowered and produced pollen more profusely as the temperature rose, enabling it to spread on to new ground. However, it cannot tolerate much shade, so it had a fairly brief heyday at the beginning of the Post-glacial, before the taller forest trees forced it into a subordinate role. The first tree to appear in the pollen record nearly everywhere in the uplands is birch. The dwarf form of this tree had been present during the Ice Age but when temperatures rose the tree birches quickly spread, establishing a light woodland canopy over most parts of England, Wales and southern Scotland. The birches thinned out further north, only colonising more sheltered valleys and coastal areas. Birch woodland was also established on the Inner Hebrides but colonisation was limited on the windier Outer Hebrides and Northern Isles. Hazel scrub grew alongside the birches. Like juniper, hazel tends to be shaded out by a tree cover, but at this early stage there were plenty of sites in the uplands where pure hazel woods could exist, like those seen today on Mull and Skye (Plate 5). Willows colonised the many wet sites and aspen was also an early coloniser but less is known about its distribution, as its pollen grains are poorly preserved.

Under the light woodland canopy or scrub, herbaceous plants survived in decreasing numbers. However, there were still plenty of open areas at this early stage, where the lack of shade allowed grasses and sedges to maintain their dominance. Wetland sites were common, including lakes and marshes, created by the melting ice-sheets. They were colonised by various types of mire and aquatic vegetation, and some of them were gradually infilled by the plant remains and became dry land. The larger lakes, such as those of the Lake District and the Scottish lochs, are still with us today, but most of them have been reduced in size since the end of the Ice Age, as plants have colonised their margins. As the woodland spread, the typical tundra animals died out, unable to migrate northwards from Britain because the sea formed a barrier. They were gradually replaced by temperate animals, which were more at

PLATE 5 Hazel scrub on Mull, Inner Hebrides. This vegetation type was common in the early Post-glacial period

home in a woodland environment, such as deer and wild cattle. Species which could adapt to the new conditions, such as wolves, survived by changing their prey to woodland species.

By about 8000 years ago, Scots pine had replaced birch as the dominant tree in parts of the uplands. Spreading from south and east England, it gradually migrated into the birch and hazel woods, to form a mixed coniferous/deciduous woodland. The climate at this time is thought to have been slightly warmer than today but drier and more continental in nature, which may have favoured this northern or 'boreal' tree. Indeed, the period from about 9500 to 7000 years ago is sometimes referred to as the Boreal period (Table 5). Pine regenerates well after fire and there may have been natural fires at this time in some parts of the uplands, started by lightning strikes. However, pine never succeeded in colonising the Scottish islands, which retained their scrubby cover of birch, willow and hazel.

Other trees were also invading and in many places they gradually ousted pine from its dominant position. These were the more warmth-loving deciduous species, such as elm, oak and lime. They spread into England and Wales shortly after pine and proved to be more successful in competition with it, being better adapted to the climate and soils. Over the next few centuries, pine was gradually out-competed by them and eventually became extinct in England and Wales. The deciduous trees also successfully replaced pine around the coasts of Scotland and in the valleys. However, in the Scottish Highlands, pine and birch retained their dominance. The more severe climate and the less fertile soils there were more suited to the pine and birch woods than to other species. Alder was another important deciduous tree, which immigrated towards the end of the Boreal period and quickly became established in the deciduous woodlands. It is well adapted to wet sites, so its presence may be over-emphasised on pollen diagrams, as these are usually from lakes or bogs which would favour local alder growth. However, there can be little doubt that it soon became a widespread tree, as its pollen is found at sites throughout upland Britain.

The middle Post-glacial period

By about 7000 years ago, a woodland cover was established over most of upland Britain (Figure 6). The major trees which had immigrated in the early Post-glacial had extended their ranges and competed with one another, the best adapted species becoming dominant in each region. In England, Wales and southern Scotland there was a mixed deciduous woodland, with oak and hazel as the most important species, whilst pine and birch remained dominant in the Scottish Highlands. Skye and the north of Scotland were mostly covered in birch scrub, but in the north-east tip of Caithness, the Outer Hebrides and the Northern Isles, there were only occasional patches of woodland in sheltered localities, most of the ground retaining an open herbaceous vegetation cover.

The tree-line seems to have been at about 700 to 800 metres in England and Wales, falling towards the north until it was less than 300 metres above sea level in the north of Scotland. Thus there were no extensive areas above the tree-line south of north Wales at this time. Further north, woodland gave way on high ground to sub-arctic herbaceous vegetation, such as grassland or heath. Other open areas would have included coastal cliff sites, marshy ground and natural clearings caused by fallen trees or unstable ground. Most of upland Britain, though, was wooded and most of its animals and plants were adapted to the woodland environment. Shade-loving plants, such as ivy, holly and dog's mercury, increased. In the space of some 5000 years, the herds of reindeer and bison grazing on open tundra vegetation had given way to forest animals, such as deer and wild boar, browsing the undergrowth in dense woodland.

All this time, the great ice-sheets had been melting and returning their water to the oceans. Sometime between 8500 and 7500 years ago, the rise in sea level severed the last land link between Britain and the continent and over the next few centuries the coastline assumed its present shape. This made further immigration of species, particularly plants, more difficult, so it forms a convenient point at which to distinguish native from non-native species. Any plant or animal species for which there are reliable records before 7500 years ago is regarded as native, whereas species not recorded until after this date are assumed to have been introduced by humans. Table 6 lists the tree and shrub species thought to be native to upland Britain. Some species native in the south of Britain did not manage to spread to the north without human help. For example, beech and hornbeam were two of the last

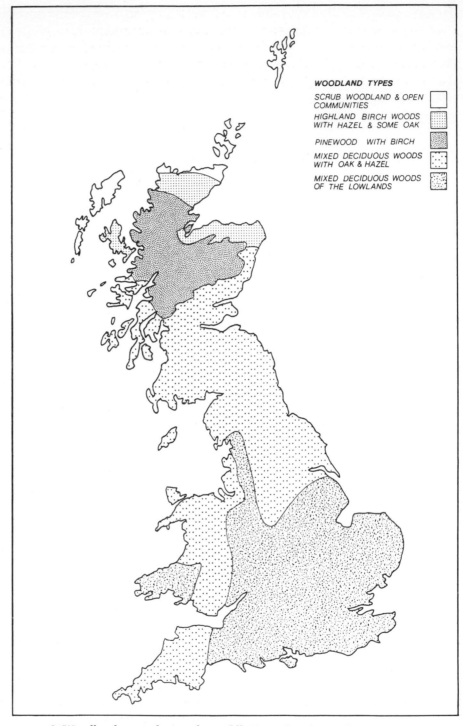

FIGURE 6 Woodland cover during the middle Post-glacial period (Reconstructed from the work of Rackham[16] and others)

tree species to enter Britain but were scarce and largely confined to areas south of the Lake District until later deforestation opened up new habitats to them. Other species achieved a more widespread distribution but were limited in abundance in the middle Post-glacial, an example being ash. Others, such as lime, reach their present climatic limit within northern England, although they may have been native a little further north in the middle Post-glacial.

TABLE 6 Trees and shrubs native to upland Britain

Species	English name	Native status and distribution
Acer campestre	Field maple	Probably native in England and Wales, introduced in Scotland
Alnus glutinosa	Alder	Native throughout uplands except Northern Isles
Betula nana	Dwarf birch	Native only in Scottish Highlands. N Scotland and Upper Teesdale today but formerly more widespread
Betula pendula	Silver birch	Native throughout uplands except Northern Isles
Betula pubescens	Downy birch	Native throughout uplands
Buxus sempervirens	Box	One Post-glacial record of pollen from Lake District, otherwise not native to uplands and confined to S England today
Cornus sanguinea	Dogwood	Native only as far north as S Lake District and Durham but introduced elsewhere
Corylus avellana	Hazel	Native throughout uplands
Crataegus monogyna	Hawthorn	Native everywhere except Northern Isles
Cytisus scoparius	Broom	Probably native throughout uplands except Northern Isles
Euonymus europaeus	Spindle	Very few records for past distribution but found today in English and Welsh uplands and introduced to S Scotland
Fagus sylvatica	Beech	Probably native in uplands only in SW England but widely planted elsewhere except Northern Isles
Frangula alnus	Alder buckthorn	Native to England and Wales but rare in Scotland and not common in uplands
Fraxinus excelsior	Ash	Native throughout uplands except Northern Isles
Ilex aquifolium	Holly	Native throughout uplands except NE Caithness and Northern Isles.
Juniperus communis	Juniper	Native to uplands except SW England but modern distribution concentrated in Scotland and Isles, Lake District and NE England

Species	English name	Native status and distribution
Ligustrum vulgare	Wild privet	Native to English and Welsh uplands but probably introduced in Scotland
Malus sylvestris	Crab apple	Native except in Scottish Highlands, Caithness and Outer Isles
Pinus sylvestris	Scots pine	Native throughout uplands except Scottish Isles in past but now confined to Highlands but widely planted elsewhere
Populus tremula	Aspen	Native throughout uplands
Prunus avium	Wild cherry	Native except in Scottish Isles but also widely planted
Prunus cerasus	Dwarf cherry	Possibly native to SW England, Wales and Lake District but introduced elsewhere
Prunus padus	Bird cherry	Native to uplands except SW England and Outer Isles
Prunus spinosa	Blackthorn	Native except in Outer Isles but absent from most of Scottish Highlands
Quercus petraea	Sessile oak	Native throughout uplands except Outer Isles but often hybridises with *Q robur*
Quercus robur	Pedunculate oak	Native throughout uplands except Outer Isles but often hybridises with *Q petraea*
Rhamnus cathartica	Buckthorn	Native to England and Wales except NE and SW England, but not common in uplands
Salix alba	White willow	Probably native except in Outer Isles but uncommon in uplands and sometimes planted
Salix arbuscula	Mountain willow	Rare native of Scottish mountains
Salix aurita	Eared willow	Native throughout uplands
Salix caprea	Goat willow	Native throughout uplands but uncommon or absent in Outer Isles
Salix cinerea	Grey willow	Native throughout uplands
Salix fragilis	*Crack-willow*	Native except in N Scotland and Outer Isles
Salix herbacea	Dwarf willow	Native to W Scotland, Scottish Isles and Lake District; very rare in Wales
Salix lanata	Woolly willow	Rare native in Scottish Highlands only
Salix lapponum	Downy willow	Rare native in Scottish Highlands, N Scotland and very few other sites
Salix myrsinites	Whortle-leaved willow	Rare native of Scottish Highlands
Salix myrsinifolia	Dark-leaved willow	Uncommon but native in N England and parts of Scotland

Species	English name	Native status and distribution
Salix pentandra	Bay willow	Uncommon but probably native from Wales northward to the E Highlands. Planted elsewhere
Salix phylicifolia	Tea-leaved willow	Uncommon but native in N England and Scotland except Shetland
Salix purpurea	Purple willow	Native except in Outer isles but often planted
Salix repens	Creeping willow	Native throughout uplands
Salix reticulata	Net-leaved willow	Very rare native of Scottish and Welsh mountains
Salix triandra	Almond willow	Uncommon native of uplands as far N as SE Scotland
Salix viminalis	Osier	Native throughout uplands but also widely planted
(Note: *Salix* spp are notorious for hybridising)		
Sambucus nigra	Elder	Native throughout uplands except Northern Isles
Sorbus aria agg.	Common whitebeam	A rare native tree scattered throughout uplands except for Scottish Isles
Sorbus aucuparia	Rowan	Native throughout uplands
Sorbus rupicola	Rock whitebeam	Rare native of calcareous sites, eg in SW England, Wales, Pennines and Skye
Sorbus torminalis	Wild service-tree	Native south of Lake District but uncommon
Taxus baccata	Yew	Native to uplands of Wales and N England but rare elsewhere. Absent from Scottish Isles. Probably never common
Tilia cordata	Small-leaved lime	Native to English and Welsh uplands but not Scottish ones
Tilia platyphyllos	Large-leaved lime	Probably native in Wales and N England and in past in Galloway. Pollen not always distinguished from that of *T cordata*
Tilia × *europaea*	Hybrid lime	Occurs very occasionally as natural hybrid between above two species but much more commonly planted throughout uplands
Ulex europaeus	Gorse	Not recorded before Neolithic but probably native throughout uplands
Ulex gallii	Western gorse	Not usually distinguished from above species in fossil records but probably native in W England and Wales and SW Scotland, rare elsewhere in Scotland and absent from Isles

Species	English name	Native status and distribution
Ulmus glabra	Wych elm	Native throughout uplands except Northern Isles
Ulmus minor	Small-leaved elm	Native in uplands only in SW England
Viburnum opulus	Guelder-rose	Native throughout uplands except Outer Isles

Source: Nomenclature after Stace, C, *New flora of the British Isles*, Cambridge University Press, Cambridge, 1991.

The other major effect of Britain becoming an island was a climatic change towards higher rainfall and greater humidity. The middle Post-glacial is sometimes known as the Atlantic period for this reason. The mean annual temperature was 2 or 3°C warmer than at present, enabling some species to extend their ranges towards the north, and woodland cover reached its greatest extent in Britain.

Human impact in the early and middle Post-glacial

The development of vegetation outlined so far has been presented as a natural process, brought about by the interplay of climate and soils with factors of plant dispersal and competition. Although the broad picture of woodland types and their distribution was probably similar to that which would have developed in the absence of any human impact, people were already having marked effects on the vegetation cover of some areas. The traditional terms for the various cultural periods and their approximate dates in the uplands are shown on Table 7. The early and middle Post-glacial periods correspond to the long period known as the Mesolithic, during most of which people were at the hunter–gatherer stage, although herding may well have developed towards the end. The change in vegetation cover during this period, from tundra to woodland, must have led to tremendous readjustments to both the hunting techniques and the diet of Mesolithic people. A greater emphasis on vegetable components may have been one consequence, as the early woodlands would have been rich in edible nuts, fruits and berries.

Although the numbers of people involved were small by comparison with later periods, evidence is accumulating that they had a considerable impact on the upland vegetation cover. Layers of charcoal in some peat profiles suggest fire was being used, certainly in a domestic context but probably also as an aid to hunting. Fire may have been used to drive game in a particular direction, to clear sight-lines or even to promote a fresh bite of grass and attract wild animals to certain clearings. Pine trees may have been burned but standing deciduous trees are very difficult to set alight, so it was probably the undergrowth which was burned in most cases. This would have made for easier movement through the woodlands and enabled Mesolithic people to prevent regrowth of trees in any natural clearings. On pollen dia-

TABLE 7 Cultural periods and their approximate dates

Approximate dates	Cultural period
Eighteenth century on	Modern
Sixteenth and seventeenth centuries	Tudor and Stuart
Eleventh to sixteenth centuries	Medieval
Ninth to eleventh centuries	Viking
Fifth to ninth centuries	Anglo-Saxon/Dark Age
First to fifth centuries AD	Roman
1200 BC to first century AD	Iron Age
1850–1200 BC	Bronze Age
4000–1850 BC	Neolithic
10,000–4000 BC	Mesolithic
Ice Age	Palaeolithic

grams from Dartmoor, the Pennines and the North York Moors, there are temporary increases in the pollen of grasses and other herbaceous species, which may be a record of these Mesolithic activities. The new clearings may also have caused hazel to fruit more profusely, which would have provided an additional source of food in the form of hazelnuts. Alder is another species which may have benefited from the openings in the canopy, and the large amounts of both hazel and alder pollen on some pollen diagrams have been tentatively linked to Mesolithic manipulation of the vegetation[13]. Although not conclusive, these lines of evidence do hint at the fact that hunter–gatherer cultures may have had a far greater impact than was previously thought.

The late Post-glacial period

About 5000 years ago, there was a sudden decrease of elm pollen, seen on pollen diagrams throughout north-west Europe. A climatic cause is unlikely, as elm is the only species consistently affected, so an outbreak of a disease, such as Dutch elm disease, seems a more probable explanation. In 1984, the remains of the elm bark beetle, a carrier of the disease, were found in British deposits of this age, providing at least circumstantial evidence to support the theory[14]. However, another contributory factor could have been human activities. During the fourth millennium BC, farming techniques spread to Britain, at the beginning of the Neolithic cultural period. As well as pursuing wild game through the woodlands, Neolithic people kept their own domesticated stock – cattle, sheep, goats and pigs. It has been suggested that branches of elm might have been lopped from the trees to feed to these animals, as elm is one of the most nutritious of the native trees. In this way, the flowering of elm might have been restricted and less pollen would have been produced. It seems unlikely that Neolithic people could have been responsible for the total decrease of elm at this time, but it is possible that their activities might have helped the spread of Dutch elm disease.

Another possibility is that elm trees occupied the very sites which were most prized by Neolithic people for arable cultivation. The development of farming led to an increase in population and a shift in the distribution of people on to the soils which were easiest to cultivate with the primitive implements available. Of particular importance were the light, well-drained calcareous brown earths of areas such as the southern North York Moors, southern Lake District and parts of the Pennines, Wales and south-west England, and these may have been the soils where elm was most abundant. At sites on the margins of these areas, the first cereal pollen grains appear on the pollen diagrams around the time of the elm decline, accompanied by pollen of typical agricultural weed species. These were mostly native plants, such as ribwort plantain, common sorrel and daisy, some of which had been common at the end of the Ice Age but had decreased during the forest maximum. As time went on, they were joined by introduced species, such as common poppy, charlock and black mustard.

It is probable that Neolithic people practised shifting cultivation, whereby a small area of forest would be cleared, its undergrowth burned and cereals planted. After a few years the fertility of such small plots would be exhausted. The farmers would clear new plots, leaving the abandoned ones to re-colonise with native vegetation before they returned to re-clear them many years later. In this way, the deciduous woodlands were gradually opened up by small temporary clearances. The species which were best able to take advantage of the clearings were light-loving trees and shrubs, such as hazel, ash and birch, together with grasses and weeds, whilst bracken occupied sites at the woodland edges. The pollen diagrams show increases of these species from Neolithic times onwards. At some archaeological sites, finds of even-sized wooden poles suggest that woodlands were being systematically managed to provide a regular supply of wood. This was the beginning of a long history of woodland management, which will be described more fully in chapter 5.

In Bronze Age times, the exploitation of metals allowed the population and impact on the environment to increase[15]. Some upland areas have archaeological evidence for considerable Bronze Age activity, which would have been made easier by the relatively warm climate at the time. Although settlement sites are rare, there is evidence for a mixed agricultural economy, with arable land in the valleys and grazing land on the higher ground. This agriculture led to more and more openings in the forest canopy, especially on higher ground, where the woodland cover was more scrubby and forest regeneration slower than in the more sheltered valleys.

A serious deterioration in climate took place during the first millennium BC. A decrease in temperature and an increase in rainfall and humidity led to the development of peat bogs on many uplands and made the occupation of the higher areas less attractive. From Iron Age times onwards, settlements tended to concentrate on the margins of the uplands, in some cases on sites which have been continuously occupied since that time.

In many parts of England and Wales, large-scale, sustained clearances of deciduous woodland took place in the Iron Age. Pollen diagrams record a substantial decrease in tree pollen, as is well-illustrated on the pollen diagram from the North York

Moors (Figure 5), as woodland was cleared to grow crops or graze livestock. Even without deliberate clearance, grazing pressure would have resulted in the conversion of some woodlands to grasslands or moorlands, as the animals prevented the trees from regenerating. The exploitation of iron provided the first cheap and widely available metal implements, such as stronger ploughs to cultivate heavier soils. The smelting of iron required charcoal, so some woodlands were managed as coppices to provide a regular supply of fuel. Most deciduous trees are capable of being coppiced – that is, they will sprout again from a felled stump – but few of them will reach the flowering stage on a regular coppice cycle. This means that they would no longer be producing pollen and this would be seen on the pollen diagrams as a decrease in the graphs for these trees. Other uses for wood included domestic fuel and the building of wooden huts, as well as a host of minor uses for fencing, utensils, etc.

The onslaught on the woodlands continued into the Roman period, when agriculture and industry were organised on a larger scale than previously. Villas and farms south of the Antonine Wall would have needed more land to grow crops and graze stock, more timber for new buildings and more wood as fuel for their baths and under-floor heating systems. Written records suggest that the climate was milder during the Roman occupation, which was a great boost to arable agriculture. We know that the Romans introduced many new crops to Britain, although most of them were more important in the lowland zone. The population of Roman Britain has been estimated as about four million[15], so it is not surprising that the impact on the vegetation should have been so great. By the time the Romans left in the early fifth century AD, the woodland cover of areas such as the higher parts of Dartmoor, the Pennines and the North York Moors had gone for ever.

Northumbria and Scotland were less affected by these changes, being largely outside Roman influence. Here the pollen diagrams do not show evidence of widespread clearance until the fourth or fifth centuries AD, and even then the Highland pine and birch woods were little affected. Further south, a decrease in population is thought to have occurred during the Anglo-Saxon period, owing to agricultural recession and possibly to outbreaks of plague. Most agricultural land was probably maintained in cultivation but a lack of systematic woodland management in areas away from settlement sites allowed some woodlands to regenerate. Population gradually increased again and new settlers arrived in the Viking period. Place-names and archaeological evidence in northern England suggest that the uplands were exploited as grazing land and valley woodlands were cleared for crop growing. Increasingly sophisticated agricultural implements allowed the cultivation of the heavier gleyed soils.

Domesday Book (1086) provides us with the first systematic account of land use in England. Rackham calculates that the proportion of woodland ranged from about 26 per cent in Derbyshire and perhaps 12–16 per cent in west and north Yorkshire to only 3 or 4 per cent in Devon and Cornwall[16]. The rest of the uplands were covered with grasslands, croplands, moorlands or bogs. Wales and Scotland are not covered by Domesday Book; they probably retained a higher proportion of their woodland at this stage, although the impact of prehistoric and early historic cultures should not be under-estimated.

The climate was warm during the early medieval period[17] and population numbers expanded until reversed by the Black Death in the fourteenth century. More and more woodland was cleared in the valleys and those higher areas not already stripped of their tree cover. Anderson describes the period from AD 1097 to 1400 in Scotland as 'one in which the process of clearing Scotland's forests went on more speedily than at any time before or since'[18]. In addition, some woodlands were cleared deliberately as a security measure. Woods were notorious as the harbourers of outlaws and highwaymen in medieval times. In Wales, both the Romans and the Normans had complained that the Welsh tended to take cover in the woods, and much felling took place to try to dislodge them, for instance, during Edward I's reign. Two famous Welsh resistance leaders, Llewelyn the Great and Owain Glyndwr, both took refuge in woods in Snowdonia[19]. The elaborate fortifications built by the English in their attempts to subdue the Welsh would also have required a great deal of timber, leading to more clearance of woodland. Linnard estimates between 400 and 500 ha of woodland were felled to build the 48 km road from Chester to the River Conwy in 1277[20].

The early Medieval period was also one of particularly heavy grazing pressure. The large monastic houses were big landowners and are known to have run large flocks of sheep and herds of cattle on the uplands. These maintained and extended the areas of grassland, as shown by increases for the pollen of grasses and grassland weeds on the pollen diagrams. Rabbits caused an additional grazing pressure in some areas. Introduced by the Normans, they became a popular source of food from the fifteenth century onwards and warrens occupied large areas. After the Dissolution of the monasteries, the climate became colder, and the period between AD 1550 and 1850 is known as the Little Ice Age. Farming became more difficult and there was a decrease in the number of sheep and cattle grazed on the uplands. This, coupled with increased leaching and gleying of soils, gave heathers a competitive advantage over grasses, and moorland extended at the expense of grassland.

Some parts of the uplands were set aside as Forests for hunting purposes. The term 'Forest' was a legal one and did not necessarily imply woodland, although many Forests were wooded originally. Forests seem to have been a Norman introduction and several English ones are recorded in Domesday Book. They came later to Scotland, the first being the Forest of Ettrick in 1136. There were at least 16 Royal Forests in the uplands of England in medieval times, and several in Scotland. Their primary function was to supply meat for the monarch and his entourage. Beasts of the Forest were the native red deer, roe deer and wild boar and the introduced fallow deer. Other animals could be hunted under licence from the monarch, such as hares, foxes, badgers or wolves. There were also private forests or chases, where aristocratic landowners held private hunting rights. They were particularly common in Wales. Lower down in status were warrens and parks. The total number of Forests, chases, warrens and parks was enormous by the end of the medieval period. The existence of these areas acted as a brake on the process of woodland clearance but grazing, poaching and illegal assarting (making enclosures for cultivation) gradually increased. By the time they were formally disafforested (mainly between 1770 and 1850), most of them had long since lost most of their woodland cover.

The demand on the remaining woodlands for fuel to smelt iron and other metals increased through time, putting considerable strain on the coppice system in England and Wales. Some of the iron-working companies moved up to Scotland in search of extra supplies of wood. There is evidence to suggest that some of them took a rather cavalier attitude towards the woodland resources, leading to local shortages of wood, and some companies went out of business fast[19]. Most pressure was put upon the deciduous woodlands of southern Scotland but from the eighteenth century onwards some of the pinewoods were also exploited. As Scots pine will not coppice, the effects on these woods were dramatic. Large areas of pinewood were also felled to provide timber for the navy and as part of the English reprisals against the Highlanders after the 1745 Jacobite Rebellion. Within a few centuries, the forests of the Highlands had been destroyed.

In the early nineteenth century, the widespread and devastating Highland Clearances took place, in which thousands of people were evicted by their landlords and replaced with large flocks of sheep. For example, the ruined villages of Achanlochy and Rosal are all that remains of a population of some 3000 people in Strath Naver. Any scrub woodland remaining at that time would have been destroyed by the sheep flocks within a few years. Many of these areas in northern Scotland were converted into deer forests in the nineteenth century, when shooting became popular. As deer numbers have increased, they have posed problems for regeneration of the remaining woodlands. In other parts of Scotland and in England and Wales, the heather moorlands have been managed as grouse moors since the middle of the nineteenth century. This involves the rotational burning of the moors and has led to an increased dominance of heather, which is seen near the top of many pollen diagrams (Figure 5).

From the seventeenth century onwards, men such as Arthur Standish and John Evelyn had been exhorting landowners to make plantations to reinstate some of the lost woodland cover. Planting in Scotland was established in the seventeenth and eighteenth centuries by landowners such as the Dukes of Buccleuch and Atholl. Some of these plantations are still very fine, such as those in the Tay valley near Dunkeld. Exotic species were included, such as Wellingtonia or copper beech, but they were often intermixed with native trees. Plantations were made from the eighteenth century onwards in England and Wales, too, the trees chosen reflecting the fashion of the period: beech was popular in the eighteenth and nineteenth centuries; hornbeam, European larch and sycamore in the nineteenth century, and an enormous range of coniferous species in the twentieth century. The use of non-native species and the blanketing of parts of the uplands with conifer plantations have met with considerable opposition from the general public. However, these are merely the latest in a long series of changes in the uplands over the past 15,000 years, and they are unlikely to be the last.

References

1   Gelling, M, *Place-names in the landscape*. Dent, London, 1984.
2   Sheail, J, *Historical ecology: the documentary evidence*. Institute of Terrestrical Ecology, Cambridge, 1980.
3   Darby, H C, *Domesday England*. Cambridge University Press, Cambridge, 1977.
4   Turton, R B, *Honor and Forest of Pickering*. North Riding Record Society, New Series, Vols I-IV, 1894.
5   Ousby, I, *James Plumptree's Britain*. Hutchinson, London, 1992.
6   Andrews, C B and Andrews, F, *A selection from the tours of the Hon. John Byng (later Fifth Viscount Torrington) between the years 1781 and 1794*. Eyre and Spottiswoode, London, 1954.
7   Pennant, T, *A tour in Scotland; 1769*. Melven Press, Perth, Scotland, 1979 (first published 1774).
8   Defoe, D, *A tour through the whole island of Great Britain*. Penguin Classics, Harmondsworth, Middlesex, 1986. (first published 1724–6, London).
9   Hill, D, *In Turner's footsteps*. John Murray, London, 1984.
10 Shackley, M, *Environmental archaeology*. George Allen and Unwin, London, 1981.
11 Godwin, H, *History of the British flora* (second edition). Cambridge University Press, 1975.
12 Gray, J M and Lowe, J J (eds), *Studies in the Scottish Late-glacial environment*. Pergamon Press, 1977.
13 Smith, A G, The influence of Mesolithic and Neolithic man on British vegetation: a discussion. In Walker, D and West, R G (eds), *Studies in the vegetational history of the British Isles*, pp 81–96. Cambridge University Press, Cambridge, 1970.
14 Girling, M A, The bark beetle *Scolytus scolytus* (Fabricius) and the possible role of elm disease in the early Neolithic. In Jones, M (ed), *Archaeology and the flora of the British Isles*, pp 34–8. Oxford University Committee for Archaeology, Oxford, 1988.
15 Spratt, D A and Burgess, C, Upland settlement in Britain. The second millennium BC and after. *British Archaeological Reports*, British Series 143, Oxford, 1985.
16 Rackham, O, *Trees and woodland in the British landscape* (revised edition). Dent, London, 1990.
17 Lamb, H H, *Climate: Present, past and future*, 2 vols. Methuen, London, 1977.
18 Anderson, M L, *History of Scottish forestry*, vol 1. Thomas Nelson and Sons Ltd, London and Edinburgh, 1967.
19 Hinde, T, *Forests of Britain*. Gollancz, London, 1985.
20 Linnard, W, *Welsh woods and forests: history and utilization*. National Museum of Wales, Cardiff, 1982.

3

The mountain tops

Those mighty mountains mystical, that loll
And brag in space, and pay not any toll
To bat-eyed time. . . .

F V Branford

The physical environment

Nowhere is the impact of the physical environment on plant and animal life felt more keenly than on the tops of the highest mountains and hills. Here the effects of climate, slope and altitude combine to produce some of the severest and most challenging habitats for wildlife. Montane habitats lie above the potential limit of tree growth; the main areas are in the Scottish Highlands, with a smaller area in Snowdonia and fragments on the Southern Uplands, the Lake District and the northern Pennines.

Climate is the over-riding factor controlling plant growth and animal life at high altitude (Plates 6 and 7). British mountains are unusual in having very steep temperature lapse rates, caused by high humidity and cloudiness. Low winter temperatures pose a danger of frost damage to plant tissues, so only the hardiest plants can survive on exposed sites and much of the ground is bare. Plants prefer the insulation of a snow or ground cover during the coldest spells, most species surviving either as low-growing woody shrubs or as bulbs or corms. Another problem during the winter months is physiological drought as, although precipitation is high, much of it is in the form of snow or ice and not available to plants until it melts. The lack of water is exacerbated by the strong winds, which cause plants to lose moisture through transpiration. Many montane plants are adapted to resist drought, such as roseroot, which has a thick, fleshy rootstock.

In such an extreme climatic regime, the details of topography take on a critical role in providing variations in microclimate, such as shelter from the prevailing wind, a hollow where snow may collect or an aspect open to the summer sunshine. Slope is particularly important in affecting soil and moisture supply. The steepest slopes tend to have truncated soils, where material is removed from the surface as fast as it accumulates. Drainage is often excessive, especially on coarse-textured, porous rocks, such as sandstone. Vegetation grows most profusely where springs or late snow patches provide additional moisture.

As the temperature often falls below 0 °C in the winter, cycles of freezing and

PLATE 6 Summer in the Cairngorms. Arctic-alpine plants grow in clumps between the granite boulders. Late snow-patches persist in north-facing corries

PLATE 7 Winter in the Cairngorms. Plants survive under an insulating blanket of snow

thawing are common. They cause frost heave and move the soil particles around, sometimes upending larger stones. Many summit areas have frost-shattered rock debris and a mass of unsorted stones on the surface but some have patterned ground. On steeper slopes, solifluction takes place. This disturbs plant roots but may contribute valuable nutrients to replace those washed away by erosion. Larger rock fragments form screes on the steep slopes below eroding crags such as Glyder Fawr and Glyder Fach in Snowdonia. Instability and lack of organic matter make it very difficult for plants to survive.

The nutrient status of the soil is an important factor determining the richness of the mountain flora. Acidic rock types, such as sandstone, quartzite and granite, have a less diverse flora than those which are calcareous, as calcium is one of the key nutrients for plant growth. In the Scottish Highlands, the most varied plant growth occurs on the Dalradian limestones and schists of the Grampian Highlands, which include the exceptionally rich site of Ben Lawers, with its many botanical rarities. The limestone outcrops at Durness also have a rich calcareous flora. Serpentine rock has high levels of magnesium, which is toxic to most plants at such concentrations, so interesting and unusual plants may be found in areas like the Keen of Hamar on Shetland, where plants such as arctic sandwort and northern rock-cress grow. Calcareous sites are also found on some of the volcanic rocks of Snowdonia and on the metamorphosed sugar limestone of Upper Teesdale.

In the present climate, the potential limit of tree growth is about 600 metres in England and Wales, falling to near sea level on the north coast of Scotland, but factors such as grazing pressure mean that the actual tree-line is usually lower than the theoretical one. Plant communities similar to those found on the highest mountain tops may be found at much lower altitudes in the north-west of Scotland and some of the islands, such as Mull and Skye. Species such as dwarf birch, mountain sorrel and moss campion grow near sea level in northern Scotland and at high altitude inland. The wind is another important factor, reducing summer temperatures and limiting competition from other plants.

The present vegetation communities

There is a rich variety of plant communities in montane areas. The general zonation with increasing altitude is sub-montane scrub, followed by dwarf shrub heath or acidic grassland, giving way to snow-beds or arctic-alpine vegetation on the exposed summits (Figure 7). However, there are very few places where this sequence can still be seen. The most recent and comprehensive account of these vegetation types is provided by the National Vegetation Classification[1], but earlier descriptions include those of McVean and Ratcliffe[2], Tansley[3], Burnett[4] and Ratcliffe[5].

As woodland gives way to scrub vegetation, the trees become stunted and deformed in shape, especially where the wind is strong, and the canopy becomes more and more open to light. This enables the understorey shrubs to flourish, chief amongst which is juniper. The western seaboard of the Northern Highlands is the

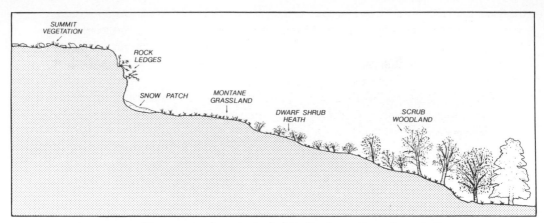

FIGURE 7 Diagram to show typical altitudinal zonation of vegetation

stronghold of the dwarf form, but it also grows on the Grampian Highlands. An unusual juniper scrub on calcareous soils occurs near Braemar in the Morrone Birkwoods National Nature Reserve. Juniper is uncommon elsewhere but it occurs sporadically on the Pennines, in the Lake District and in north Wales, mostly on cliff faces. Juniper scrub will not survive under prolonged snow cover, so thrives on areas blown clear of all but a few centimetres of snow in winter. Willows can also dominate the scrub vegetation and there are four species which are particularly characteristic of the Scottish Highlands. Unlike juniper, they can tolerate a fairly long snow cover in winter as well as a high degree of exposure. However, they are obviously susceptible to grazing, as most surviving examples of this vegetation type grow on inaccessible crags and ledges, for example in the Glen Clova region (Plate 8).

On acid soils the next altitudinal zone is usually dominated by dwarf shrub heaths. Many of them are grazed by sheep or red deer and some are shot over for grouse but the rotational burning, which is characteristic of grousemoors at lower altitudes, is practised less frequently on these high areas. This allows a greater variety of plant species to thrive alongside the dominant heather, including crowberry, bearberry, mountain bearberry, cloudberry, wavy hair-grass, deergrass and a ground layer of mosses and lichens. With increasing altitude, the heather adopts a prostrate growth form and other species gradually assume dominance, particularly bilberry or crowberry. Bilberry is deciduous and can survive even under prolonged snow cover. On blocky scree or areas of bare rock, the evergreen crowberry is more often dominant but bilberry may well grow alongside it. Crowberry is a tough woody shrub which can spread to colonise new ground as a low-growing mat. Most dwarf shrub heaths grow on acid rocks but one particularly interesting type occurs on calcareous soils over the Durness limestone. It is dominated by the attractive little white-flowered shrub, mountain avens (Plate 3). Very sensitive to grazing, this vegetation type is highly restricted today. Fragments occur on cliff ledges on the calcareous strata in the Breadalbane–Clova area and there is also an isolated occurrence on sugar limestone in Upper Teesdale.

PLATE 8 Rock ledge vegetation in Glen Clova, dominated by downy willow, with roseroot, great wood-rush, lady's-mantle, grasses and ferns over a carpet of mosses

The alternative to dwarf shrub heath in the montane zone is vegetation domi-nated by grasses, sedges or rushes. The commonest grass dominant is the mat-grass, whose pale, wiry stems give a bleached appearance to many of the grassy mountain tops. It grows in small tussocks and is not very palatable to domestic stock, so at lower altitudes its abundance is usually a sign of over-grazing. In montane habitats, its ability to withstand low temperatures and prolonged snow cover give it a competitive advantage. It is the dominant grass at all altitudes from 600 to 1200 metres and covers large areas in the Highlands, the Southern Uplands and the Lake District. It covers many high plateau areas in the Cairngorms, where it forms important winter fodder for mice and voles, which graze it beneath the snow cover. On wetter soils at high altitude the tufted hair-grass takes over dominance, forming large tussocks. It is particularly characteristic of the wetter western parts of the Highlands and also occurs in the Southern Uplands. Other areas are dominated by stiff sedge. Like the mat-grass, it can tolerate long snow-lie and occurs mainly in the central Highlands and the Cairngorms. In areas where strong winds allow only a light cover of snow to form, three-leaved rush may be dominant. It can tolerate a fair degree of instability in the soil. It is sometimes accompanied by viviparous sheep's-fescue, which can repro-duce vegetatively from small plantlets formed on the ends of stems – a useful strategy in habitats where pollination must be a chancy affair.

The climate of the tops of the highest mountains is often so extreme that grasslands and heaths give way to areas dominated by mosses, club-mosses or lichens. The woolly fringe-moss forms carpets on many Scottish mountain tops above 900 metres, sometimes being the only plant species present. It can withstand very low temperatures and very strong winds but will not tolerate a deep snow cover. Where the moss carpet is broken up by wind or frost, other plants have an opportun-ity to compete. They include some very rare species, such as diapensia and Iceland-purslane. Topographic hollows, such as corries where deep snow accumulates, pro-vide habitats for a range of snow-bed communities, usually dominated by mosses. As some of these snow-beds do not melt until mid-summer (June to August), the grow-ing season is too short for most plants. The melting snow provides moisture, so that the moss communities are usually saturated. The stronghold for these plant commu-nities is the Cairngorms, where they occur at altitudes between 900 and 1250 metres. Higher plants which can withstand these conditions are few but they include bilberry, stiff sedge and the dwarf willow, whose catkins appear on the prostrate shoots as soon as the snow melts.

Animal life

The native fauna of the mountain tops is limited by the severe winter climate and is generally much poorer than that of habitats at lower altitudes. Many of the larger animals are more characteristic of moorlands or woodlands and only occasionally stray on to montane areas. Mammals, birds, amphibians, reptiles and insects are all reasonably mobile and so are able to exploit a number of areas. The only truly montane mammal species in Britain is the mountain hare. Originally a native of the Scottish Highlands, it was introduced into the Hebrides, Northern Isles, Southern Uplands, Cheviots and the Peak District from the 1880s on, although the Grampian Highlands are still its main stronghold. Shorter and stockier than the brown hare, it has blue-grey fur in summer but sports a white coat in winter. This is an obvious camouflage device against its main predators, which are the golden eagle, fox and wild cat. It feeds mainly on heather shoots, so its distribution is linked to that of the dwarf shrub heaths.

Red deer are commonly to be seen in the lower part of the montane zone, although they were originally woodland animals. Large areas of the Highlands are deer forests, where herds are managed primarily as a sporting resource with the bonus of venison. Population numbers are usually strictly controlled by annual culling nowadays, which is necessary in the absence of natural predators such as the wolf. Most large Hebridean islands also have deer herds, one of the best studied being on Rhum[6]. Feral goats are also found on Rhum and also in Snowdonia, parts of Galloway and the Cheviots. The fox is an inhabitant of many different habitats and is the only widespread predator of the montane zone. Other large mammals which sometimes occur include the roe deer, rabbit, stoat, weasel, polecat, badger, pine marten and wild cat, but all are commoner at lower altitudes.

Small mammals are abundant in all areas up to 900 metres and can even thrive in late snow-beds. The field vole, bank vole, common and pygmy shrews, mole and wood mouse have all been recorded frequently. The common lizard has been recorded up to altitudes of 760 metres and the common frog up to 900 metres but amphibians and reptiles are not generally characteristic of the mountain top habitat. Many invertebrate groups include montane species, such as the mountain ringlet butterfly, netted mountain and Kentish glory moths (Colour plate 2).

The bird life of the uplands has received more attention than other animal groups[7]. Only three species are truly montane. The snow bunting nests in screes or rock crevices, while the dotterel prefers exposed plateaux and ridges. The ptarmigan nests in a variety of mountain habitats and, like the mountain hare, changes colour in the winter to avoid detection on snow-covered areas. Other bird species are not restricted to montane areas; for instance, many birds of prey include montane areas within their ranges. Perhaps the one which most people associate particularly with the mountains is the golden eagle. It nests mainly in the Highlands but there are a few pairs in Galloway and one pair has nested regularly in the Lake District since 1969, under guard from conservationists. The snowy owl nests on Shetland and is occasionally seen in the Cairngorms. Other raptors, such as the peregrine falcon, suffered decreases in numbers because of the use of pesticides in the 1950s and 1960s but their numbers are now recovering. Another characteristic bird of mountain tops throughout Britain is the raven (Plate 9), which nests on crags. In the Western Highlands, the hooded crow is common. Many other birds are characteristic of the dwarf-shrub heaths but are commoner on moorland areas below the potential tree limit.

PLATE 9 The raven, a characteristic bird of the mountain tops

The origin of the montane wildlife

As we have seen, some plants and animals are very restricted in their distributions today, being confined to habitats above the potential limit of tree growth. However, most of them were far more common and widespread in the Late-glacial period, when Britain experienced a colder climate and soils were skeletal. There is little direct evidence for animal groups other than beetles, but pollen analysis provides ample evidence for plants. Many species which today may only be found at high altitude, such as purple saxifrage or Iceland-purslane, grew in the lowlands as well as the uplands between 15,000 and 10,000 years ago. The severe climate and the lack of shade from trees and shrubs allowed them to compete successfully with other plants which would today prevent them from flourishing.

As the climate became warmer and soils stabilised in the early Post-glacial, the typical Late-glacial plants were replaced in most of Britain by woodland species and the only open habitats where arctic-alpine species could survive were above the tree-line. Later, when people began to clear the woodlands, grazing pressure from domestic stock prevented the montane plants from extending their range. Throughout the Post-glacial, they have been confined to the mountain tops, where the severe climate provides the nearest modern equivalent to Late-glacial conditions. However, there are notable differences, especially the greater degree of leaching of the soils and the higher grazing pressure. This has resulted in the concentration of some species in areas where erosion or frost heave enrich the soil with nutrients or on ledges and cliff faces inaccessible to grazing animals. Thus, in the montane flora today we see the surviving remnants of the once widespread flora of the Late-glacial. However, in many cases these relic communities have fewer species than their predecessors, as the reduction in habitat over the past 10,000 years has inevitably taken its toll.

The fragmented distributions and rarity of the surviving communities make them very vulnerable and many of them are under great threat today. The rare mountain top habitat which has allowed them to survive is very attractive to winter sports enthusiasts and rock climbers. The situation is most worrying in the Cairngorms, where major tourist developments have occurred since 1960 and further ones are proposed. Erosion has occurred on the ski runs and attempts at artificial regeneration have not been successful at high altitudes, as plant growth is very slow in such a marginal environment. The chair-lifts give access to the mountain tops in summer as well as winter, and trampling by walkers destroys plant growth and causes erosion on the most heavily used footpaths. The track to the summit of Cairngorm has had to be artificially reinforced. Walkers and cross-country skiers also disturb mammals, such as red deer, and nesting birds, such as ptarmigan and dotterel. In winter, this disturbance is particularly damaging, as animals can ill afford to expend energy in running away.

Thus the relics of the Late-glacial flora and fauna, which have managed to survive through the Post-glacial period in dwindling numbers on scarce mountain top habitats, are coming under increased pressure at the very time when people are beginning to appreciate their value. They represent a living link with the past – a precious resource which we should endeavour to preserve for the future. We shall close this chapter by considering two special areas where the montane flora has been studied in detail and where recent research has thrown light upon the origins of the plants and the factors necessary for their survival.

The Isle of Skye

The Isle of Skye is one of the best places in Britain to see montane habitats today and it includes many plant species which are Late-glacial relics. Despite its northerly latitude, temperatures are no lower than those of the foothills of Snowdonia, owing to the influence of the North Atlantic Drift. Mean monthly temperatures at sea level range from 1 to 15°C, with recorded extremes of −9 and 28°C, while temperatures on the mountain tops are about 6°C colder. Annual rainfall ranges from about 1400 mm to 3400 mm, increasing with altitude, but snowfall is notably lower than in the Cairngorms or Snowdonia. One of the most important limiting factors for plant growth is wind; gales are recorded on at least 20 days a year at sea level and up to 200 days a year on the mountain tops. Areas open to the prevailing westerly winds suffer a much greater degree of exposure than those sheltered by being to the east of higher ground. Thus, the climate is marginal for tree growth, and this allows herbaceous plants which are shade-intolerant or poor competitors to survive at relatively low altitudes. Where the effects of climate are combined with those of high altitude, some of Britain's rarest arctic-alpine species are found.

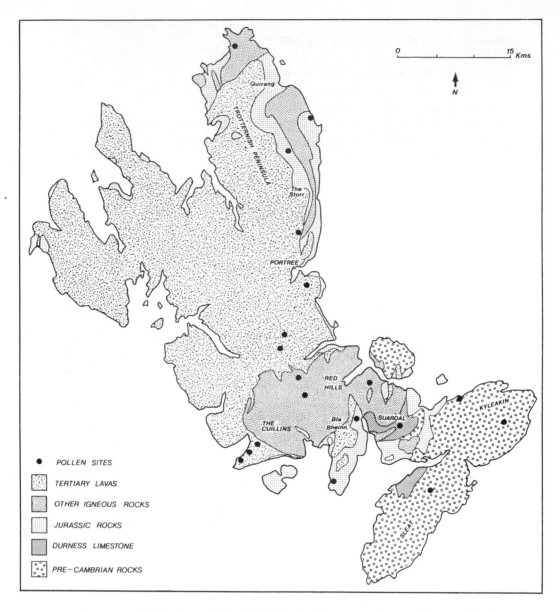

FIGURE 8 Geology of Skye (Solid circles show sites where pollen analysis has been carried out)

For an island of only 172,000 hectares, Skye has a tremendous range of geology and landforms (Figure 8). Most of the northern part of the island is composed of Tertiary volcanic rocks (basalt and gabbro), which dip towards the west from an impressive escarpment running north from Portree to the Storr and Quirang. Differences in the hardness of the various basalt layers give rise to an unusual stepped

PLATE 10 The impressive east-facing volcanic escarpment of the Trotternish peninsula, Skye

PLATE 11 Blanket bog and lochan in the Cuillins, Skye

topography (Plate 10). Underlying Jurassic sediments are exposed along the east coast of the Trotternish peninsula and in parts of central Skye. The mountainous core of the central part of the island is also composed of igneous rocks, but these are younger than the plateau lavas of the north, rising to 1000 metres in the Cuillins. In central Skye is a lower-lying area of Durness limestone, known as Suardal, which includes a few small areas of limestone pavement. The rolling hills of the Sleat peninsula and Kyleakins in south-east Skye are formed from older Pre-Cambrian rocks.

In the Ice Age, the Cuillins supported their own ice cap, which was sufficiently well developed to deflect ice flowing out from the Scottish mainland. Much of northern Skye is covered with glacial drift and there are also extensive areas of Post-glacial peat (Plate 11). The glacial history of the island has been studied by many workers, from 1846 to the present day. Not surprisingly, Skye has also attracted the attention of historical ecologists. Birks[8] carried out an intensive study of the past and present vegetation, a study built upon by more recent work[9]. From the results of pollen analyses carried out at 19 sites (Figure 8), it is possible to reconstruct much of the vegetation history of Skye from the Late-glacial period onwards.

During the early stages of the interstadial, pioneer communities of grasses and sedges covered most of the ground, with woody plants only existing in very sheltered spots. As temperatures rose, dwarf-shrub heath developed, dominated by crowberry, heathers and juniper. In areas sheltered from the strong westerly winds, birch and willow trees were able to grow. During the Loch Lomond stadial, ice covered approximately 180 square kilometres of south-central Skye and the Kyleakins. Glaciers flowed out from the mountains towards the coast, in some cases extending beyond the present coastline. Most of the woody plants died out and tundra vegetation was re-established, as in other parts of Britain.

The climate began its Post-glacial amelioration about 10,000 years ago. Pollen diagrams from Skye show a similar sequence of events to those seen in Scottish mainland sites, with tundra grassland replaced by crowberry heath, then juniper scrub and finally by birch–hazel woodland within about 1500 years. Again, shelter was an important factor and the most wooded parts of the island were the Sleat peninsula and Kyleakin Hills in the south-east, where the trees may have grown at altitudes of up to 610 metres in the middle Post-glacial. The limestone area of Suardal had ash–hazel woods on rich calcareous soils. Elsewhere, however, woodland was confined to isolated favourable areas, and the vegetation of much of northern Skye was heath, grassland or blanket bog.

This incomplete Post-glacial woodland cover enabled many of the Late-glacial plants to survive, particularly on the higher ground. Montane communities may be found today above 500 metres in the Kyleakins and Cuillins, and some montane species, such as mountain avens, descend to sea level. The diversity of rock types and relief gives rise to local variations in the flora, the basalt cliffs in the north being particularly rich in species, with tall-herb communities on cliff ledges, ferns and mosses in crevices and arctic-alpine plants in nooks and crannies on the cliff faces. As the snowfall is not particularly high, snow-patch vegetation is limited , but moss-heaths and sedge-heaths on exposed summits are more widespread. Gravel flushes on high ground in Trotternish form a habitat for the rare arctic plant, Iceland-purslane. Montane grasslands are widespread but usually species-poor, as soils are leached and acid. Dwarf juniper scrub occurs above 520 metres in the Cuillins and Red Hills of central Skye.

In these various montane habitats, 49 arctic-alpine species have been recorded[10]. The pollen or seeds of at least eleven of these have also been found in the peat/sediment cores from the Late-glacial period, which provides strong evidence for their survival on Skye throughout the Post-glacial period[8]. They include several familiar montane plants, such as the parsley fern, mountain avens, Iceland-purslane, dwarf willow, mountain sorrel and four species of saxifrage. They can be found growing now in situations where they have grown for the past 10,000 years.

Today, Skye provides a rare opportunity to study the sort of plant communities which were common at the end of the Ice Age, because so much of the island is inaccessible and lacks modern developments. The slopes in the Cuillins, for instance, are not suitable for skiing; there are few roads, so visitors can only penetrate the mountains by walking for several hours. Although much of the original scrubby woodland has been cleared over the centuries, farming is mainly traditional and non-intensive and there are many areas of semi-natural grassland and blanket bog with a rich plantlife. The greatest change is being brought about by afforestation, which is transforming much of central Skye into conifer forest. However, tourism is developing fast and is a very important source of employment now. Plans to link Skye with the mainland via a road bridge are well advanced, so the number of visitors is likely to increase rapidly over the next few years. The degree of disturbance to some of the montane habitats, especially those on the Trotternish peninsula, may pose a threat to the future survival of some of the rarities. In 1865, Smith wrote: 'to visit Skye is to make a progress into the dark backward and abysm of time. You turn your back on the present, and walk into antiquity[11]'. This is still true today but for how much longer?

Upper Teesdale

Our second case-study comes from an altitude of less than 700 metres in Upper Teesdale National Nature Reserve on the Pennines. A remarkable combination of climate, geology and human history has resulted in a unique set of ecosystems, elements of which can be traced back directly to the Late-glacial period. Here can be found one of the best juniper woods outside the Scottish Highlands and some of the rarest plants in Britain[12].

Whilst the climate cannot rival that of the Scottish Highlands, it is nevertheless severe. Mean monthly temperatures vary from 0 to 12.5°C but daily minima of −4°C are common as late as May and the lowest recorded temperature is −28°C. Ground frosts can occur in any month of the year. The area lies in the rain shadow of the main Pennine escarpment, receiving between 1000 and 1500 mm of precipita-

PLATE 12 The spectacular waterfall of High Force, formed by the Whin Sill, in Upper Teesdale

tion a year, much of which falls as snow in winter. Strong wind is another factor, posing problems of exposure for plants and animals and making the climate feel more extreme than it really is. This effect is exacerbated by the largely treeless nature of the present landscape, which has been produced by human activities, especially within the last 3000 years.

The underlying solid rocks date from the Lower Carboniferous period and consist of extensive limestones with sandstones, grits and shales and occasional thin coal beds. The large volcanic intrusion of the Whin Sill forms several dramatic water-falls, such as High Force (Plate 12) and Cauldron Snout, and cliffs, such as Falcon Clints. It has also altered the other rocks with which it came into contact, changing the limestone to a coarse crystalline marble, known as sugar limestone, the sandstones to white quartzite and the shales to a porcelain-like rock, known as whetstone. Mineral veins associated with this metamorphism include lead, zinc, fluorspar and barytes, and there was a thriving mining industry in Teesdale in the late nineteenth century.

Thick deposits of boulder-clay cover the solid rocks in the valleys. Soils differ according to the depth of the drift cover. Where it is more than 60 cm deep, they tend to be podzolised, with surface peaty layers, whilst over a thinner drift cover they are generally brown earths. Where there is less than 30 cm thickness of drift, the soils relate closely to the solid rocks below. Over limestones, thin calcareous soils are produced, whereas those on the Whin Sill outcrops are rich in bases, such as calcium and magnesium. On old mining spoil heaps, soils are contaminated with heavy metals, which provides a habitat for particular plant species tolerant of these conditions.

PLATE 13 Juniper scrub, a survivor from the Late-glacial period in Upper Teesdale

In this unusual physical environment, several interesting plant communities may be found. Juniper grows in an area of about 100 ha on the Whin Sill outcrop, varying from dense impenetrable scrub to isolated bushes (Plate 13). There is no apparent relationship with soil or topography but most of it is on the north-facing slope of the main valley, probably because this land was less valuable for growing agricultural crops. The juniper wood was used traditionally for thatching, as fire-lighters and to form the bases of hay-stacks. Many of the stands are even-aged and originated about AD 1900 but the part near High Force is of mixed ages and includes some bushes at least 200 years old[13]. This area has a fern-rich ground flora, reminiscent of juniper woods in the Scottish Highlands. None of the stands seems to be regenerating today, except occasionally by layering, when branches break, bend to the ground and take root. It may be that juniper needs burning in order to regenerate from seed, as has been shown in some of the Scottish woods. Experiments are being carried out to test the effects of various management practices, including burning, coppicing and dragging out cut branches, in the hope of discovering the secret of good regeneration.

The flora of Upper Teesdale has long been famous for its rarities. Pigott listed 75 species, many of which were already known by 1805[12]. One, the shrubby cinquefoil, was mentioned by John Ray in 1670. Baker listed 32 rare species in 1868 and others were discovered in the late nineteenth century, including some which have since disappeared. The twentieth century has seen the addition to the list of species such as the rare spring-sedge and dwarf birch, together with several rare hawkweeds, lady's-mantles and mosses. The rarities are known collectively as the Teesdale assemblage. About a third of them may be described as arctic-alpine or alpine species, such as mountain avens and spring gentian (Colour plate 4). For some northerly species, Teesdale is their southernmost location in Britain, whilst others have continental or southerly distributions. For the Teesdale sandwort, this is the only British station. What factors have led to this extraordinary assemblage of species, growing together in Upper Teesdale today?

Godwin was the first to suggest that the Teesdale assemblage might be a relic of the Late-glacial period, when the unusual climate, immature soils and lack of shade enabled the species to grow together. Over twenty pollen diagrams have been published from peat deposits in the area, the earliest dating from the end of the Late-glacial period[14]. Grasses and sedges dominated an open herbaceous vegetation, the only woody species recorded being juniper, dwarf birch and willows. Over 30 other pollen types included several of the rare species, such as mossy saxifrage, starry saxifrage and moonwort. By about 8800 years ago, the juniper woodland had been replaced by birch and hazel, with pine spreading from the Tees basin on to the fells. Other trees then immigrated, including oak, elm and alder. By about 8000 years ago, woodland was well established up to altitudes of 760 metres, as is confirmed by tree trunks buried in the peat on the fells. On limestone areas, hazel was probably the most abundant species, but the area now occupied by the Cow Green reservoir was a stronghold for pine. The rare spring-sedge, which still grows nearby today, is a pinewood species.

By 5000 years ago, pine had more or less died out, oak and alder were becoming more important and blanket peats were starting to spread on the higher ground. There is some evidence on the pollen diagrams for minor effects on the local forests from mesolithic people using fire as part of their hunting activities. The first cereal pollen grains are recorded soon after 5000 years ago and a major forest clearance is seen at many sites about 3000 years ago. By the Iron Age, most of the woodland on the fells had been replaced by grassland or heath and blanket bog was spreading further. Despite a minor regeneration of woodland in Roman times, the landscape remained basically open from then on. The upper dale was part of the Royal Forest of Teesdale in medieval times, but it was also used for grazing stock. The grazing pressure and occasional use of burning led to the maintenance of grasslands and heaths on the higher ground, the impact increasing from the seventeenth century onwards.

Thus the range of habitats available for plant growth has changed considerably over the last 10,000 years. For species which were common in the Late-glacial, the biggest problem of the Post-glacial was the development of the forest cover. However, the pollen diagrams show tree pollen comprising no more than 50 per cent of the total pollen, which suggests that closed woodland did not cover the whole area. Even at the period of maximum forest development, between 8000 and 5000 years ago, records have been found for some of the rare species, including dwarf birch, mountain avens, spring gentian and hoary rock-rose. Juniper is also recorded from the mid-Post-glacial.

Many rarities are found today on the sugar limestone, where the thin, easily eroded soil may have given a competitive advantage to species such as the spring gentian and Teesdale violet. Others, such as Scottish asphodel, bird's-eye primrose and Teesdale sandwort, may have survived on marshy ground. As the impact of grazing gradually increased over the past 5000 years or so, grasslands and moorlands spread, enabling some species to extend their ranges. For instance, there are pollen records from the past 5000 years for sea plantain, alpine bistort and cloudberry. Other plants, such as Teesdale violet and alpine penny-cress, have found a niche on the mining spoil heaps. As a result of all these factors, the Teesdale rarities have survived and may indeed be more abundant today than at any time since the Late-glacial period.

However, the area faced a major threat in the late 1960s, when the growth of industry on Teesside led firms such as ICI to seek additional sources of water. Upper Teesdale was eventually chosen as the most suitable site for a new reservoir, despite protests from environmentalists. The issue became a major controversy and, owing to the inexperience of the conservation lobby and the lower profile which nature conservation had in those days, the industrialists won the day. However, money was made available for research before the area was flooded and a great deal of extremely valuable work was carried out, including pollen analyses from sites which were later flooded, vegetation mapping, and research into the reproductive potential of some of the rare plants. Populations of some of the rarities were transplanted to botanic gardens for further experimental work and propagation. In 1970, the dam was finished and a 4.8 km stretch of the River Tees at Cow Green was flooded. The reservoir destroyed 8.5 ha of the unique mosaic of habitats in Upper Teesdale, comprising up to 10 per cent of the limestone grassland communities and significant proportions of the plants which grew in the sedge marshes and on mining spoil heaps. The scheme also had other effects on the flora; for instance, the reduced frequency of flooding downstream from the dam has adversely affected the spread of the shrubby cinquefoil, which grows on shingle banks and alluvium and relies on floods to transport its seeds to new areas.

It is ironic that within a few years industrial recession had hit Teesside and a vast new reservoir had been built in the Kielder Forest of Northumberland, which could have supplied all the water needed for the remaining industries. The flow of the River Tees over the High Force waterfall has been less spectacular since the dam was built but the Cow Green reservoir itself has formed an alternative tourist attraction. As the wind whips across the water, it erodes from the banks yet more of the precious sugar limestone grasslands. Nature trails, car parks and toilet blocks have been constructed to help the general public enjoy the remaining areas of interest. But for some of the plant communities which had survived 10,000 years of changing climate, soils and vegetation cover, 1970 marked the end of an era.

References

1   The National Vegetation Classification is published in 5 volumes: Rodwell, J (ed), *British plant communities*. Cambridge University Press, 1991 *et seq.*
2   McVean, D N and Ratcliffe, D A, *Plant communities of the Scottish Highlands*. Monographs of the Nature Conservancy 1, HMSO, London, 1962.
3   Tansley, A G, *The British Islands and their vegetation*. Cambridge University Press, 1939.

4   Burnett, J H (ed), *The vegetation of Scotland*. Oliver and Boyd, 1964.
5   Ratcliffe, D A, *A nature conservation review*. Cambridge University Press, 1977.
6   Clutton-Brock, T H and Ball, M E, *Rhum: the natural history of an island*. Edinburgh University Press, 1987.
7   Ratcliffe, D A, *Bird life of mountain and upland*. Cambridge University Press, 1990.
8   Birks, H J B, *Past and present vegetation of the Isle of Skye*. Cambridge University Press, 1973.
9   Walker, M J C and Lowe, J J, A reinterpretation of the Lateglacial environmental history of the Isle of Skye, Inner Hebrides, Scotland. *Journal of Quaternary Science*, 3, pp 135–46, 1988. Walker, M J C and Lowe, J J, Reconstructing the environmental history of the last glacial-interglacial transition: evidence from the Isle of Skye, Inner Hebrides, Scotland. *Quaternary Science Reviews*, 9, pp 15–49, 1990.
10 Murray, C W and Birks, H J B, *The botanist in Skye*, (2nd edn). Botanical Society of the British Isles, 1980.
11 Smith, A, *A summer in Skye*. Nimmo, Hay and Mitchell, Edinburgh, 1912.
12 Clapham, A R (ed), *Upper Teesdale: The area and its natural history*. Collins, London, 1978.
13 Gilbert, O L, Juniper in Upper Teesdale. *Journal of Ecology*, 68, pp 1013–24, 1980.
14 Turner, J et al, The history of the vegetation and flora of Widdybank Fell and the Cow Green reservoir basin, Upper Teesdale. *Philosophical Transactions of the Royal Society of London*, Series B, 265, pp 327–408, 1973.

Fen Bog, North York Moors, one of the key sites for pollen analysis

The Kentish glory, a rare moth of the Scottish Highlands

Purple saxifrage in the Brecon Beacons, a Late-glacial plant now confined to montane habitats

The spring gentian, one of the best known of the Late-glacial relics in Upper Teesdale

A carpet of bluebells in a typical coppiced woodland

Gnarled old oak trees over bracken and mossy boulders in Wistman's Wood, Dartmoor

Heather moorland, North York Moors. Purple bell heather and pink cross-leaved heath flower in the foreground. Heather in the background has been burned in patches. A narrow strip of closely grazed grassland adjoins the road

The green hairstreak, a common butterfly on moorlands, feeding on bilberry

4

Scottish pinewoods

All through the forest, which then measured in extent nearly twenty square miles, small rivers ran with sometimes narrow strips of meadow land beside them ... up towards the mountains the mass of fir broke into straggling groups of trees at the entrance of the Glens which ran far up among the bare rocky crags of the Grampians. Here and there upon the forest streams rude sawmills were constructed, where one or at most two trees were cut up into planks at one time ... nearer to the Spey the fir wood yielded to banks of lovely birch ... yet over all hung the wild charm of nature, mountain scenery in mountain solitude beautiful under every aspect of the sky.

Elizabeth Grant of Rothiemurchus, 1807

Extent and distribution

The Scottish Highlands are the only parts of Britain where it is possible to see native coniferous forest, dominated by the Scots Pine. With its tall reddish trunk, blue-green foliage and irregular outline, it forms a characteristic and much loved element of the traditional highland landscape. However, as we shall see, its present distribution is much reduced from its former extent and the pinewood community is very different from the 'Great Caledonian Forest' in its heyday.

In 1959, Steven and Carlisle published a detailed and systematic account of the native pinewoods of Scotland, which has become the classic work of reference[1]. By consulting historical records from the sixteenth century onwards and studying the present woodland composition and structure, they were able to identify 35 pinewoods which they considered to be native, that is, derived from the natural woods of the past. Later work by McVean and Ratcliffe [2], Burnett[3] and Bunce[4], has confirmed the native status of these sites and their approximate extent. In the denser stands, the tree canopy forms up to 70 per cent cover, but in other woods it may be as little as 25 per cent[5]. If a fairly loose definition is used, including marginal areas and other habitats within the general area of pinewood, the area of land covered is approximately 10,720 ha, but only about 1600 ha consist of relatively dense stands of woodland.

Some of these are isolated woods in the midst of heather moorland or grassland, such as those on the shores of Loch Maree; others are surrounded by modern coniferous plantations, such as those in Glenmore. The distribution of the main

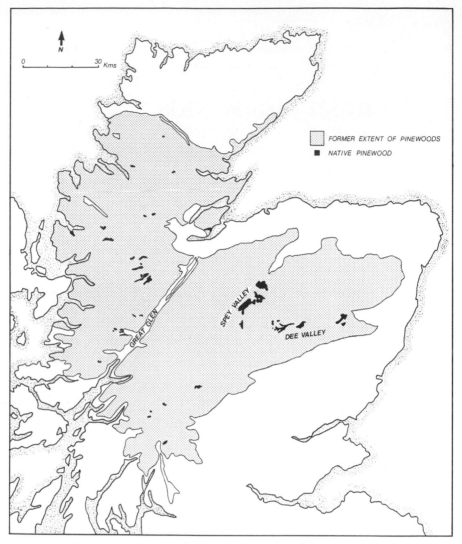

FIGURE 9 Surviving remnants of native pinewood, and former approximate extent
in Scotland (Based on the work of McVean and Ratcliffe,[2] O'Sullivan[7] and others,
and information from P R Cundill)

native remnants is shown in Figure 9, which sets them in the context of the area
thought to have been formerly covered by native pinewood. The greatest extent of
such woodland remnants lies in the valleys of the rivers Spey and Dee, with the
largest blocks surviving in Abernethy Forest. Another group of pinewoods is to be
found in the Great Glen, while smaller patches exist in the Northern Highlands. Some
of these woods are managed by the Forestry Commission but most are in private
hands; many of them are now afforded some degree of protection as Sites of Special
Scientific Interest or nature reserves.

Plant and animal life

The range of variation within the vegetation of the pinewoods is comparatively small, and all are now grouped into one category in the National Vegetation Classification[5]. However, McVean and Ratcliffe recognised two distinct types, based on the ground flora. In moderately dense pinewoods, where occasional birch or rowan are the only other trees, the ground flora is usually dominated by bilberry and mosses, with cowberry and wavy-hair grass. A particular feature of many of these woods (and of some pine plantations) is creeping lady's-tresses, an attractive orchid with white flowers arranged spirally up the stem. In more open woods with a mixture of pine and birch, sometimes with holly and juniper, the main ground flora species are heather and bilberry (Plate 14). The heather is often tall and woody and interspersed with hummocks of *Sphagnum* mosses in wetter patches. Where the trees are even less dense, this type of woodland gives way to pine heath vegetation, with scattered trees over a well-developed ground flora of heather moorland species (Plate 15).

The total number of plant species in the pinewoods is not high compared with that in deciduous woodlands. Several grasses and ferns occur, together with herbs such as wood-sorrel, wood anemone, common cow-wheat and chickweed wintergreen. Boggy patches have cottongrasses, rushes, bog-myrtle and mosses. There are several rarities, many of which are also associated with pinewoods in Scandinavia, such as coralroot orchid, twinflower and one-flowered wintergreen. The soils underlying pinewoods are usually podzolised, with a thick layer of mor humus at the surface. Sometimes there is a fragmentary iron pan, but this is less well developed than under heather moorland, as the pine roots tend to break it up.

The fauna of the pinewoods overlaps considerably with that of other habitats but there are some species particularly associated with this vegetation type. The mammal fauna is less diverse than formerly, mainly owing to human activities. The commonest large mammals today are the otter, fox, roe deer and red deer. Some of these, particularly the red deer, are so common nowadays that they pose a serious threat to the continued existence of the pinewoods. There are over 300,000 red deer in Scotland and they have to be controlled by culling. Less common are the pine marten, red squirrel, badger and wild cat. Small mammals, such as field vole, wood mouse, stoat and weasel, are more plentiful, partly because some of their predators have been eliminated or reduced in numbers.

Over 70 species of bird regularly breed in the Scottish pinewoods but many of them depend on habitats other than the trees, such as clearings, boggy patches or open water. The commonest birds are the chaffinch and the wren, followed by the goldcrest, coal tit, robin and willow warbler, all of which are widespread species in the uplands. However, there are three species for which the pinewoods form more or less the only habitat, namely the capercaillie, the crested tit and the Scottish crossbill, the only endemic British bird species. The siskin is also very characteristic of the pinewoods and has recently been expanding its range into coniferous plantations in other parts of Britain.

PLATE 14 Native Scots pine over juniper, with a ground flora of heather, Rothiemurchus Forest

PLATE 15 Scots pine regenerating on pine heath, Rothiemurchus Forest

There has been less research on the invertebrates but the beetles have received some attention. A survey in the 1970s found 129 species associated mainly with pine in Great Britain, 106 of which occurred in Scotland[6]. Forty-four of these species were restricted mainly to native pinewoods and some of them were very rare. For most of them, it is the wood itself which is the most important habitat, including trunks, branches, twigs and rotting stumps, and some are particularly attracted to burnt wood. The survival of these species is bound up with woodland management practices and they find modern plantations far less attractive, owing to the lack of old and dead trees.

The pollen record

As we saw in chapter 2, by about 7000 years ago, pine had been out-competed by deciduous trees such as oak and elm in England, Wales and southern Scotland but survived in the Scottish Highlands. Much work has been carried out in recent years to discover the reasons for this. Pollen analysis is the most useful tool and pollen diagrams now exist for practically all areas of Scotland, including many of the islands[7]. The key period seems to have been the early Post-glacial. Scotland was probably the last part of Britain to gain a woodland cover, being furthest away from the sources of immigration of most tree species. The climate was also cooler and wetter than further south, so there was considerable potential for leaching of the soils in the thousand or so years before tree roots were present to counteract it. Pine expanded its range and established itself in the Scottish Highlands in the relatively warm and dry period between about 8000 and 6500 years ago, being well suited to the climate and leached soils. It successfully maintained dominance there and out-competed most deciduous trees, except alder, which spread locally on to wet ground beside lochs and in river valleys, reaching its maximum extent between 7000 and 5000 years ago.

Thus, in the middle Post-glacial, when most of Britain was covered with deciduous woodland, the Scottish Highlands were still dominated by pine and birch, with alder in wet areas and trees such as rowan, aspen, willow and bird cherry playing a subordinate role. This was the heyday of the Scottish pinewoods and they covered a greater extent than before or since. Buried pine stumps (Plate 16) show that the woodland grew up to an altitude of about 700 metres in the Cairngorms, with isolated trees reaching at least 770 metres. This is considerably higher than the present tree limit of about 550 metres, with stragglers to 640 metres. McVean and Ratcliffe attempted to map the former extent of the pine forest, based on tree stump evidence and pollen diagrams. More recent work has led to refinement of their map (Figure 9). Pinewoods extended in the north-west of Scotland as least as far as Loch Sionascaig and in the north-east to about the latitude of Helmsdale. In the extreme north of Scotland they gave way to birch woodland and finally to open herbaceous communities. For a short time about 4800 to 3900 years ago, pine may have extended even further north, as tree stumps of this age have recently been discovered

PLATE 16 Pine stumps buried beneath blanket peat, Galloway

as far north as Loch Strathy. However, there is little evidence to suggest that pine was ever important on the Scottish islands, although some pine stumps have been reported from Lewis.

The last 4000 years have seen a decrease in the area dominated by pinewoods, especially in the Northern Highlands. Here, blanket peat started to form in the wet climate of the middle Post-glacial and pine found it increasingly difficult to regenerate. It is this spread of blanket peat which has led to the preservation of some of the pine stumps, as the stumps will rot away unless covered by peat within a fairly short time. A deterioration of the climate in the first millennium BC led to the further increase of peat in the Northern Highlands at the expense of pine. Only a few pinewoods remained in particularly favourable spots, such as well-drained sunny slopes and sheltered valleys, as at Coulin, Shieldaig and the lower slopes of Beinn Eighe. Thus, pine cannot really be regarded as the natural vegetation cover in most of the Northern Highlands today, as its demise has been a largely natural process.

In the Grampian Highlands, on the other hand, the situation is different. Here, the climate is not so conducive to the development of blanket bog, and pine forest would still be dominant over most of the area, had it not been for human intervention. It is not known whether Mesolithic people had any effects on the pinewoods, but, if they were using fire in their hunting activities, this may have aided the regeneration of pine (see below). From late Neolithic times onwards, the first indications of woodland clearance appear on the pollen diagrams, but most effects are on the deciduous forests of lowland Scotland, which offered the best soils for agriculture. Generally, the effects of prehistoric people on the pinewoods are less marked than is the case with deciduous woodlands further south, suggesting that the Scottish Highlands were not particularly attractive areas for prehistoric settlement and agriculture.

Historical records

The first documentary record of the Scottish Highlands is a map drawn by Ptolemy in the second century AD, which shows a woodland area, labelled 'Caledonia Silva', between Loch Long and the Beauly Firth. This map is not noted for its geographical accuracy but it does at least show that the Romans knew of the existence of a distinctive type of woodland in the area beyond their jurisdiction. Some effects on the pinewoods may have been felt from the activities of the Picts and Scots who inhabited the area but there is very little evidence. From the Dark Ages onwards, the human impact gradually increased, as population and agriculture expanded. In medieval times, large areas of land, including areas of pinewood, were granted to monasteries, such as the abbeys at Dunkeld, Elgin and Arbroath. However, it was still the lowland deciduous woodlands which were most attractive for both agriculture and exploitation as firewood. Indeed, fourteenth century sources describe the Highland pinewoods as being full of wild animals, and they were probably avoided until lack of resources elsewhere forced people to turn to them. In the seventeenth century, General Monk ordered woods near Aberfoyle to be cut down because they were harbouring both wolves and thieves, and other woods, for example in Rannoch, Atholl, Lochaber and Loch Awe, were also partly destroyed because of the supposed prevalence of wolves[8].

A greater threat to the pine forests came from the spread of the iron industry to Scotland in the seventeenth century. Shortages of wood further south led the iron-masters to turn their attention to Scotland. In 1609, an Act of Parliament was passed restricting the activities of the iron mills but this led to a thriving black market[9]. Despite the law, bloomeries were established as far north as Strath Naver and Loch Maree, and large iron works at Carron and Falkirk also took wood from the Highlands. Oak and birch made better charcoal but pine was used as well and the effects on the pine trees must have been dramatic, as they do not regenerate from felled stools as deciduous species do. The felling increased after the Jacobite Rebellion of 1745 was put down. Many Highland estates were forfeited to English lords and some of them sold off their woods for smelting purposes – an early example of asset stripping. The iron industry continued to make inroads into the pinewoods until the early nineteenth century.

Meanwhile, other uses had also been found for the pine trees. In the seventeenth century it was discovered that the tall straight pine trunks were ideally suited as masts of ships for the navy. Areas near Loch Arkaig and Ardgour were amongst those to be exploited, the logs being floated down the rivers and into the sea-lochs for export. Canals, lochs and log collection basins were constructed. Elizabeth Grant of Rothiemurchus described the development of the timber industry in the Spey valley from the 1790s onwards[10]. The peak of exploitation was reached during the Napoleonic Wars, when there was a high duty imposed on foreign imports, and many of the Speyside and Deeside forests were felled. The advent of the railways brought further devastation to some areas, as sparks from the locomotives caused fires in the remaining woodlands. Other woods were deliberately destroyed to improve the sheep grazing. Finally, in the twentieth century, inroads into the surviving fragments of pinewood were made during the two world wars, for example in the Spey valley and at Kinlochewe, whilst Locheil Old Forest was destroyed in commando training.

It is, perhaps, surprising that any areas of pine forest have survived the impact of the last four hundred years. However, such remnants as those in Abernethy Forest have avoided destruction, as is shown by a pollen diagram from a site in one of them, where a clear dominance of pine is shown for the last 8000 years, with only a short-lived clearance phase in the early nineteenth century[7]. The proportion of heather on some pollen diagrams shows a gradual increase over the last few centuries, indicating a change in the ground flora within the woods or the spread of heather moorland on areas outside them.

The pinewoods today

As a result of this long history of natural change and exploitation, the pinewoods have not only been vastly reduced in extent but also greatly modified in nature, so that the surviving remnants of native pinewood differ in several important ways from their predecessors. Firstly, their age-structure is usually different from that of a natural woodland, owing to felling activities in the past and grazing pressure limiting regeneration. The original woodlands would have had an uneven age structure, with many seedlings and saplings, as well as mature trees and some senescent ones. However, today it is unusual to find more than two age classes present and many populations are very top-heavy with an unnaturally high proportion of mature and old trees. McVean and Ratcliffe found three common age structures[2]. The first was more or less even-aged stands, where all the trees had regenerated at one time, perhaps following clearance or a severe forest fire or storm. The second type had two generations present, typically a small number of trees more than 150 years old and a larger generation 80 to 100 years old. Thirdly, there were the pine heaths, where the trees tended again to be all of one age class. Sites with a greater mixture of ages are rare, but notable examples occur in Abernethy Forest, in Glen Tanar on Deeside and in the Kirkconnell Flow National Nature Reserve in Galloway.

Another difference from natural woods is the proportion of dead wood present. In the original pine forests, there would have been dead standing timber as well as plenty of dead wood lying around on the ground, providing a habitat for a wide range of fungi, ferns and invertebrates and nesting sites for birds such as woodpeckers. Many surviving remnants of native pinewoods are managed as nature reserves but, where they have been subsumed in modern plantations, modern management practices tend to remove much of the dead wood. One survey conducted in the 1970s found an average of only 6 per cent dead wood present[11].

Today, pine is dominant over all other tree and shrub species, and some pollen diagrams from Deeside show a similar pattern throughout most of the Post-glacial. However, in other areas, pollen analysis suggests that this dominance was less marked in the past. Although pine may have been the commonest tree species, it was nearly always accompanied by birch, so that most of the forests of, say, 6000 years ago were really mixed rather than coniferous ones. As well as birch, there were other deciduous trees, such as aspen, rowan, willow and bird cherry, and some woods had a shrub layer of juniper or holly. Occasional remnants of these more mixed woods survive at places such as Morrone near Braemar and Tullich Glen on Deeside.

Under the original mixed pine–birch woodlands, soils would have been more fertile than they are under the pure pine stands of today. Scots pine tends to promote podzolisation, with its acid litter, relatively shallow roots and heath-type ground flora. However, the deciduous trees would have counteracted this, with their more extensive root systems and richer ground flora to recycle nutrients from the sub-soil. Some sort of acid brown earth soils would have developed, and the loss of nutrients through leaching would not have been very great. Although there might have been a slightly acid layer of leaf litter, including pine needles, on the surface, it is unlikely to have been the deep mor humus layer that is characteristic of most pinewoods today. Pollen analysis and radiocarbon dating have shown that the mor humus layer in Abernethy Forest is at least 1000 years old[7]. It has been gradually building up over the centuries, locking up many of the valuable plant nutrients, such as phosphorus. In places, its water-retaining capacity has led to the development of a real peaty layer at the soil surface, colonised by bog plants and mosses. Thus, although the soils of the Scottish Highlands were always marginal for trees such as oak and elm, they were only mildly acidic in the past, whereas today podzolised and gleyed profiles are widespread.

Changes to animal populations

Alongside the changes in the vegetation and soils of the pinewoods, alterations to the animal populations were occurring. The large mammal fauna of the original pinewoods included several species which are now extinct there. One of the early casualties was the European lynx, which may have suffered from prehistoric hunting activities, as its bones have been found in a cave site near Inchnadamph in association with Neolithic hearths. The elk died out about AD 1300, owing to destruction of its habitat and hunting. The brown bear and wild boar lingered on until the seventeenth century in northern Scotland, long after they had become extinct further south. The beaver was hunted for its skin and also became extinct in the seventeenth century[12].

The native polecat is now extinct in Scotland, although modern escaped ferrets occupy a similar niche. The wolf was exterminated as a perceived danger to man and the last one was killed in the late eighteenth century. Wolf hounds were used for hunting until the sixteenth century and wolf skins were exported from ports such as

Inverness. Other mammals have suffered reductions in their populations, including the badger and pine marten, although the latter is spreading in modern coniferous plantations. The wild cat is a rare sight nowadays but is holding its own in the more remote pinewoods. Feral domestic cats sometimes inter-breed with it and constitute a threat to its survival as a distinct species.

Birds have also suffered from the changes in the pinewood habitat. The capercaillie became extinct in the 1770s but was successfully re-introduced in the nineteenth century. Numbers of many birds of prey, such as golden eagle and common buzzard, were severely reduced by gamekeeping from the nineteenth century onwards, the birds being trapped, shot or poisoned to reduce their predation on game-bird chicks. The use of pesticides in the twentieth century also took its toll, but numbers of most raptors are now increasing, following legislation to protect them.

As many of the predatory mammals and birds declined, numbers of their prey species often expanded, upsetting the ecological balance. Red and roe deer have both increased and the former is now threatening the very survival of many pinewoods. Deer not only browse the foliage but also fray and eat the bark of young pine trees. Documentary evidence illustrates the rise in red deer numbers in the pinewoods on the Mar estate, near Braemar[13]. The diaries of the Earl of Fife from 1783 to 1792, together with estate records for the nineteenth and twentieth centuries, show that deer numbers increased rapidly from the late eighteenth century onwards, following eviction of sheep farmers to improve the shooting value of the estate. Most pine trees in the area originated between about 1760 and 1820, when deer numbers were still moderate, and there has been virtually no regeneration since then except within fenced areas.

Problems of regeneration

Grazing by sheep and deer is a very important factor limiting the regeneration of many pinewoods today. Small mammals, such as voles and mice, also play their part, eating pine seeds or seedlings, and squirrels and crossbills attack the pine cones. The reduction in numbers of species near the top of the food chain has meant that populations of grazers and small mammals are no longer controlled. Experiments have shown that Scots pine produces plenty of viable seed in the Highlands, but the high predation rates at the seed, seedling and sapling stages make it very difficult for the tree to regenerate[14]. Areas which have been fenced to exclude at least the larger grazers, have shown good regeneration not only of pine but also of its companion species, such as birch, rowan and willow. Examples can be seen in the forests of Abernethy, Rannoch, Crannach and elsewhere. However, the high cost of deer fencing is often prohibitive and many woods remain unfenced and therefore unable to regenerate.

Other factors add to the grazing pressure to limit regeneration, particularly the podzolised soils and thick mor humus layer. Where the ground flora is dominated by bilberry and mosses, the deep layer of mor humus and moss is not ideal for germination and seedling survival. In dry weather it becomes desiccated, whereas in wet weather it may be waterlogged. In woods where the ground flora is dominated by bilberry and heather, the latter tends to out-compete pine seedlings for essential nutrients, especially phosphorus, which is often in short supply. Where heather is dense, neither pine nor birch can readily regenerate. Growth of pine seedlings is usually aided by infection of their roots by a particular fungus, which helps to supply nutrients to the young trees, but if the fungus is absent pine growth is slow.

In the past, natural forest fires may have limited the build-up of the ground flora and mor humus. By removing competing species and recycling nutrients, fire creates a perfect seedbed for pine and good regeneration has been observed to follow three to five years later. Many other species of pine, especially the North American ones, are dependent on fire, their cones only opening to release the seeds after fire temperatures have been experienced. It seems likely that Scots pine is at least partly fire-adapted, too, regenerating best after fire, although capable of releasing its seeds without it. Lightning may have created fires, especially in the warmer, drier period when pine showed its main expansion in Scotland. Lightning or accidental fires have sometimes been a feature of pinewoods in more recent times; for instance, there is evidence of six major fires in Glen Tanar between 1688 and 1920[12]. However, the modern tendency is to control fires, and this may work to the disadvantage of pine by facilitating the build-up of large quantities of flammable ground vegetation. When accidental fires do occur, they may be so severe that even the mature trees are killed, as happened near Carrbridge in 1976.

Lastly, the even-aged structure of many modern pinewoods poses yet more problems for regeneration. Pine seedlings are dependent on light and do not grow well under the dense, dark canopy of mature pine trees. In the natural mixed forests, the areas under deciduous trees, together with clearings where old trees had fallen, would have provided opportunities for pine seedlings to become established. It is probable that the boundaries of the original pinewoods shifted with time, giving a mosaic of mature forest, clearings and areas of regeneration. The fact that many of the surviving pinewood remnants are hemmed in by modern plantations or agricultural land may make it virtually impossible for the present generation of trees to replace themselves.

The outlook for the surviving native pinewoods is not a particularly rosy one, despite the fact that most of them are Sites of Special Scientific Interest or nature reserves and they have been the subject of recent appeals, such as the Findhorn Foundation's 'Trees for Life' project. Not only have they been reduced to a fraction of their former extent but their characteristics and associated wildlife have been so modified over the years as to make it very difficult for them to regenerate successfully. Their fragmentation also means that populations have become isolated and their gene-pools are thus limited. Research on the genetic variation between pine trees in Scotland has established that there are several distinct groups of pinewoods, including a north-western group, a south-western group and two groups on Speyside[15]. Pine trees in surrounding plantations, often grown from foreign seed, pose a threat to the native stock through the potential which they provide for hybridisation. Exclusion zones have now been established to try to prevent such genetic mixing but, without some drastic management measures, it may not be possible to claim for much longer that there are any true survivors of the native pinewoods which were once the glory of the Scottish Highlands.

References

1   Steven, H M and Carlisle, A, *The native pinewoods of Scotland*. Oliver and Boyd, 1959.

2   McVean, D N and Ratcliffe, D A, *Plant communities of the Scottish Highlands*. HMSO, London, 1962.

3   Burnett, J H (ed), *The vegetation of Scotland*. Oliver and Boyd, 1964.

4   Bunce, R G H, The range of variation within the pinewoods. In Bunce, R G H and Jeffers, J N R (eds), *Native pinewoods of Scotland*, pp 10–25. Institute of Terrestrial Ecology, Cambridge, 1977.

5   Rodwell, J S (ed), *British plant communities: vol. 1, Woodlands and scrub*. Cambridge University Press, Cambridge, 1991.

6   Hunter, F A, Ecology of pinewood beetles. In Bunce, R G H and Jeffers, J N R (eds), *Native pinewoods of Scotland*, pp 42–55, 1977.

7   O'Sullivan, P E, Vegetation history and the native pinewoods. In Bunce, R G H and Jeffers, J N R (eds), *Native pinewoods of Scotland*, pp 60–9, 1977.

8   Anderson, M L, *History of Scottish forestry*, vol 1. Thomas Nelson and Sons Ltd, London and Edinburgh, 1967.

9   Carlisle, A The impact of man on the native pinewoods of Scotland. In Bunce, R G H and Jeffers, J N R (eds), *Native pinewoods of Scotland*, pp 70–7, 1977.

10   Elizabeth Grant of Rothiemurchus, *Memoirs of a Highland lady: vol. 1, 1797–1885*. Canongate Classics, 1988.

11   Goodier, R and Bunce, R G H, The native pinewoods of Scotland: The current state of the resource. In Bunce, R G H and Jeffers, J N R (eds), *Native Pinewoods of Scotland*, pp 78–87, 1977.

12   Callander, R F, The history of native woodlands in the Scottish Highlands. In Jenkins, D (ed), *Trees and wildlife in the Scottish uplands*, pp 40–5. Institute of Terrestrial Ecology, Abbots Ripton, Hunts, 1986.

13   Watson, A, Eighteenth century deer numbers and pine regeneration near Braemar, Scotland. *Biological Conservation*, 25, pp 289–305, 1983.

14   McVean, D N, Ecology of Scots Pine in the Scottish Highlands. *Journal of Ecology*, 51, pp 671–86, 1963.

15   Forrest, I, Fingerprints of the Caledonian pine. *Forest Life*, issue no. 7. Forestry Commission, Edinburgh, 1990.

5

Deciduous woodlands

A delightful walk it was: for it was a pleasant afternoon in June, and their way lay through a deep and shady wood, cooled by the light wind which gently rustled the thick foliage and enlivened by the songs of the birds that perched upon the boughs. The ivy and the moss crept in thick clusters over the old trees, and the soft green turf overspread the ground like a silken mat.

Charles Dickens, 1837

Historical development

Deciduous woodland formed the natural vegetation cover of much of upland Britain and most of the flora and fauna were woodland species. It has also played a large part in human history, featuring in folklore, literature and song. It has provided building materials, furniture, fuel and food, and it has a high amenity value. It is a cherished resource, the more so because of its historical links. To quote just one example, there is an exceptionally large oak tree on the banks of the Tay at Dunkeld, which is protected as the supposed last survivor of the Birnam Wood mentioned in Shakespeare's *Macbeth* (Plate 17).

Different types of deciduous woodland have originated at particular periods. Woods resembling the early Post-glacial birch and juniper woods survive today only in parts of Scotland, such as Glen Finan. Many of them probably had a greater mixture of species in the past but they have been impoverished by grazing pressure or timber extraction. Hazel woods survive on Skye and Mull, where the trees are gnarled and wind-pruned but apparently natural. Woods with birch, hazel and aspen may also be found in Scotland. In Inverkirkaig Woods in north-west Scotland, the hazel grows over large mossy boulders, while birch and some aspen form the canopy. In many other places in the Scottish Highlands, where steep slopes or rocky terrain make grazing difficult, scrub woodlands dominated by birch survive (Plate 18). They have all probably been exploited at some time for fuel or have suffered some grazing pressure, but they are the nearest we have to the early Post-glacial woods of the uplands.

Oak woodland was dominant in the middle Post-glacial over most of southern Scotland, northern England, Wales and south-west England. The two native species overlap in their distributions and often hybridise, but the sessile oak was generally more characteristic of shallow acid soils in the north and west, whilst the pedunculate oak favoured the deeper, richer soils. It is still possible to find examples of oak

PLATE 17 The Birnam Oak, Dunkeld. This tree is popularly believed to be a survivor of the wood mentioned in Shakespeare's *Macbeth*

PLATE 18 Highland birchwood at Craigellachie National Nature Reserve, Speyside

woodland at the extreme ends of this former distribution. In Dartmoor, there are several relic oakwoods, such as Wistman's Wood (Colour plate 6) and Black Tor Copse, dominated by pedunculate oak. In northern Scotland, the same species of oak extended right up the coast and still regenerates freely in the absence of grazing at Loch a' Muillin Wood National Nature Reserve. Many other species were intermixed with the oak, such as wych elm, hazel and alder. Elm was particularly common in Wales, south-west England and parts of the Pennines. Other trees were important locally, such as ash on limestone rocks, small-leaved lime and occasionally large-leaved lime on more fertile soils from the Lake District southwards, and even beech in a few woods in south-west England. Alder was a widespread tree of wet sites through-out the country. Its importance is often exaggerated on pollen diagrams, however, as it so often grew immediately around lakes or bogs.

There were other less common trees, such as bird cherry, wild cherry and field maple, and understorey shrubs, such as guelder-rose, hawthorn, holly and black-thorn (Table 6). These would have been locally frequent wherever there was more light, for instance under gaps in the tree canopy, near the coast, on cliffs or beside lakes and rivers. The ground flora also flourished wherever there was enough light, although its distribution would have been patchy in the dense middle Post-glacial woods. Pollen from ground flora species is rarely recorded on pollen diagrams but 19 species have been recorded as pollen or seeds in upland Britain (Table 8).

This, then, was the 'wildwood'[1], which reached its maximum extent in the middle Post-glacial (Figure 6). There are no British woods like the wildwood surviv-ing today – all have been managed and modified. The nearest equivalent is probably somewhere like the Bialowieza National Park in eastern Poland, where the structure of the forest is thought to resemble that of natural woods. The trees can live for 500 years or more and they rise to 40 metres in height, casting a dense shade. Fallen trees create gaps in the canopy which are colonised by herbaceous plants and young trees. Many of the original woodland animals survive, too, including elk, bison, wild boar and wolf. Although an imperfect analogy, Bialowieza gives us a glimpse of what a natural wood was like.

Some deciduous woodlands originated later and are known as secondary woods. On the Pennines, for instance, the middle Post-glacial woods were dominated by oak and hazel, but when they were cleared the light-loving ash was able to spread and is now the dominant tree. In some cases, the secondary woods are very ancient and date from prehistoric or early historic times; in other cases they are compara-tively recent, as in parts of the Derbyshire Dales, where they grew up after AD 1800. Ash and oak grow together in many areas today, a good example being Colt Park Wood, Ingleborough, where trees grow out of limestone pavement and there is a very rich ground flora in the grikes. Many of the birch woods seen today in the uplands, other than those of the Scottish Highlands, are also of secondary origin. Birch, like ash, is a fast coloniser and rapidly fills any gaps in the canopy or spreads on to felled areas. It is a short-lived tree and in most cases a generation or two of birch will be succeeded by longer-lived species, such as oak or elm. This is well illustrated in

TABLE 8 Pollen and seed/fruit records of woodland ground flora species

Osmunda regalis	Royal fern
Pteridium aquilinum	Bracken
Athyrium filix-femina	Lady-fern
Phegopteris connectilis	Beech fern
Gymnocarpium dryopteris	Oak fern
Polypodium vulgare	Polypody
Trollius europaeus	Globeflower
Silene dioica*	Red campion
Stellaria holostea*	Greater stitchwort
Oxalis acetosella	Wood-sorrel
Potentilla sterilis	Barren strawberry
Fragaria vesca	Wild strawberry
Geum rivale/urbanum	Water/wood avens
Circaea lutetiana*	Enchanter's-nightshade
Hedera helix	Ivy
Sanicula europaea	Sanicle
Angelica sylvestris	Wild angelica
Mercurialis perennis	Dog's mercury
Digitalis purpurea	Foxglove
Ajuga reptans	Bugle
Lonicera periclymenum	Honeysuckle
Hyacinthoides non-scripta	Bluebell

*probable identification

Source: Pollen and seed/fruit records based on Godwin, H, History of the British flora. Cambridge University Press, Cambridge, 1975. Nomenclature after Stace, C, New flora of the British Isles. Cambridge University Press, Cambridge, 1991.

Garbutt Wood on the North York Moors, where a sizeable birchwood sprang up through natural regeneration on an area felled during the First World War. The trees are now dying off and being replaced by oak, rowan and holly. Other woods have been planted, mainly during the last few centuries. They often include non-native trees, such as sycamore, as well as native species, such as beech, growing outside their natural limits in Britain.

Plantlife and soils

The wide range of deciduous woodlands means that there are many different ways of classifying and describing them[2,3,4]. However, they have certain common features in their ecology. A complex vertical structure exists in most woods, with plant growth being limited by the available light. Up to six layers may be recognised, although they will not all be well developed in any one wood. The main tree canopy layer may have an understorey of younger trees, beneath which there may be a layer of lower-growing woody shrubs. The ground flora also consists of up to three layers: a tall herb layer of plants such as bracken or bramble; a layer of shorter herbs, such as bluebell and primrose; and a layer of mosses or lichens growing on fallen trunks or boulders. Where the tree canopy is dense, the lower layers will be sparse, as plants compete for light. Any well-developed layer will limit the layers beneath it; for instance, a thick shrub layer is likely to have poorly developed ground flora layers. In a natural wood, the growth of all layers below the tree canopy depends on gaps created by fallen trees or other natural openings, but in a managed wood such clearings are often created artificially.

The ground flora species have evolved various strategies to enable them to compete for light. Many species flower early in the year, before the trees come into leaf, when there is the maximum amount of light and the greatest number of insect pollinators. Conspicuous early flowerers are lesser celandine and wood anemone but dog's mercury also flowers in early spring, its less showy flowers depending on the wind rather than insects to pollinate them. Later in the spring, other familiar woodland flowers have their turn, such as primrose, wood-sorrel, lords-and-ladies, violets and bugle, to be followed still later by bluebell, ramsons and yellow pimpernel. Other species adopt a climbing habit to search out the light, such as ivy and honeysuckle. Species like foxglove, which have not evolved such strategies, are dependent on growing in clearings. The closing of a gap in the canopy prevents them from flowering and they must either spread into another clearing or else survive the shade in vegetative form or as buried seed until another gap occurs overhead.

An established woodland creates its own microclimate. Less rainfall reaches the woodland floor than reaches the ground outside the wood, as the trees intercept some of the rain and it is evaporated back into the atmosphere from their leaves. Temperatures tend to be more even in the shady conditions within the wood and wind speeds are much reduced. However, for many woodland plants the most important factor in their survival is probably the lack of competition from more aggressive species which cannot tolerate the shade.

Some ground flora species are almost entirely confined to sites with a known history of continuous woodland cover for several centuries[3]. In the uplands these include wood anemone, primrose, herb Paris, early-purple orchid and lily-of-the-valley. Where these are found outside the woodland canopy, they indicate that the site was wooded until quite recently. The reason for this strong association between certain plants and ancient woodlands seems to be their poorly developed powers of seed dispersal. Within the woods, most of these plants depend on vegetative spread and, if seeds are produced, they only travel short distances. This means that these plants have great difficulty in colonising new woods unless they can make the journey via a wooded corridor or hedgerow. They are effectively imprisoned in their own woods and, as the area of woodland in Britain has decreased, populations of these plants have become more and more isolated.

Many species of fungi are characteristic of deciduous woodlands. Some are specific to particular trees, such as King Alfred's cakes on ash or Jew's ear on elder. Others, such as Dryad's saddle, grow on a variety of trees. Some bring colour to the woodland floor, such as the fly agaric. Very little is known about the history of these fungi or how quickly they can colonise new woods, but fungal spores are generally freely dispersed by the wind. Other very important fungi are those which infect the roots of trees and aid the uptake of nutrients, especially in acid soils. Without these unseen members of the woodland flora, the growth of many trees would be less vigorous.

The soils underlying deciduous woodlands are usually of the brown earth type but in the uplands most are acidic, as a result of the underlying geology and the effects of leaching. Typically, these soils show no clear horizons but are a brighter orangey colour and more clayey in the subsoil than the topsoil. The roots of deciduous trees can penetrate more than 3 metres in depth, forming an efficient means of recycling nutrients and thus preventing too much leaching. Some upland soils are very thin and the trees are rooted in stony ground between large boulders, as in many of the Highland birch woods or in Wistman's Wood on Dartmoor (Colour plate 6). Valley woods, on the other hand, often grow on gleyed soils, which experience seasonal or permanent waterlogging. Tree species tolerant of waterlogging in the soil include alder, birch and aspen.

Animal life

The animal life has been much impoverished since the days of the middle Post-glacial, when bison (Plate 4), wild ox, wild cattle, wild boar, brown bear, lynx and wolf roamed through the undergrowth. Some of these, such as the wild ox, died out as a result of the changing climate; hunting undoubtedly caused the demise of others, such as the wild boar and wild cattle. The wolf was deliberately persecuted as a perceived threat to humans and rewards were given for killing it in the medieval period. It was common until the thirteenth century and then was gradually wiped out from England and Wales, hanging on longest in remote parts of the Peak District. After that it survived only in the Scottish pinewoods. Today, the only large wild animals are deer. In the absence of large carnivores, control of deer is a major problem in some areas. Smaller mammals include badger, fox, stoat, weasel, mice, voles and shrews. The native red squirrel survives in the Lake District and parts of Scotland; elsewhere it is the grey squirrel which predominates, causing much damage to trees by stripping their bark. This species was introduced from North America in the nineteenth century and has spread to many parts of the uplands, proving to be a more successful competitor and more flexible in its diet than the native red squirrel. Several species of bat also inhabit woodlands, hibernating or roosting in trees. They include the pipistrelle, which is common nearly everywhere, the noctule, the common long-eared, Natterer's and Daubenton's.

Birdlife is plentiful, although the birds of prey, such as the red kite and the common buzzard, are undoubtedly rarer than in the past, owing to the use of poisons. Some bird species are particularly associated with deciduous woodland, including the green woodpecker, woodcock, treecreeper, nuthatch and tree pipit. The upland woods are the main habitats for the common redstart and pied flycatcher. Many summer migrants also visit the deciduous woodlands, especially species of warbler, such as the garden warbler and chiffchaff. Many other British bird species, while not confined to the woods, use them for part of the year or nest in them. They include familiar species, such as the robin, blue tit and blackbird. Although most of these must have been woodland birds originally, many of them have adapted very successfully to other habitats, such as hedgerows and gardens. Their greater mobility gives them a major advantage compared to woodland plants.

Over half of all British insect species use deciduous woodlands. On the oak tree alone, over 100 moth caterpillar species have been recorded, common examples being the buff-tip and winter moths. There are comparatively few woodland butterflies in the uplands, but the purple hairstreak and speckled wood occur in England and Wales and parts of Scotland and the meadow brown is common throughout Britain. Amongst the many other insects, the gall wasps are often noticeable by their effects on trees. For example, common galls to be found on oak include spangle galls and marble galls. Some 650 beetle species are associated with woodlands, whilst other woodland invertebrates include many spiders and nearly half the British list of molluscs. There has been little work on the history of most of these groups of invertebrates in the uplands but research indicates that some groups have potential as indicators of ancient woodland sites. For example, some wood-boring beetles are associated with very old trees, and some slug and snail species also seem to be diagnostic of ancient woods.

Woodland management

Woodland was a valuable commodity in the past and practically all the surviving deciduous woods show signs of former exploitation. All settlements needed access to woodland or woodland products, although in particular areas some substitutions could be made, such as coal or peat for fuel or stone for building material. The arts of woodmanship were at their peak in medieval times, when a distinction was made between timber and wood. Timber was the tree trunks used for major constructional purposes, while wood or 'underwood' was the smaller branches or twigs. In addition, the ground flora of the woodland was a resource for grazing animals, wild and domesticated. These three major commodities, timber, wood and pasture, required different management techniques, although more than one technique was often applied in a single wood[5].

The commonest form of management was coppice-with-standards, where the standard trees provided the timber and the coppiced trees the wood (Plate 19). The density of standards was between 12 and 100 per ha and the vast majority were oak. The main requirement was for timber beams for houses, the commonest length being 20 feet (6.2 metres), so the base of the canopy was at this height and trees were generally less than 100 years old. Longer beams were needed for larger buildings or the shafts of windmills, so some trees were allowed to grow taller. In order to ensure a continuous supply of timber, trees in different parts of the woodlands would be of

PLATE 19 Coppice-with-standards, Witherslack Woods, Lake District

different ages, although individual compartments might be treated in a uniform manner for convenience. Another major use of timber was in shipbuilding, where oak was used for almost all parts except the masts. Hundreds or even thousands of trees were needed for the largest ships but the total demand was far less than that for house timbers. Shipbuilding increased in importance with time, reaching a peak in the early nineteenth century.

The wood was provided by the regrowth of the coppiced trees between the standards. Any deciduous species would do, including hazel, elm, ash, birch, lime, aspen, alder, willow and any oaks not needed as timber trees. They were all cut back to around ground level or just above, from which point they would spring again (hence the name 'spring wood' applied to many coppiced woods). Far from harming the trees, this form of management actually prolonged their lives. It is known that coppiced stools can live for at least 1000 years, compared to perhaps 400 or 500 years for an oak tree grown to maturity. Some woods contain very large coppiced stools many hundreds of years old. The coppice was usually cut on a short cycle of four to eight years, which provided many poles of small diameter. Often the timber would belong to the lord of the manor but the peasants would have rights to take underwood for defined purposes. These rights were known as hedgebote, cartbote, housebote, firebote, etc – each referring to a specific use of the wood.

Some woods were grown as pure coppices, producing wood for particular industries, foremost among which was the iron-smelting industry. The only way to supply the large quantities of charcoal needed by a medieval furnace over a period of several years was to manage an area of woodland surrounding the furnace on a rotational basis. For instance, in the fourteenth century, the Bishops of Durham employed a forester to manage oakwoods in the Hamsterley area for charcoal production. Coppices are also known to have been set up in conjunction with other ironworks, as at Pickering in 1541. Other metals were also smelted, especially lead, copper and zinc, in central Wales, Derbyshire, the Yorkshire dales and elsewhere. Longer rotations were better for charcoal, so the length of time between coppicing increased as iron working gained in importance; for instance, rotations of 16 to 17 years were used in Wales[6]. Coppices for charcoal were widespread in the uplands, and in many woods the traces of the old charcoal-burning platforms may still be seen as roughly circular areas about 10 metres across, cut into the hillside, with a scree-like deposit of charcoal debris downslope.

As time went on, other uses for wood developed. An important one in many woodlands in south-west Scotland, Cumbria and Wales was the production of oak bark for tanning in the leather industry. Longer rotations were needed here of 15 to 30 years, and even 60-year rotations are recorded, although intermediate thinnings were carried out. So valuable was the bark that some oak coppices were planted especially for this purpose. Other trees had their particular uses, too; for example, birch was used for making reels and bobbins and alder was suitable for gunpowder charcoal and clog-making. However, the commonest coppice species overall was undoubtedly hazel, which had a multitude of domestic and agricultural uses.

Coppicing eventually died out in most parts of the uplands as demand for its products declined in the nineteenth and twentieth centuries. Most woods ceased to be coppiced regularly between 1900 and 1930, although a few in the Lake District and southern Scotland continued to be cut until the middle of the twentieth century. Recently there has been a revival of coppicing in some areas, partly as a source of fuel for wood-burning stoves and partly as a conservation measure. The popularity of barbecues has also created a market for charcoal, which is being filled by new companies working in areas such as the southern North York Moors. Other potential markets now being developed include fertilisers and leaf-silage (brushwood converted to protein-rich animal feed)[7].

The effects of these management practices on the woodland ecology were dramatic. The managed woodland had a lower and lighter canopy than the wildwood, which allowed much more light to reach the woodland floor, particularly in the first year or so after coppicing. This was a great boost to the woodland ground flora, which flowered profusely, carpeting the ground with sheets of wood anemones, primroses or bluebells (Colour plate 5). However, the ground flora also had to cope with the shade phase, when the coppice poles grew tall and blocked out most of the light. Strategies which had been used in the wildwood were employed, such as maintaining slow vegetative growth until the light returned, seeding into newly coppiced areas or surviving as buried seeds in the litter layer.

Insect species also benefited from the lighter canopy woodland, finding in the newly coppiced sections of the wood a habitat reminiscent of natural glades in the wildwood. Insectivorous birds, such as the tree pipit or pied flycatcher, would have taken advantage of the increased number of insects, although the absence of old trees in the typical coppiced wood must have led to a shortage of suitable nest sites for hole-nesting species. Small mammals also found food supplies increased and the absence of large predator species in the managed woods enabled their numbers to increase. The demise of the coppice system resulted in other changes for the woodland flora and fauna. The last generation of poles grew up and competed with one another, unchecked by further cutting. The strongest few poles from each coppiced stool formed mature trunks, creating a dense shade. This has led to the impoverishment of many woods, which now lack the spectacular displays of spring flowers and the abundance of insect life they enjoyed under traditional management.

Wood pasture

The other major use of woodlands was as pasture for beasts (Plate 20). Cattle, sheep, goats, pigs, horses, ducks and geese were all pastured in woods at various times. Pig grazing (right of pannage) was particularly common in the autumn, when the acorn crop was ripe. Grazing pressure is not conducive to good timber or wood production, as the animals eat not only the ground flora but also any young trees and sometimes gnaw the bark of older trees as well. One strategy for overcoming this problem was to pollard the trees at about 2 metres high. They would then sprout again from the top of the cut trunk and produce wood in a similar fashion to coppiced stools. Harvesting this wood was less convenient than with poles growing from ground level and pollarding was not a common form of woodland management. However, it was often used for trees on the edges of woods, on boundaries and in Forests and parks. Holly, being evergreen, was pollarded as winter feed for cattle, especially in the Pennines and Cumbria. Former pollards may be recognised by their branching trunks at about 2 metres high, from which the last generation of pollarded poles has grown up to maturity, giving the trees a top-heavy appearance. The timber of pollards was not of much use, so they were usually pollarded many times, producing very old trunks.

Some of these pollards played host to other organisms, especially lichens and beetles, and old woodland indicator species have been recognised amongst both these groups[8]. Up to 40 lichen species may occur on a single tree at the richest sites, the best host species being oak, ash, beech and elm. The invertebrate fauna living in the bark can also be useful indicators of ancient wood pasture and can make up 20 per cent of the total fauna of a woodland. The greatest numbers of insects and mites are found on willows, oak and birch. The ground flora of wood pastures was usually less diverse than in coppiced woods, being dominated by grasses and bracken. Typical woodland flowers which cannot tolerate grazing, such as primrose or bluebell, were absent and the flora resembled that of a grassland or heath. Young trees could occasionally grow up in the shelter of holly or hawthorn bushes but otherwise regeneration was limited.

A second strategy for reconciling wood production with grazing was to fence compartments of the woodland in rotation for so many years after coppicing. This

PLATE 20 Wood pasture, Longsleddale, Lake District

meant a reduction in the area of pasture but prevented most damage to the coppice crop. The overall effect on the woodland ecology was to produce a version of coppiced woodland with an impoverished ground flora, due to the grazing in the later years of the coppice cycle. The choice between pollarding and fencing depended on the relative importance and value of grazing and wood production, but the balance between the two approaches was not always achieved easily. Pressure from grazing on timber and wood production led to the passing of a number of Acts of Parliament in the fifteenth and sixteenth centuries, requiring owners of woods to fence them after coppicing.

The Lake District woodlands

The impact of management on the native woodland cover of the uplands is well illustrated in the Lake District. The region has an exceptional variety of landscape, climate, vegetation and soils. The Skiddaw Slates and rocks of the Borrowdale Volcanic Group form the mountainous core of the region, contrasting with the gently rolling topography of the Silurian rocks and the rim of Carboniferous limestone (Figure 10). There are classic glacial erosion features in the central part, with truncated soils on the steep slopes and brown earths and gleys in the valleys. Calcareous soils are found over the limestone and there are extensive limestone pavements, as in Gait Barrows National Nature Reserve.

This physical diversity was reflected in the great variety of woodland types

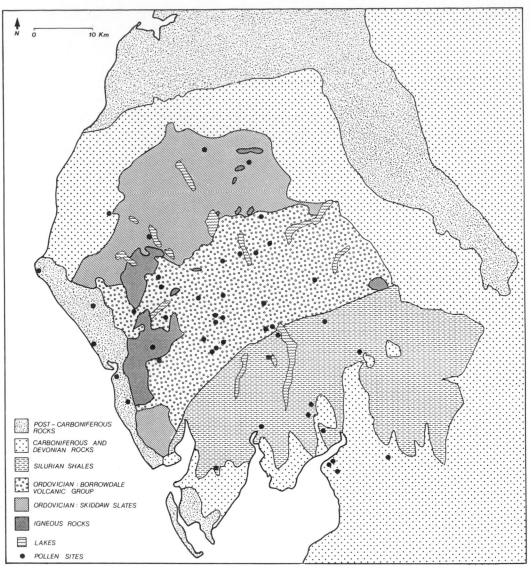

POST – CARBONIFEROUS
ROCKS

CARBONIFEROUS AND
DEVONIAN ROCKS

SILURIAN SHALES

ORDOVICIAN : BORROWDALE
VOLCANIC GROUP

ORDOVICIAN : SKIDDAW SLATES

IGNEOUS ROCKS

LAKES

● POLLEN SITES

FIGURE 10 Geology of the Lake District (The solid circles show sites from which pollen diagrams have been published)

which had developed in the area by the middle Post-glacial. A mixed woodland dominated by oak covered most of the ground up to an altitude of at least 650 metres. Birch and hazel grew where the canopy was not too dense and pine persisted on some of the higher fells. Elm and lime were frequent on the rich calcareous soils of the southern part of the region, along with less common trees, such as ash, bird cherry, wild cherry, yew, spindle and alder buckthorn. Alder grew around the many lakes and tarns, in the river valleys and around the peat bogs. We know a great deal about the woodland history of the Lake District, as over 60 pollen diagrams have been published from the area (Figure 10). Some are from lakes, varying in size from Windermere to small corrie tarns; others are from blanket peat on the fells and lowland bogs near the coast. Amongst the many workers in the region, Pennington has made an outstanding contribution [9].

The clearance of the native woodlands is recorded on the pollen diagrams from Neolithic time onwards. The Bronze Age, Roman and Viking periods were all ones in which the woodland cover decreased considerably and, by the medieval period, many of the upland fells had already been grasslands or moorland for several centuries. However, dense woodlands survived in many of the valleys and some of these were managed as coppices or coppice-with-standards by the Cistercian abbeys. For instance, in the twelfth century, Furness Abbey held land in the Grisedale–Furness area and was coppicing on a fourteen year rotation, using birch, holly, oak, ash and alder. The Cistercian abbey of Holm Cultrum also managed coppiced woodlands for charcoal production [10].

There were also areas under Forest law in the Lake District. In the Royal Forest of Inglewood in the north-east, sources of income in addition to the hunting of deer included grazing, pannage, fishing, sales of stray animals and fines for poaching or making enclosures in the Forest. These activities imply that there were large areas of wood pasture management but there must also have been areas of coppice-with-standards, as wood was sold for charcoal and bark for tanning. Timber was sold frequently, for example for rebuilding in Carlisle after a serious fire in 1391 [10]. In the private Forests of Copeland Chase and Derwent Fells, there were large cattle farms (vaccaries), and some settlements were allowed. Parts of the Forests were sold off, so that most of the western side of the Lake District had been disafforested by the thirteenth century and parts of the north were disafforested in the fifteenth.

By the late sixteenth century, there was virtually no natural woodland left in the Lake District. The higher fells had been stripped of their woodland cover in prehistoric or early historic times and the valleys were either agricultural land or managed woodlands. There are Duchy of Lancaster records in the sixteenth century for both coppicing and former wood pasture, for example in Elterwater Park and in Borrowdale [3]. From AD 1600 to 1900, the rural economy of much of the lower ground depended on wood production. Oak was coppiced for charcoal on rotations of 14 to 25 years length. New coppices were planted and Hawkshead became a centre for local woodland crafts. Coppicing for charcoal was widespread, especially in High Furness, and remains of the charcoal burners' huts and pitsteads may be seen, for example in Roudsea Wood National Nature Reserve.

Bark for tanning was another important woodland product, and was more valuable than either timber or sheep in the nineteenth century. Some wood was used for shipbuilding in the shipyards at Whitehaven and Maryport. Another important use of wood was for making bobbins for the Lancashire cotton industry. The first bobbin mill was built at Staveley in 1797 and by 1850 there were 64, concentrated in the Windermere–Coniston area, and bobbins were sold far and wide. Ash and birch were the most important types of wood but many other trees were also used, including planted beech, chestnut and sycamore. The last bobbin mill, at Stott Park, closed in 1971 but has since been re-opened as an industrial museum.

The woodlands today

With the decline of the traditional markets for coppice products, most coppices were abandoned sometime early in the twentieth century. By 1980, only 134 ha of active coppice and 89 ha of coppice-with-standards remained. As former coppices were neglected, the last generation of coppiced poles grew up tall and cast a dense shade. Boundary walls were not repaired and sheep and cattle gained access to the vast majority of woodlands, turning them into unofficial wood pasture. A grassy ground flora developed, with bracken and brambles in some areas, and many of the traditional woodland wildflowers were suppressed. Examples of such woods are to be seen all over the region, such as the woods near the head of Borrowdale, in Longsleddale (Plate 20), in Swindale, in Naddle Low Forest and near Brothers Water. There are other woods which have been managed as wood pasture for many centuries, and these usually have a more varied wildlife. For example, Seatoller Woods are one of the richest sites in western Europe for Atlantic mosses and liverworts and also have interesting beetle and mollusc species. Great Wood, near Keswick, has a very rich lichen flora[11].

There are some old coppiced woods which have escaped regular grazing, such as Spring Hag Wood, near Staveley, whilst Witherslack Woods have some very good examples of coppice-with-standards (Plate 19). Formerly coppiced woods on the limestone areas in the south-east are dominated by ash and oak, with yew, birch, hazel, small-leaved lime, sycamore, holly and beech, and a very diverse ground flora. A few examples survive of the former high-level woods of the Lake District, notably the Keskadale and Birkrigg oaks, which lie at an altitude of 400 to 500 metres on a very steep slope (30 to 40 degrees) on the side of the Newlands valley. They have been coppiced in the past for charcoal production and are gnarled and stunted in growth. Despite this, they regenerate freely when fenced against sheep. On the east side of Martindale, there are remnants of mixed woods dominated by alder at an altitude of 300 to 350 metres. The surrounding area was managed as deer forest and the alder may have survived here as its foliage is not favoured by deer. Above Watendlath Tarn there is a high-level birch wood at an altitude of 300 to 380 metres, which was grazed in the past but is now regenerating where fenced. Many woods in the Lake District are now owned or managed by conservation bodies, including the National Trust, the Woodland Trust and the Cumbria Wildlife Trust. Management at several of these sites involves reinstatement of the coppicing regime, as in Dorothy Farrer's Spring Wood, near Staveley, and Brigsteer Woods.

Lastly, there are many ornamental woodlands, dating from the eighteenth and nineteenth centuries. The species chosen depended on fashion and the whim of the landowners; for instance, in the 1780s, Agnes Ford of Grizedale planted 77,000 trees, mostly oak and ash[12]. Elsewhere on the Grizedale Hall and Muncaster estates, larch, beech and sycamore were planted. William Wordsworth recorded some of the introductions of the late eighteenth century, including beech, larch, lime and fir trees[13]. Many woods include some conifers or ornamental trees amongst older coppiced woodland; for example, Whitbarrow woods and the woodlands around Ullswater. Although a far cry from the wildwood of the Lake District, these ornamental mixed plantings are of great amenity and landscape value and provide valuable additional habitats for woodland wildlife.

References

1   Rackham, O, *Trees and woodland in the British landscape* (revised edition). Dent, London, 1990.
2   Rodwell, J S (ed), *British plant communities: Vol 1, Woodlands and scrub.* Cambridge University Press, Cambridge, 1991.
3   Peterken, G F, *Woodland conservation and management.* Chapman and Hall, London, 1981.
4   Bunce, R G H, *A field key for classifying British woodland vegetation. Part 1.* Institute of Terrestrial Ecology, Cambridge, 1982.
5   Rackham, O, *Ancient woodland: Its history, vegetation and uses in England.* Edward Arnold, London, 1980.
6   Linnard, W, *Welsh woods and forests: History and utilization.* National Museum of Wales, Cardiff, 1982.
7   Everett, R D, Farm Woodlands. In Adamson, J K (ed), *Cumbrian woodlands – past, present and future,* pp 62–4. Institute of Terrestrial Ecology symposium no. 25. HMSO, London, 1989.
8   Harding, P T and Rose, F, *Pasture-woodlands in lowland Britain.* Institute of Terrestrial Ecology, Abbots Ripton, 1986.
9   Pennington, W, Vegetation history in the north-west of England: A regional synthesis. In Walker, D and West, R G (eds), *Studies in the vegetational history of the British Isles,* pp 41–79. Cambridge University Press, Cambridge, 1970.
10   Satchell, J E, The history of woodlands in Cumbria. In Adamson, J K (ed), *Cumbrian woodlands – past, present and future,* pp 2–11, 1989.
11   Pearsall, W H and Pennington, W, *The Lake District.* Collins, London, 1973.
12   Voysey, J C, The management of woodlands in Cumbria. In Adamson, J K (ed), *Cumbrian woodlands – past, present and future,* pp 18–20, 1989.
13   Wordsworth, W, *Guide to the Lakes* (1835). Edited by E. de Selincourt. Oxford University Press, Oxford, 1977.

6

Heather moorlands

> To the student of nature these heather-clad wastes possess a fascination and interest of an unusual kind. Although woods, fields and lanes have their own peculiar charms, they have not the special charm of the moors.
>
> F Elgee, 1912

The British Isles have been called 'the world's great moorland countries'[1]. The vast sweeps of purple heather form one of the most characteristic images of the uplands. They have been the inspiration for poets from Robert Burns to Ted Hughes, the backdrop to many an artist's 'monarch of the glen', and the setting for novels, such as *Lorna Doone* and *Wuthering Heights*. Writers in former times took it for granted that moorlands were part of the natural scene – a wildscape only superficially affected by human beings[2]. Yet, as we now know, this is far from the true story. In this chapter we shall deal exclusively with those areas below the potential limit of tree growth, the vast majority of which once supported woodland. The reasons for their present treelessness have been a source of fascination to ecologists for many years.

Vegetation and soils

Moorlands are dominated by dwarf shrubs, the most important being the common heather. It has exceptional powers of regeneration and can grow to the exclusion of almost all other plants under certain management regimes. Although the individual flowers are unspectacular, when flowering *en masse* on a Scottish hillside or a Yorkshire moor in late summer, they make a glorious sight. This heather is frequently accompanied by two other members of the same family, bell heather and cross-leaved heath. Both have bell-shaped flowers, larger than those of heather, the bell heather's being a rich dark mauve and those of the cross-leaved heath a pale pink (Colour plate 7). They favour different drainage conditions, the bell heather needing a well-drained soil and the cross-leaved heath tolerating wetter situations, but all three heathers can often be found growing in close proximity. There are also many berry-bearing dwarf shrubs, commonest amongst which are the bilberry, cowberry and crowberry. Clumps of grasses, sedges and rushes often grow amongst the dwarf shrubs, and the hard-fern is common. Low-growing flowers include tormentil, heath milkwort and heath bedstraw. Many moors are also rich in mosses and lichens[3].

Other species add to the plantlife in various parts of Britain. In south-west England and Wales, the western gorse creates bright yellow patches, which make a colourful contrast to the purple of the heathers. On well-drained sandstones and grits, bilberry is often dominant. Other plants of dry situations include common cow-wheat and chickweed wintergreen. In parts of the Pennines and Lake District, the dwarf shrubs are found growing in an intimate mixture with acid-tolerant grasses, such as mat-grass, sheep's-fescue, common bent, and wavy hair-grass. The green-ribbed sedge sometimes forms large tussocks and another common plant is heath rush, which can tolerate much drier conditions than most other rushes.

Wetter sites have different plant communities, which grade into true bog communities on deep peat. Here plants such as the cottongrasses and *Sphagnum* mosses are to be found, and cross-leaved heath is often more abundant than heather. Vast areas of western Scotland are covered with wet moorland, where the heathers share dominance with deergrass or purple moor-grass, and other species include bog asphodel and the heath spotted-orchid. Small boggy patches are a feature of most moorland areas and add to the diversity of the habitat for animal life. With increasing altitude, montane species appear, such as cloudberry, bearberry and dwarf cornel.

Moorland soils are nearly always acid and most show signs of podzolisation and gleying. Many of the nutrients are locked up in the litter layer and others are leached down the soil profile, so there is a gradual impoverishment of the soils. Moorland plants are tolerant of low nutrient status but grazing animals often suffer deficiencies of minerals, such as copper or boron. Soil horizons are sharply delimited and sometimes include a thin iron pan, which may form an obstacle to root pene-tration and impede drainage. This may lead to waterlogging of the top-soil, inhibiting the decomposition of plant litter. A thick mor layer builds up on top of the mineral soil, and the thicker it becomes the more acid and waterlogged it gets, so the process is a self-reinforcing one. The mor layer may develop into peat, with all the plant roots growing in it, out of contact with the mineral soil below. Thus, moorland soils form a continuum from freely drained podzols through to poorly drained peats.

Animal life

The moorlands are home to a distinctive assemblage of wild animal species as well as to several introduced ones, such as sheep, cattle and ponies. The largest of the native mammals which regularly use the moors is the red deer. There are herds on Exmoor, in the Lake District and the Southern Uplands but the greatest numbers are to be found in the Scottish Highlands. As we saw in chapter 5, they were originally crea-tures of the woodlands but, as the area of woodland decreased and management of it intensified, they were forced to adapt to the moorland habitat instead. The nutrition and shelter offered by open moorland are far less good than in the woodlands, and this has resulted in a decrease in size of about 50 per cent, as can be seen by com-paring modern red deer with skeletons from archaeological sites[4]. When Scottish red deer were exported to New Zealand and re-introduced to a woodland habitat, they

PLATE 21 Red grouse in breeding plumage, North Yorkshire

regained their original size within 50 years[5]. In most parts of Scotland today, numbers are controlled by culling or sporting activities. Elsewhere, herds are limited by food supplies, as most of their natural predators have been eliminated. Experiments on Rhum show that they tend to breed later and suffer higher rates of mortality, especially amongst calves, when numbers increase[6].

Other mammals include the rabbit, brown hare, stoat, weasel, wood mouse, bank vole and field vole. Population explosions of the last named species have been recorded in the Southern Uplands from time to time. Foxes frequently exploit moorlands as part of their territories. Reptiles and amphibians are also to be found on moorlands; the most distinctive species is the adder, which is widespread on drier moors, along with the common lizard. The common toad and common frog both use moorlands in addition to other habitats, sometimes depositing their spawn in unsuitable situations, such as temporary pools or bogs which dry out.

Insects are important grazers of moorland plants and some can have devastating effects. For instance, the heather beetle can defoliate large areas of heather. There are many bugs and other invertebrate feeders on plants, as well as the caterpillars of butterflies and moths. The number of butterfly species on moorlands is small; typical species include the meadow brown, small heath, large heath, dark green fritillary and green hairstreak (Colour plate 8). Moth species, on the other hand, are very plentiful on moorlands. Amongst them are the emperor moth, northern eggar, fox moth, ruby tiger, wood tiger and true lover's knot. There are also many carnivorous insects and spiders, as well as invertebrates feeding on larger animals – sometimes with disastrous results for humans and their livestock. Both sheep and cattle are affected by a range of parasites, the best known of which is the sheep tick, and they also suffer attacks from clegs and horse-flies. But perhaps the most notorious insect pests of the moorlands are the midges, which not only plague humans but also drive the red deer to higher ground in late summer.

The most famous moorland bird is the red grouse, a sub-species of the willow grouse found nowhere but in the British uplands (Plate 21). It feeds on heather, except for the first few days of its life, and its original habitat would have been heather glades within the woodlands. As the heather increased at the expense of the trees, grouse numbers increased until it is now established in all areas, albeit the populations on Dartmoor and Exmoor have been introduced deliberately[7]. Its numbers today bear little relationship to natural factors, as they are kept artificially high by careful game management, and most of its natural predators have been eliminated. The black grouse has a more restricted distribution and is characteristic of the margins of moors, as it needs the cover of trees or shrubs. It is best known for its spectacular communal courtship displays on traditional sites, known as 'leks'. It was formerly widespread but has disappeared from most southern parts of its range and is now only to be seen on the northern Pennines and in Scotland.

Several waders breed on the moors, including the golden plover, dunlin and curlew. Smaller birds are also plentiful, especially meadow pipit, whinchat, stonechat, wheatear and skylark. The moorlands have their own special member of the thrush family, the ring ouzel, with black plumage and a distinctive white collar. The carrion crow is widespread but in north-west Scotland it is replaced by the hooded crow. The raven is found on some moorlands in the west of Britain. Other birds use moorlands for nesting, an interesting example being the Canada goose in places like Nidderdale on the Pennines.

Birds of prey are at the top of many moorland food chains and there is an overlap of species with the montane zone (chapter 3). The short-eared owl is widespread (Plate 22); the common buzzard and peregrine falcon are reasonably common on uplands in the west of the country, while the merlin is found mainly in eastern Scotland and on the North York Moors. The hen harrier was much persecuted by gamekeepers in the past and its range was reduced to the Outer Hebrides and

PLATE 22 Short-eared owl on nest

Orkneys by the early twentieth century. Since World War II it has made a comeback, spreading into eastern Scotland by 1950, southern Scotland and the borders by 1960 and Wales and northern England by 1970. As a predator on grouse, however, it is still persecuted illegally. The golden eagle also contracted its range because of gamekeeping but is now a regular breeder again in many parts of Scotland and has a solitary outpost south of the border in the Lake District.

The origins of moorlands

There are three main lines of evidence for the historical development of moorlands: pollen analysis, the study of blanket peats, and the examination of soils buried beneath hillwash or archaeological structures. Pollen diagrams record heather pollen in large quantities, as heather uses the wind as well as a range of insects for pollination. Other heath species tend to be under-represented, as they rely mainly on insect pollinators, but their pollen grains turn up in sufficient numbers to give an indication of their presence. Pollen diagrams show that heath species, particularly crowberry, were important elements of the Late-glacial flora. As the Post-glacial forest closed in, most of these species were confined to areas above the tree-line, where they still form montane dwarf-shrub heaths today. The first signs of an emerging moorland habitat below the potential limit of tree growth come in the Mesolithic disturbances linked to the use of fire (chapter 2). The expansion of the moorlands since then has mirrored the decline of the woodlands. Clearance led initially to either grassland or arable crops, but whenever agricultural activity or grazing pressure diminished, heath plants spread on to the abandoned clearings. This suggests that soils soon became podzolised once the woodland cover was removed, giving heath plants a competitive advantage. Some grazing pressure would have been required to prevent the re-colonisation of trees, and it is likely that many uplands have been used as grazing land more or less continuously from Neolithic times onwards.

The dates of moorland expansion vary from upland to upland, depending on the periods of intensive farming activity. The growth of blanket peats is an important line of evidence, as it was often triggered by human activities. For instance, in south Wales, Neolithic pastoralists seem to have prevented trees from regenerating, which led to waterlogging of soils and the initiation of blanket peat on high ground[8]. Blanket peats in other areas of Wales and in parts of Scotland and the Pennines began to spread in the Bronze Age, after a period of intensive agricultural activity[9]. Further peat expansion followed the climatic deterioration of the first millennium BC.

The analysis of buried soils throws further light on the development of moorlands, and Dimbleby carried out pioneering work in the 1960s on the effects of Bronze Age activities on soils[10]. He investigated the soils buried underneath Bronze Age barrows on the North York Moors and elsewhere and found a range of soil types in various stages of podzolisation. Pollen grains preserved in these buried soils and in the turves of the barrows themselves showed that the landscape was a mosaic of woodland, hazel scrub and grass-heath communities. The state of podzolisation of the soils seemed to correlate with the length of time since the local woodland had been cleared, confirming the link between vegetation change and podzolisation.

Rackham believes that all our large moors existed by the end of the Iron Age, although they were not as extensive as today[1]. During the Dark Ages, many moorlands expanded to reach approximately their present dimensions, as shown by a major rise in the pollen curve for heather on many pollen diagrams. Later periods saw minor changes in the areas of moorland. The boundary between the enclosed land in the valleys and the moorland beyond fluctuated through time, according to economic prosperity. In times of agricultural expansion, such as in the early medieval period or during the Napoleonic Wars, more land was taken into cultivation and the moorland edge moved upslope. In periods of economic depression, the boundary moved down again, leaving abandoned fields to be reclaimed by heather or bracken. Such old fields can be seen around the fringes of all the large moorland areas, their boundaries picked out by tumbled stone walls or deserted drainage ditches.

Moorland management

Two main management techniques are used to maintain the heather moorlands: grazing and burning. Many different animals grazed on the moors in the past, including cattle, sheep, goats, ponies, pigs, ducks and geese. However, in the nineteenth century, sheep came to predominate, when selective breeding produced hardy varieties, such as the Cheviot and Scottish blackface, which could be wintered out on the open moors. The new breeds spread rapidly and soon replaced the other grazing animals. This caused various changes to the moorland ecology, which were not noticed at first but gradually led to problems. Sheep are selective feeders, preferring grass and only eating heathers when the foliage is relatively young. This led to the elimination of the highly palatable grasses and a preponderance of old, woody heather.

During the nineteenth century, regular burning was introduced to keep the heather at a palatable stage (Plate 23). Ideally, none of it would be more than about ten years old, in order to provide optimum grazing for sheep. However, sheep farming was not the only economic use for moorland areas. From about 1850 onwards, grouse-shooting became popular, aided by the development of breech-loading guns and the greater accessibility of the uplands in the railway age. Large areas of moorland were managed for grouse-shooting, particularly on the eastern side of England and Scotland. At first, burning was discouraged on grouse moors as a potential disturbance to the game birds. With the help of rigorous gamekeeping, the vast majority of the grouse's predators and competitors were eliminated and, although the grouse remained a wild bird, its numbers increased dramatically. Record bags of over 2000 birds shot on a single day were recorded on several

PLATE 23 Heather burning, North York Moors

occasions in the late nineteenth and early twentieth centuries, especially from the western Pennines, Peak District and Southern Uplands[7].

In some areas, though, grouse numbers began to fluctuate wildly, due to outbreaks of disease. So lucrative had the sport become and so influential were the upper classes who practised it, that a Committee of Inquiry was set up in 1905, under the chairmanship of Lord Lovat. A report was produced in 1911, entitled *The grouse in health and disease*, in which the chief cause of the population fluctuations was identified as infection by a parasitic threadworm. In order to kill off the parasite, regular burning of the moorlands at approximately ten-yearly intervals was recommended. The Committee also recognised the importance of providing a good diet for the grouse in order to produce a healthy population less susceptible to parasite attack, and this is now thought to be the more important consideration. As a result of the Committee's report, regular burning was introduced on most grouse-moors. This dual economy has persisted to the present day, with grouse providing a highly profitable return for the landowners and sheep supplying a more modest income for the tenant farmers.

The burning regime which evolved was a compromise between the need to provide tender young heather for the grouse and sheep to eat and the need for older heather for the grouse to nest in. Strips or patches were burned at 10- to 15-year intervals in rotation, producing a mosaic of heather at various stages of development. This works to the great advantage of heather, as it is able to sprout again from the rootstock, provided the fire is not so fierce as to burn away all the woody parts. Heather also regenerates freely from seed and seems to be fire-adapted, since germination is improved after light burning[11]. If the heather is not burned frequently enough, it becomes very woody and a large amount of litter builds up, so the fire burns at too high a temperature, sometimes igniting the underlying peaty soil as well. However, if done carefully, burning produces almost a monoculture of heather, in which all other plant species play a subordinate role.

Modern management problems

The management of grouse-moors has led to a number of unforeseen side-effects, particularly deterioration of soils, erosion of the peat and the spread of bracken. Every time an area of moorland is burned, nutrients are released from the plants, most of them falling back on to the ground in the form of ash or soot. Some of these deposits may be lost by wind or water erosion, and some nutrients are lost from the local area in the smoke. Most are replaced in the rainfall but research has shown that there is a long-term net loss of nitrogen and phosphorus[12]. When animals are sent to market there is a further small loss of the nutrients which might have been returned to the soil in their carcasses. Thus, modern management for grouse and sheep has added to the gradual, long-term decline in the nutrient status of moorland soils.

Research on the North York Moors has shown that the regular burning regime has led to the drying out of the top few centimetres of the blanket peat. This means that it is highly susceptible to being set alight by any unusually hot fire. Although most deliberate burns on grouse-moors are carefully controlled, occasionally fires get out of hand or are started accidentally. There are documentary references to unusually severe fires in particularly dry summers over the last two centuries. For example, an entry in the Ripon Millenary Record for 1827 gives a vivid description of such fires in the Yorkshire Dales:

> In the month of July the extensive moors in the West Riding of Yorkshire were in a state of conflagration, not merely on the surface, but consuming the peat down to the rock or clay. Hawksworth Moor was entirely consumed; on Ilkley Moor five hundred acres were burnt; Burley Moor, Burnsall Fell, Hebden, Grassington, Rombalds, Blubberhouses, Fountains Earth and Dallowgill Moors were all on fire. The flames and smoke together presented an imposing and formidable appearance from high grounds, whence a view of them might be obtained.

Large moorland fires have occurred in many other areas, for example in the Peak District in 1959 and on the North York Moors in 1904, 1909, 1947 and 1976. The scars from some of these fires are still visible today and long-lasting changes in vegetation have taken place. Mosses are often important in the eventual recolonisation of such areas but this may take several years or even decades, during which time the burnt surface deposits are subjected to erosion. In the early stages, individual mineral particles are removed by wind or rain, but persistent water erosion leads to the development of small channels and eventually to proper gully formation. On Levisham Moor on the North York Moors, gullies up to 3 metres or more in depth have formed, in the sides of which earlier erosion deposits are exposed. Pottery at the junction of the old soil surface and the erosion deposits is of nineteenth or early twentieth century date, linking the erosion to the period in which burning of the surrounding moorland has been a regular occurrence[13]. A great deal of research has been carried out recently into the rehabilitation of seriously burned moorlands, using various surface treatments, such as rotavation, fertilising and fencing, and sown mixtures of grasses and tree species[14].

Some people are now questioning the wisdom of continuing the regular burning of moorlands. It seems that we are now witnessing the breakdown of a system which has been operating for some 150 years but may not be sustainable indefinitely. Research is being carried out into alternative methods of producing a nutritious cover of heather, such as cutting instead of burning. There are several commercial uses for cut heather, for example as fertiliser or in sewage treatment, but these involve removal of the cut material and thus add to the long-term depletion of soil nutrients. An alternative is to use a forage harvester to cut and chop the heather and spread it on to adjoining patches of moorland. This has been done successfully on the North York Moors but is expensive and the machines are not suitable for all types of terrain, so at the moment it is only considered viable as a means of dealing with heather that has been left too long to burn safely, or as a way of creating firebreaks[14].

Other areas are suffering from problems of over-grazing. This is seen particularly on Ilkley Moor on the Pennines, which has been used as common grazing land from 1893 onwards. An early vegetation survey by Smith and Rankin in 1903 showed heather to be dominant on the higher ground with grass-heath on the lower slopes. By the time the Wharfedale Field Naturalists' Society re-surveyed the area in 1959, crowberry and cottongrass were expanding on the higher ground at the expense of heather, while bracken had replaced grass-heath on the lower slopes. Because the number of grazing animals was not controlled, there were far too many sheep on the Moor by the 1980s, and heather was being grazed out, while the unpalatable crowberry spread on the higher ground. Experimental work showed good recovery of heather in fenced off plots, particularly following light burning which controlled the crowberry[15].

The bracken problem

The encroachment of bracken on the lower slopes of Ilkley Moor is part of a much wider problem, affecting most of upland Britain today. Bracken has been described as 'the most successful international weed of the twentieth century and a serious source of land loss and of toxins which threaten the health of both animals and humans'[16]. One of the five commonest plants in the world, it can compete successfully with most other vegetation but is suppressed by tree growth. Its history in Britain is linked to the availability of open ground, which was probably at the edges of woodlands and in natural glades. It spread as the woodlands were opened up, and its spores are recorded on pollen diagrams in nearly all the early clearance phases. It seems to have been one of the first plants to invade abandoned agricultural land in the absence of significant grazing pressure.

However, its extent did not give cause for concern until the twentieth century and, indeed, it was a useful plant in former times[17]. Its fronds could be collected and used as stable bedding for cattle or other stock and it could be used as a thatch for roofs. Crushed and burnt, it was a source of potash in the glass-making industry. It was also kept in check by the trampling of cattle and horses' hooves. Since its traditional uses declined and sheep replaced the heavier beasts on the moorlands, bracken has colonised any suitable habitats. It needs a well-drained soil, so is not a problem on blanket peat areas except where they have been drained. It is particularly characteristic of steep valley sides above the enclosed land, including many areas of abandoned fields, where it often covers enormous areas to the virtual exclusion of other plant life. However, it can also compete with heathers on well-drained soils and has often seized the opportunity to expand when moorland burning has been too severe for good heather regeneration. Although it can colonise new ground from spores, it usually spreads vegetatively, advancing up to a metre or more per year and forming enormous clones which can be hundreds of years old.

The spread of bracken in the twentieth century has become the subject of numerous research projects and several international conferences[18,19]. It is a cause of concern because it has no real use in the agricultural economy today and because it harbours ticks which spread disease to both sheep and grouse. It has also been found to be poisonous to stock and carcinogenic to humans, with links to both stomach and oesophageal cancer. However, it does provide a valuable habitat for small birds and mammals, and a food source for about 40 invertebrate species, 11 of which are specific to it. A light cover of bracken may provide a partial substitute for a woodland canopy, to the benefit of such woodland plants as bluebell, primrose or wood-sorrel[20].

Estimates of the amount of land currently covered by bracken and its rate of expansion vary[21]. The rate of spread in Britain in the 1980s is thought to have been between 1 and 2 per cent per year, rising to about 3 per cent per year in the worst affected areas, such as common lands in west-central Wales. A recent estimate for the uplands of England and Wales was a rate of 0.8 per cent per year and it may be that the rate is slowing down now, as the number of remaining suitable habitats diminishes[22]. Methods of bracken control include cutting or brashing, spraying with chemicals such as asulam or glyphosate, and biological control. However, there is no doubt that the real cause of bracken's success is poorly managed farmland or over-burnt moorland and it may be that changes in agricultural or moorland management will prove to be the real solution to the problem.

Moorland conservation

Large areas of moorland have been afforested with conifers in the twentieth century, particularly in Scotland, Wales and the North York Moors (chapter 8). Other areas, especially the moorland fringes, have been ploughed out for agricultural use. For example, much of central Exmoor was reclaimed by the Knight family after the Enclosure Act of 1815[23]. Agricultural encroachment on to moorlands in the twentieth century has led to much controversy. A Committee of Inquiry was set up under Lord Porchester, which made recommendations in 1974 for the safeguarding of moorland areas. It is estimated that in total over 25 per cent of the moorland in the North York Moors and Exmoor has been lost to agriculture and forestry but the losses have been lower in most other uplands. In 1978 there were still at least 2.3 million ha of heather moorland in Britain[24].

From the conservation standpoint, moorlands are less easy to defend than more natural habitats, such as deciduous woodland or wetlands. On the other hand, their artificiality adds an extra historical dimension of interest[12]. The real question is whether or not the moorlands as we know them today are stable in the long term. Certainly, their animal life has been much depleted by gamekeeping and the diversity of their plant life has been much reduced by modern management techniques. Over the millennia, their soils have deteriorated to the point where erosion and disastrous fires have become major threats.

However, given the chance, these areas might regain much of their lost diversity and interest. Whenever grazing and burning cease, trees begin to colonise even the most barren moorland area. Birch and rowan are usually the first colonisers, followed by holly or hawthorn. They are often joined by pines, larches and other volunteer conifers from forestry plantations. As long ago as the 1950s, Dimbleby showed that birch could break up the iron pan and reverse the trend towards podzolisation within 50 or 100 years. He also initiated trials of various hardwood species at Broxa on the North York Moors to investigate the long term prospects for re-establishing a woodland cover on the moorlands. Today his plots are crowded with mature birch, oak, sweet chestnut, Scots pine and other trees, proving that the poor state of the moorland soils could be overcome by suitable fertiliser treatments and plantings. Such tree growth, whether by natural colonisation or by deliberate planting, may offer a solution to the problem of moorland stability. It may be that the moorlands will only be viable in the long term if managed as part of a lengthy rotation with woodland. Perhaps we need to re-create something like the woodland–moorland mosaic which would have been familiar to the early prehistoric inhabitants of the uplands.

To illustrate the development of heather moorlands in greater depth, we can look at two areas where, through detailed research work, it has been possible to link the ecological history with archaeological evidence for the effects of human cultures. Dartmoor and the North York Moors contrast markedly in their physical features but some interesting comparisons emerge in the way people have affected the landscape and wildlife.

Dartmoor

The popular image of Dartmoor is that of a remote, windswept moorland, beset with treacherous bogs and grazed by wild ponies. However, the landscape has witnessed many changes in management over the years, from Mesolithic hunting through to present-day military training. Remains of prehistoric settlements and farming systems are widely and abundantly distributed over all the higher ground and each cultural period has left its imprint on the environment. The underlying rock type is granite, which forms gentle domed uplands, partially separated by the valleys of the East and West Dart rivers into the North, South and East Moors. The uplands were fashioned into a series of erosion surfaces during the Tertiary period, forming extensive badly drained plateau surfaces. This erosion in a sub-tropical climate led to deep rotting of the granite and, where this is exposed on the sides of the hills, subsequent weathering during the Ice Age has enlarged the natural joints of the rock to form tors, such as Haytor and Great Mis Tor.

Dartmoor was not over-ridden by ice during the last glacial period but, in the extreme tundra climate, much weathering and erosion of the granite occurred, leaving large blocks or 'clitter' liberally spread over the valley sides, and finer deposits on their floors. There are many mineral veins associated with the granite and its surrounding metamorphic rocks. Many are of commercial value and have been exploited, including tin, copper, arsenic, lead, zinc, silver, iron, wolfram, tungsten and kaolinite. The granite itself forms good building stone and has been quarried in several places.

Dartmoor experiences a relatively high annual rainfall, averaging about 1440 mm but rising to over 2400 mm on the western side. This has facilitated the development of extensive peat bogs on the higher plateau surfaces and in the valleys. Drier plateau areas have moorland communities, some of which are dominated by heathers and western gorse and managed as grouse moors. Where sheep, cattle and ponies exert a sufficiently intensive grazing pressure, grasses are dominant. Other areas are dominated by bilberry and many steep valley sides are over-run by bracken. Woodlands are generally confined to the valleys but there are a few surviving high-level oakwoods, such as Black Tor Copse and Wistman's Wood (Colour plate 6). Forestry plantations are limited on the moors but the areas near Postbridge and Fernworthy Reservoir have substantial blocks of conifers. However, it is the moorlands which dominate the Dartmoor scene today (Figure 11).

There are several published pollen diagrams from Dartmoor (Figure 11). They show that mixed deciduous woodland was established by the middle Post-glacial, with oak and hazel as the most important trees but with elm, alder and a little ash and small-leaved lime. It is not certain whether woodland covered the whole of Dartmoor at this stage. High-level sites record some pollen from heath and bog plants but these could be from the bogs themselves, which may have been of very limited extent. On the other hand, no wood remains have been found beneath or within the peat cover on the moors above 547 metres. Probably, the woodland thinned out with increasing

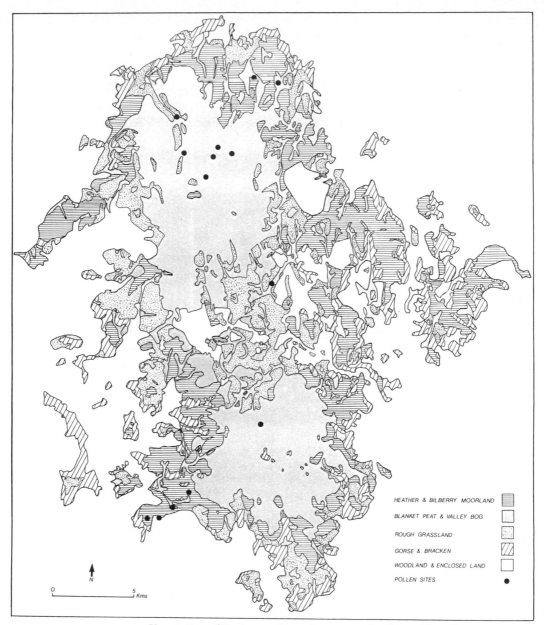

FIGURE II Vegetation of Dartmoor (Based on a map by the Field Studies Council, 1979; pollen sites are shown by solid circles)

HEATHER & BILBERRY MOORLAND

BLANKET PEAT & VALLEY BOG

ROUGH GRASSLAND

GORSE & BRACKEN

WOODLAND & ENCLOSED LAND

POLLEN SITES

ing altitude, giving way to hazel scrub. Whatever the precise position of the tree-line in the middle Post-glacial, it was soon to be affected by human activities. There is evidence for woodland disturbance in the Mesolithic period above 450 metres, where fire was most effective at the woodland edge and in areas of scrub. By enlarging naturally open areas of boggy ground and burning the undergrowth, Mesolithic hunters began the process of conversion of the Dartmoor uplands to moorland vegetation[25]. This is reflected in a gradual increase of heather pollen, together with the spread of blanket peat on to much of the higher ground.

The grazing of domestic animals began in the Neolithic and parts of Dartmoor were converted to grassland and scrub. There may have been a decrease in human impact in the later Neolithic, when pollen diagrams show a temporary regeneration of woodland, but it was followed by a period of intensive activity and population growth in the Bronze Age. Human activity on the higher parts of Dartmoor reached a peak in the early part of the second millennium BC. Settlement and farming were more intensive than at any period before or since. The remains of this early Bronze Age period are still well preserved today. Large-scale archaeological excavations have been carried out at many sites and have yielded valuable information on the soils and vegetation as well as human activities.

In the early Bronze Age, much of Dartmoor could have been described as a 'ritual landscape'. In the centuries following 2000 BC, stone circles, stone rows and single standing stones were erected, all of which are believed to have had a ritual significance. There are also abundant funerary monuments from this period, including over 130 large burial mounds around the edges of the higher land and hundreds of smaller mounds[26]. Archaeology has also revealed details of the early Bronze Age life-style. Remains of over 3000 hut circles may still be seen on Dartmoor, scattered on the slopes all around the high moors, such as in the Merrivale area or on Chagford Common. Some of them are within enclosures, as at Grimspound, or associated with field systems, as at Kestor. Some of them were probably permanent settlements while others may have been temporary summer shielings.

Pollen analysis records evidence of cereal cultivation at some sites. A mixed agriculture was probably practised, with arable fields on the lower ground and pastoralism higher up. Analysis of buried soils shows that there were brown earths on the flanks of the uplands but that soils on the higher ground were already podzolised and showing signs of surface waterlogging. The overall impression is of an intensively exploited landscape, with vegetation and soils undergoing rapid changes in the early Bronze Age. Fleming has described the scene as 'a shifting mosaic of woodland, scrub, heath, blanket bog and grassland'[27].

Between 1700 and 1600 BC, the exploitation of Dartmoor was formalised by the laying out of a system of boundary banks. Initially of earth with hedges or fences on top, they were later converted to stone walls, known today as 'reaves'. The tumbled remains of these walls, up to 80 cm high and one or two metres wide, can be traced over many miles, although they are often difficult to pick out on the ground. They are best seen from the air and with a light covering of snow, when a pattern can be distinguished of systematic subdivision of land into a number of territories. Most reaves are in the marginal zone around the high moors, at altitudes of between 250 and 400 metres. Long parallel reaves lead up the valley sides to end in terminal reaves, running along the contours and encircling the central high plateau areas.

These core areas of moorland were probably used as common grazing land for the livestock of several territorial groups. The lower parts of the valleys provided other grazing land, subdivided by more reaves. The arable land and settlements were on the upper slopes of the valleys, particularly on South Dartmoor. Fleming believes the whole way of life lasted some three or four hundred years, during which Dartmoor was an important centre of settlement and farming in south-west England. By the end of the Bronze Age, the higher parts of the moors were grass-heath areas used as common grazing land, the lower slopes and many of the valleys were farmland or settlement sites, and only the steeper slopes or deep valleys retained a woodland cover.

The climatic deterioration of the first millennium BC rendered the higher areas less attractive for farming. A shift in settlement took place towards lower land around the margins of Dartmoor during the Iron Age. Reduced grazing pressure on the high moors allowed heather moorland to spread at the expense of grassland, as illustrated by a rise in the heather curve on the pollen diagrams. However, there was still sufficient grazing to prevent the recolonisation of trees and the higher parts have remained open ever since. The moorland had by then attained approximately its present limits.

Later cultures may not have altered the overall extent of moorland on Dartmoor but they were important in maintaining the open vegetation and preventing the re-establishment of woodland. There was a brief expansion of cultivation and settlement in early medieval times on to land which has since been deserted[28]. The central part of Dartmoor was a Royal Forest from the eleventh to the thirteenth centuries, later passing to the Duchy of Cornwall as a private chase. Within the Forest there were unusually 35 'ancient tenements' of cultivated land in the valleys of the Dart rivers. Around the fringes of the Forest there were grazing lands which were common to practically the whole of Devon. Is this, perhaps, an echo of the Bronze Age common grazing tradition on Dartmoor? In the thirteenth and fourteenth centuries, the Cistercian abbeys of Buckfast and Tavistock grazed large flocks of sheep on the moors, thus continuing the age-old tradition.

The development of the tin industry from the twelfth century onwards had relatively little effect on the moorlands but led to the clearance of some alder woods in the valleys for charcoal. Tinners' charters of 1201 and 1305 mention rights to cut peat from the moorlands. Rabbit warrens were often set up in conjunction with the tin mining and the artificial warrens which were constructed may still be seen, for instance at Huntingdon Warren. The close grazing of rabbits would have converted the warren areas to grass-heaths. Other grazing animals on the moorland included sheep, cattle and ponies, the last used as beasts of burden by the tin miners.

In the eighteenth century, Dartmoor did not escape the effects of the 'age of improvement'. One improver was Thomas Tyrwhitt, who tried to introduce arable agriculture. A second wave of improvers in the mid-nineteenth century made other 'newtakes' but these were abandoned within a few decades. At the top of the pollen diagrams there is a great expansion of heather pollen, characteristic of modern moorland management and dating from the past 150 years or so. This is the latest stage in the development of the moorland habitat on Dartmoor, the origins of which we have traced over some 7000 years. Seen in this light, as a unique legacy of human impact on the landscape, the moorlands of Dartmoor assume a high priority for conservation.

The North York Moors

The North York Moors are composed of younger rocks and receive less rainfall than Dartmoor. The main expanse of moorland is on Jurassic sandstones and shales, where soils are podzolised and often gleyed, with peaty surface horizons. Deeper peat bogs occur on the flatter areas of the main watershed and in many of the valleys. The Tabular Hills in the south of the region are formed of calcareous grits and limestones. They generally have a mixture of rich farmland and woodland over brown earths or calcareous soils, although there are some patches of podzolised soils on steep slopes overlying grits. Because of its easterly position, the area has a low rainfall, even the highest land receiving little more than 1000 mm per year. There are 51,000 ha of unenclosed moorland on the North York Moors, mostly managed as grouse moors (Figure 12, Colour plate 7). Elgee differentiated 'thin' moors from 'fat moors', the

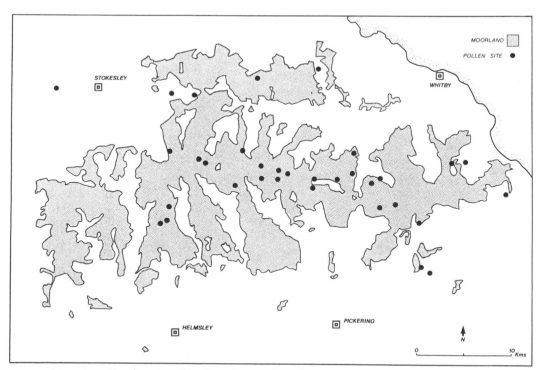

FIGURE 12 Heather moorland on the North York Moors (Based on maps by the North York Moors National Park; pollen sites are shown by solid circles)

latter developed over deeper peat [2]. Moorland vegetation may be dominated by several different species, including bracken, heathers and rushes, often growing in intimate mixtures, according to soil or drainage. As on Dartmoor, the story of the development of these moorland plant and animal communities goes back to the prehistoric period.

There are more than 30 published pollen diagrams from the North York Moors (Figure 12), spanning between them the entire Post-glacial period[29]. Sites studied include valley bogs, blanket peats, bogs behind landslips and buried soils and their distribution is concentrated on the moorland areas. The pollen diagrams reveal that almost the whole area was wooded by the middle Post-glacial, except for small areas of heath or bog vegetation on the highest land, where the woodland cover thinned out. Mesolithic hunters would have found such areas attractive and may have enlarged these natural areas of heath by burning the undergrowth. The first signs of interference in the vegetation coincide with the formation of the first blanket peats on the high watershed about 5000 BC. After this, there is evidence of recurrent burning at springhead sites on the high watershed. On Bilsdale Moor there are many charcoal layers in the peat, corresponding with at least eight separate episodes of disturbance to the local woodland. After each disturbance phase, there is a more stable phase of woodland regeneration. It is probable that pioneer trees, such as oak and hazel, were regenerating into the open areas after the burning ceased, taking advantage of the extra light. As a result of the combination of burning and grazing pressure from wild animals, the high watershed was becoming a mosaic of open woodland, scrub, moorland and bog.

There are many archaeological sites on the North York Moors to testify to these activities. Some sites have produced hundreds of flints, lying at the junction between mineral soil and blanket peat, showing that the sites were not covered with peat at this stage. Elgee gave an imaginative but charming description of what these flints tell us of the Mesolithic lifestyle[30]:

> Like stray shafts of sunshine their small imperishable flints illuminate the depths of the gloomy avenues of time. They give us glimpses of skin-clad men spearing salmon in the Esk or stalking deer over the melancholy moors; of women and children gathering roots, herbs, and berries in the forests or feeding camp fires on the heathery knolls whence craftsmen in the intervals of flint-chipping swept their eyes up over their happy hunting-grounds, an unsullied creation, rolling to distant land and sea horizons.

Neolithic farming and settlement were concentrated on the Tabular Hills and there is little evidence for agricultural activity on the high moors. It is probable that hunting continued there in the Mesolithic tradition, possibly with the addition of herding or pastoralism, as Neolithic and Bronze Age flints have been found on many Mesolithic hunting sites. Some blanket peat was initiated in the Neolithic, possibly as a result of soil degradation following many years of hunting activities. In the Bronze Age, the moors seem to have been more attractive to people, as was the case on Dartmoor. The warmer climate would have helped and soils were less degraded than they are today, as shown by analysis of buried soils under Bronze Age barrows[10]. On the Tabular Hills, there was a wide variation in soils, suggesting a period of rapid soil change. Some soils showed very little sign of podzolisation, while others had developed an iron pan and were experiencing some surface waterlogging. It should be noted, however, that some of these soils may have continued to evolve since their burial. In those soils which were already acid enough to preserve pollen, the picture is one of hazel scrub, grassland and grass-heath vegetation. On the watershed of the high moors, most soils seem to have been already podzolised and gleyed; their pollen content suggests open alder and hazel woodlands, interspersed with areas of moorland.

Pollen diagrams from most of the peat bogs record the Bronze Age impact and some of them have cereal pollen, identified as emmer wheat and barley. It seems that the economy was a mixed one, with some arable cultivation on the upper valley sides and pastoralism and hunting continuing on the higher ground[31]. Archaeological evidence consists of irregular field systems and about 70 cairnfields, the latter being clusters of clearance cairns. They are found mostly on the hillsides and spurs below 300 metres and are thought to be mainly Bronze Age in date by association with other archaeological remains. These include the many round barrows, often containing several cremations, which are conspicuous features of the high ground. No houses of definite Bronze Age date have been found on the North York Moors, in contrast to Dartmoor, so it is probable that the settlement sites were in the valleys and their remains are buried under hillwash.

The North York Moors counterparts of the Dartmoor reaves are the linear dykes of the Tabular Hills, which probably date to about 1000 BC and later[32]. They appear to constitute a subdivision of the landscape into territorial estates, the boundaries of which were marked by the dykes, rivers and escarpments. There may have been an intimate association between upland and lowland, with livestock overwintered in the valleys and taken up to the woods or pastures on the higher ground in spring and summer. Possibly some of the cairnfields represent the remains of temporary shielings in the summer pastures. However, there is no evidence yet for common grazing land like that found on Dartmoor. The fact that the dykes are best developed on the Tabular Hills indicates that soils were more productive there. It may be that by the late Bronze Age farming had already been abandoned on the higher moors.

In the Iron Age and Roman periods, settlement moved to the margins of the uplands, possibly in response to the deterioration in climate. Grazing continued on the central areas, maintaining the open nature of the plant communities. In the Dark Ages, moorland vegetation spread, as shown on the pollen diagrams by a sustained increase in the heather curve. The moorland area probably reached almost its present extent during this period. A continued grazing pressure has been maintained through the centuries to prevent tree growth on the moorlands. The balance of grass-heath and moorland has varied according to the intensity of this grazing pressure. For example, in early medieval times, there was a great deal of sheep grazing on the moors, much of it under the control of monastic houses, such as Whitby Abbey,

Rievaulx Abbey and Guisborough Priory. Most of the eastern North York Moors was the Royal Forest of Pickering, and here moorland was more limited in extent, although grazing from deer and sheep gradually converted most of the woodland to open vegetation types.

The 'age of improvement' resulted in a few abortive attempts to grow cereals on the moorland but the chief land use was rough grazing until the advent of the modern management for grouse and sheep. This is clearly seen on the pollen diagrams as a massive rise in the heather curve towards the top. It resulted in the decline of birds such as the raven, merlin, hen harrier, buzzard and kestrel, as recorded by Canon Atkinson in 1891[33]. There were several large rabbit warrens on the Tabular Hills, established in the eighteenth century, such as the Dalby warren. Afforestation has been responsible for most of the recent losses of moorland. Since 1950, 18.2 per cent of the moorland has been lost to plantations and 6.4 per cent to agricultural reclamation, mainly for improved pasture.

Thus, the study of ecological history in both Dartmoor and the North York Moors shows the present moorlands to be the result of several millennia of environmental degradation by human beings. Ironically, in the eyes of the general public, these same moorlands are a cherished wild landscape, encapsulated in the words of St Aelred of Rievaulx in the twelfth century: 'Everywhere peace, everywhere serenity and a marvellous freedom from the tumult of the world.'

References

1   Rackham, O, *The history of the countryside*. Dent, London, 1986.
2   Elgee, F, *The moorlands of north-eastern Yorkshire: Their natural history and origin*. A Brown and Sons, London, 1912.
3   Rodwell, J S (ed), *British plant communities: vol 2, Mires and heaths*. Cambridge University Press, Cambridge, 1991.
4   Chaplin, R E, The ecology and behaviour of deer in relation to their impact on the environment of prehistoric Britain. In Evans, J G, Limbrey, S and Cleere, H (eds), *The effect of man on the landscape: The Highland Zone*. Council for British Archaeology Research report No. 11, pp 40–2, 1975.
5   Pearsall, W H, *Mountains and moorlands*. Collins, New Naturalist Series, London, 1950.
6   Clutton-Brock, T H and Ball, T H, *Rhum: The natural history of an island*. Edinburgh University Press, Edinburgh, 1987.
7   Ratcliffe, D A, *Bird life of mountain and upland*. Cambridge University Press, Cambridge, 1990.
8   Moore, P D, The development of moorlands and upland mires. In Jones, M (ed), *Archaeology and the flora of the British Isles*, pp 116–22. Oxford University Committee for Archaeology Monograph No. 14, Oxford, 1988.
9   Spratt, D A and Burgess, C, Upland settlement in Britain: the second millennium BC and after. *British Archaeological Reports*, British Series No 143. British Archaeological Reports, Oxford, 1985.
10   Dimbleby, G W, The development of British heathlands and their soils. *Oxford Forest Memoirs*, No 23, Oxford, 1962.
11   Gimingham, C H, *Ecology of heathlands*. Chapman and Hall, London, 1972.
12   Gimingham, C H, *Introduction to heathland ecology*. Oliver and Boyd, Edinburgh, 1975.
13   Curtis, L F, Landscape periodicity and soil development. In Peel, R, Chisholm, M and Haggett, P (eds), *Processes in physical and human geography*, pp 247–65. Heinemann, 1975.

14   North York Moors National Park, *Moorland management programme, 1985–90*. North York Moors National Park, Helmsley, 1991.

15   Smith, R T and Atherden, M A, Recent vegetative change and the management of Ilkley Moor, West Yorkshire. *University of Leeds School of Geography working paper* No. 414, Leeds, 1985.

16   Taylor, J A, The relationship between land-use change and variations in bracken encroachment rates in Britain. In Smith, R T (ed), *The biogeographical impact of land-use change: Collected essays*, pp 19–28. Biogeographical Monographs 2, Biogeography Study Group, Leeds, 1985.

17   Rymer, L, The history and ethnobotany of bracken. *Botanical Journal of the Linnean Society*, 73, pp 151–76, 1976.

18   Smith, R T and Taylor, J A (eds), *Bracken: Ecology, land use and control technology*. Parthenon Press, Carnforth, 1986.

19   Thomson, J A and Smith, R T (eds), *Bracken biology and management*. Australian Institute of Agricultural Science, occasional publication No 40, Sydney, 1990.

20   Nature Conservancy Council, *Bracken in Wales*. Nature Conservancy Council, Bangor, 1988.

21   Taylor, J A, The bracken problem: a global perspective. In Thomson, J A and Smith, R T (eds), *Bracken biology and management*, pp 3–19, 1990.

22   Lawton, J H, Developments in the UK biological control programme for bracken. In Thomson, J A and Smith, R T (eds), *Bracken biology and management*, pp 309–14, 1990.

23   Miller, G R, Miles, J, and Heal, O W (eds), *Moorland management: A study of Exmoor*. Institute of Terrestrial Ecology, Cambridge, 1984.

24   Bunce, R G H (ed), *Heather in England and Wales*. Institute of Terrestrial Ecology research publication No 3, HMSO, London, 1989.

25   Simmons, I G et al, A further pollen analytical study of the Blacklane peat section on Dartmoor, England. *New Phytologist*, 94, pp 655–67, 1983.

26   Dartmoor National Park, *Archaeology of Dartmoor*. Dartmoor National Park Dept. Exeter, 1978.

27   Fleming, A, *The Dartmoor Reaves*. Batsford, London, 1988.

28   Weir, J (ed), *Dartmoor National Park*. Countryside Commission official guide. Webb and Bower, Exeter, 1987.

29   Simmons, I G et al, Prehistoric environments. In Spratt, D A (eds), *Prehistoric and Roman archaeology of north-east Yorkshire*, pp 33–99. British Archaeological Reports, British Series No. 104, 1982.

30   Elgee, F, *Early man in north-east Yorkshire*. John Bellows, Gloucester, 1930.

31   Spratt, D A (ed), *Prehistoric and Roman archaeology of north-east Yorkshire*, 1982.

32   Spratt, D A, *Linear earthworks of the Tabular Hills, Northeast Yorkshire*. J R Collis, University of Sheffield, 1989.

33   Atkinson, J C, *Forty years in a moorland parish*. Macmillan, London, 1891.

7

Wetlands

What would the world be, once bereft
Of wet and of wildness? Let them be left,
O let them be left, wildness and wet;
Long live the weeds and the wilderness yet.
G M Hopkins

Of all the habitats in upland Britain, it is perhaps the wetlands which most closely approach the idea of wilderness. The mountain streams, deep lakes and vast expanses of peat all seem to be moulded by forces beyond the control of humans. Certainly, the majority of the wetlands are of natural origin, although in some cases river courses have been altered, reservoirs have been created or drainage impeded artificially. However, wetlands have been used and abused by humans throughout the entire Post-glacial period, and the impact of modern technology has posed major threats to their plant and animal communities. There is a great range of wetlands, including rivers, canals, lakes, reservoirs, fens and peat bogs. They form a continuum from aquatic to terrestrial habitats, and changes from one type to another can be triggered by variations in climate, sedimentation or plant growth. Wetlands are unusual in that the record of these changes is preserved because of the waterlogging. They form a rich source of information for the historical ecologist, allowing the pattern of changes through time to be reconstructed in fuller detail than is usually possible for other habitats.

Open water habitats

It is estimated that there are nearly 200,000 streams in Great Britain, many of them wholly or partly in the uplands, ranging in size from tiny headstreams to major rivers like the Spey or Wharfe[1]. There are also thousands of lakes, varying from small lochans or corrie tarns to major lakes or sea lochs several hundred metres deep. The total number of water bodies in the uplands is estimated to be over 39,000[1]. They are most frequent in northern Scotland and the Outer Hebrides, where they cover over 5 per cent of the area.

As well as the natural water bodies, there are artificial canals and reservoirs, which form important additional wildlife habitats. The only upland area where canals are significant is the Pennines, where several east–west routes were built in the eighteenth and nineteenth centuries to link river systems either side of the Pennines, some of them including tunnels. The Huddersfield canal, the Rochdale canal and the Cromford canal are good examples. There are many reservoirs; some are merely enlarged natural lakes, such as Thirlmere in the Lake District, while others are new sites on flooded former farmland. Ladybower reservoir in the Peak District drowned the villages of Derwent and Ashopton, whilst the ruins of the former village of Mardale may be seen in Hawes Water in the Lake District when the water level is unusually low.

Rivers form very unstable and challenging habitats for wildlife. The headwaters usually have steep gradients, and bands of hard rock often cause waterfalls, which form obstacles for migrating fish such as salmon and trout. The streams tend to have rocky bottoms strewn with large boulders, as the water carries the smaller particles away downstream. In the middle and lower sections of rivers, meanders are usually well developed and the river beds have alternate deeper pools and shallower 'riffles', providing a variety of conditions for plant and animal life. Sudden and dramatic changes of level are experienced by some rivers, notably those on the Pennines, such as the Ure and the Swale, and this poses problems for marginal plant growth. More stable conditions are found in cut-off meanders or 'ox-bow lakes', where a marshy flora is soon established.

Lakes and canals tend to be more stable habitats than rivers, although wave erosion may be severe along some shores and, where inflowing streams enter lakes, the mixing of waters creates turbid conditions, with mineral material suspended in the water. Reservoirs usually show a clear zone at their edges between the normal upper and lower water levels, which is difficult for animals and plants to colonise. In deep lakes and reservoirs, organisms face problems of light and temperature variations. Light penetration decreases rapidly with depth, so that below 3 or 4 metres there is insufficient light for plants to photosynthesise in most lakes. Vegetation is confined to the surface layers and the margins but animal life is more widely distributed, as dead organic matter sinks down to provide a food source for organisms in the lower layers of water. The water in shallow lakes is mixed by the action of the wind, so that temperature is more or less uniform throughout. In deeper lakes and reservoirs, only the top layers are affected by wind action. Below them there is a sudden and steep decrease in temperature to a layer of much colder water, which stays at around 5°C all year round. Lakes vary considerably in their productivity, according to the type of material washed into them, some being nutrient-rich whilst others are nutrient-poor. Lakes in limestone areas may be alkaline, with a pH as high as 9.0, whereas the 'dubh lochans' of northern Scotland are very acid and have a pH of only 4.2.

Research in the Lake District has shown how the productivity of lakes can vary over time[2]. From studies of the sediments washed into the lakes in the early Post-glacial, it is apparent that fresh glacial drift was being eroded, rich in minerals such as calcium and magnesium. The remains of diatoms in the sediments show that nearly all the lakes were very productive at this stage, irrespective of their underlying geology. By the middle Post-glacial, woodland was established in the Lake District and changes took place in the chemical nature of the sediments and the diatom flora indicating that soils were becoming leached and waters less productive. The quantity of sediment arriving in the lakes increased as the surrounding land was deforested and exploited for agriculture. The more recent sediments of the lakes vary. In some cases, such as Esthwaite Water, a change is seen towards greater productivity. It is thought that this enrichment has been caused by agricultural run-off and the input of sewage from settlements like Hawkshead. Algal blooms have occurred in Esthwaite Water in recent years as a result of this enrichment, which is accentuated by the shallowness of this lake. Other lakes with less agricultural catchments and deeper waters, such as Wastwater or Ennerdale, do not show this modern change and still have clear, unproductive waters.

Plant life in rivers and lakes

Plants in rivers have to be able to contend with the current, either by being firmly attached to one spot or by floating in or on the water. Most plants are found towards the banks, where the current is weakest. In the upper reaches of rivers, mosses and leafy liverworts usually dominate the plant life. Stones and boulders provide habitats for lichens and algae, and a few flowering plants, such as floating sweet-grass or brooklime, can grow in silt trapped between the boulders. In the middle and lower reaches, Canadian waterweed is widely naturalised and grows in the deeper water, while the leaves of water-starworts, duckweeds and yellow and white water-lilies float on the surface. Stoneworts grow in limestone areas, incorporating calcium carbonate in their structures.

Plants such as monkeyflower, water mint and amphibious bistort grow on the insides of meanders. In the wet mud by the side of the river, other species may be found, including yellow iris, lesser spearwort or meadowsweet. Willows and alder are the commonest trees of the river banks. Underneath them there may be marsh plants which can tolerate regular flooding, such as marsh-marigold and butterbur. Some plants rely on the current to distribute their seeds to new areas, particularly the introduced Indian balsam, which is well established in northern England and Wales and spreading into Scotland.

Plants growing in canals, lakes and reservoirs have fewer problems associated with water movement. Plants are arranged in zones according to water depth. In the deep water of the central lake, only submerged and free-floating plants are found, such as algae, stoneworts and Canadian waterweed. In water up to about 3 metres deep, water-milfoils, pondweeds and quillwort may grow. There are also some submerged mosses and liverworts. As the water becomes shallower, plants grow rooted on the bottom and with most parts under water but the tops of their stems penetrating the surface. The water lobelia, with its delicate, pale lilac flowers projecting above the water on long stalks, is an attractive feature of many Scottish lochs and Lake

District lakes. Another plant sometimes found with it is the bladderwort, which has tiny yellow flowers and catches invertebrates in underwater traps on its stems or leaves.

In water less than a metre deep, it is possible for plants to be rooted in the mud and have nearly all their leaves and flowering parts floating on the surface. The water-lilies are the prime examples, and there are extensive beds of the white one in sheltered bays in the shallower Scottish lochs and some Lake District lakes. They are accompanied by pondweeds and bogbean. As the water level decreases to a few centimetres, another group of plants takes over, with their lower shoots in the water but the upper parts projecting into the air above. Around many lakes, extensive reedswamps are established, dominated by the common reed, with other grasses and sedges beneath. Other areas of the lake shore may have a carr woodland community, composed of alder, willows or birches, with reedswamp species growing underneath the trees. In some places, a floating mat of *Sphagnum* mosses may extend outwards from the lake shore over the open water.

The boundaries between these zones of vegetation are not always sharp, one plant community merging gradually into another as the water gets shallower towards the edge of the lake. Because the plants are so finely adjusted to water depth, it is not possible for them to develop around the edges of artificial reservoirs, unless the water level stays constant for long periods of time. The vegetation zones around lakes may be seen to some extent as a time sequence, with the deep water communities representing early stages in plant succession and the reedswamps, carr woodland or floating mats of *Sphagnum* mosses representing the later stages. Such a series of vegetation zones is known as a hydrosere; through time the hydrosere may convert open water to dry land, as the remains of dead plants build up to form peat and inflowing streams deposit sand and silt.

Some formerly large lakes have been divided into two by the development of hydroseres associated with streams flowing into the middle of their valleys. Examples are the double lakes of Buttermere and Crummock Water and of Derwent Water and Bassenthwaite in the Lake District. More typically, lakes have hydroseres at one or both ends. In some cases, small relatively shallow lakes have been completely infilled during the Post-glacial period. An example is Bowscale Moss in the Lake District, which was a lake in the Late-glacial period and is now an acid peat bog, having gone through the intervening successional stages of reedswamp and carr woodland.

Animal life in open waters

The invertebrate life in rivers and lakes ranges from microscopic organisms to large molluscs and crustaceans. The smaller creatures float in the water in great numbers and are the food for larger invertebrates and fish. The larger organisms are often good indicators of the acidity or nutrient status of the water. For instance, *Tubifex* worms can tolerate low levels of oxygen, so they are sometimes the only organisms surviving in very polluted rivers. Fresh-water mussels and snails, on the other hand, are commonest in unpolluted hard water, so are most likely to be found in limestone areas, such as the Pennines or southern Lake District. Some of the commonest crustaceans are the tiny water fleas, which are food for many fish, amphibians and larger invertebrates. The fresh-water shrimp is found in fast-flowing hard water rivers, where it is eaten by fish, crayfish and birds. The fresh-water crayfish is one of the largest invertebrates in fresh waters but is now uncommon, as it was caught frequently for food in the past.

A great many insect species have larval stages which are aquatic. They include stoneflies, caddis flies, lacewings and midges. Some spend most of their lives in the water, only emerging for the brief and final reproductive stage. The most extreme examples are probably the mayflies, which spend one or two years as aquatic larvae but only a few minutes as adults. The only moth species with aquatic larvae are the china-mark moths. Amongst the most beautiful of the insects with aquatic larvae are the damselflies and dragonflies, which are hunters near slow-flowing rivers and lakes. Other insects are wholly aquatic, such as the water crickets, pond skaters, water boatmen, whirligig beetles and the water spider.

Chief consumers of the rich invertebrate life in rivers and lakes are the fish. Some species spend their whole lives in fresh water but others are mainly marine and migrate up rivers for breeding purposes. Their present numbers are probably controlled by fishing rather than by food supply or predation. The most important fish economically are the salmon and the trout. Particularly good salmon rivers include the Tay, the Tweed and the Spey, where the young fish feed on invertebrates for the first two years of their lives, before migrating to sea. They return to the river of their birth some years later for spawning and their dramatic passage upstream, fighting against the current, involves the well-known leaps up waterfalls. Sea trout spend most of their lives at sea, returning to their own rivers to breed, like the salmon. They are merely a migratory form of the brown trout. The non-migratory form lives in nearly all fast clean streams in the uplands and only migrates within the river system itself at breeding time. Common eels are the other main migratory species, breeding in the Sargasso Sea (mid-Atlantic) and migrating up coastal rivers only in adolescent form[3].

Amongst the common resident fish of the upper reaches of rivers are the grayling, the bullhead and the minnow. In the middle reaches, the three-spined stickleback and pike are fairly common. Several other species are found in fresh waters in the uplands of England and Wales but are uncommon or absent in Scotland, including the gudgeon, perch and roach. One fish of particular interest is the arctic char, which is considered to be a relic from the Ice Age and is confined to deep, cold lakes in the Lake District and Scotland. It ventures into rivers only to spawn in the winter. The fresh-water herring is another relic species found in a few Scottish lochs, such as Loch Lomond.

Three species of newt occur in lakes, and the common frog and common toad are more or less ubiquitous. Amphibians are vulnerable to pollution and destruction of their breeding habitats, although numbers have decreased less in the uplands than in the lowlands. Mammal life consists of relatively few species. Smaller mammals include the water shrew, water vole and bank vole. Unfortunately, these species have been ousted from some river systems by the North American mink, which was introduced for the fur industry in 1929 and escaped to establish itself in the wild in the mid-1950s. It is an aggressive competitor with no real predators and has had a devastating effect on the riverine wildlife in some areas. Attempts to control its spread have met with mixed success.

The otter is a native river and sea loch mammal, which has declined alarmingly since 1960. There are several factors involved, including pollution, disturbance, competition for food and deliberate persecution by fishermen. It is now rare in England and Wales, although reasonably common still in Scotland. It is gradually making a comeback under legal protection, reinforced by a captive breeding programme, and otter havens have been set up on several relatively undisturbed rivers and stretches of coastline. For instance, a 48 km stretch of the River Till in Northumberland has been fenced off to allow otters to breed in peace, while 18 km of coastline are managed as an otter haven at Kylerhea on eastern Skye. In the past, the beaver was a member of the fresh-water fauna but it was extinct by about the twelfth century[4]. We can only guess at the dramatic impact it must have had on some of the upland river systems.

Although a large number of birds include upland rivers within their territories, only a few species are dependent on rivers for their main source of food or breeding sites. In the upper reaches of many streams, the dipper feeds underwater, catching insect larvae while walking along the river bed. It prefers clear, shallow streams with stony or gravelly bottoms. The kingfisher and sand martin both nest in river banks and the oyster-catcher nests on gravel banks in the lower reaches of some rivers. The grey heron is common on the middle and lower reaches of rivers throughout Britain. It nests in colonies on tree tops and is vulnerable to hard winters, as it lays its eggs as early as February. The grey wagtail feeds on invertebrates at the edges of rivers, whilst the reed bunting feeds mainly on seeds in the reedbeds.

Many duck species, such as pochard and tufted duck, may be found on upland lakes particularly in winter. Goosanders have been spreading in rivers and lakes for the past century. They nest in hollow trees, holes in banks or rock cavities. The red-breasted merganser is also found in lakes but nests on moorland areas. Practically every lake has its resident coot and the dabchick is also common. The mute swan is a common resident species but the whooper swan is a winter visitor, gathering in flocks on upland lakes. Many waders and gulls use lakes, particularly in winter, when they offer more shelter than the coasts.

The bird of prey most directly connected with the open waters is the osprey, which specialises in fish. It was a common species in Scotland until the early nineteenth century but then fell prey to the attentions of naturalists and egg collectors. Its numbers decreased and it was extinct by the beginning of the twentieth century. In the 1950s, one pair returned to Scotland and others followed in subsequent years. The Royal Society for the Protection of Birds (RSPB) launched one of the most successful conservation campaigns ever with its 'Operation Osprey' in the 1970s, which involved mounting guards over nests and even providing artificial nest sites on suitable tree-tops. The nature reserve at Loch Garten on Speyside was a well publicised site, where hundreds of people could observe the birds each year without disturbing them. Despite repeated attempts at theft of the eggs, the breeding was a success and the number of pairs gradually built up in many parts of Scotland. Recently the Scottish Wildlife Trust has provided visitor facilities at the Loch of Lowes nature reserve, near Dunkeld, where the ospreys successfully reared chicks in 1991 for the first time in seven years.

Problems of human impact

Rivers and lakes have been important to humans from prehistoric times onwards. They have been used as a source of drinking water and food; as lines of communication and defence; as sources of power; for cleaning and waste disposal; and for recreation. As the scale of exploitation has increased, so has the impact on their wildlife. Water-based recreation, such as canoeing, sailing and swimming, causes disturbance to wildlife, especially to sensitive species like otters. On large lakes, motor-boats can cause pollution as well as disturbance. Modern river management, such as dredging and straightening, also disturbs animals and often destroys the bankside vegetation.

Acid rain, caused by atmospheric pollution, is a serious problem in some areas. Aquatic organisms are adapted to specific ranges of acidity (pH) and some species are particularly sensitive to changes. Once the invertebrates and fish begin to die out, those organisms which feed on them, such as birds or mammals, are also doomed. The acidity of the rainwater also leads to the release of heavy metals in the soil, especially aluminium, large quantities of which are toxic to aquatic organisms. The distribution of acid rain over Britain reflects both meteorological patterns and the location of industrial areas. Although the most acid rainfall falls in south-eastern Britain, the higher rainfall amounts in the uplands mean that the areas worst affected are south-west Scotland, the Lake District and north Wales[5].

Another problem of pollution is the run-off from farmland. Increasing amounts of fertilisers have been applied to farmland. They are only partly recovered by the crops or grasses, the rest draining off into the river systems and lakes and enriching them with nitrates or phosphates. This has the effect of causing blooms of algae, which deplete the oxygen supply, leading in extreme cases to the death of other organisms, such as fish. Rivers are less prone to algal blooms than lakes, as the constant movement of water in rivers provides a source of oxygen from the air. Dissolved nitrates in the water are poisonous to many creatures, including humans. Enrichment by agricultural run-off, sewage and industrial effluents has affected many lakes in the Lake District, such as Windermere.

Fishing has been practised since Mesolithic times and fishermen have been leaving their fish-hooks around to prove it. However, some of the modern equipment can pose serious problems for wildlife. The use of lead weights by fishermen is now banned, although old stocks and existing lead in the environment still cause problems. The worst effects are on water birds, such as swans, which accidentally ingest the lead weights and suffer lead poisoning. Nylon fishing lines can also be dangerous to larger birds or mammals, which can get entangled in them and are unable to free themselves because the nylon is so strong. Other effects of fishing include the former persecution of predator species, such as otters and herons, and the concentrated effluents from some fish farms.

Mires, fens and bogs

In the later stages of hydroseres there is no open water left, the substrate being a waterlogged mineral soil or peat. Similar habitats develop on land, where drainage collects in natural hollows or valleys. In some, the main source of water is the groundwater table; in some it is seepage from springs, and in others it is rainwater. All these habitats tend to change through time, as peat builds up or more mineral material is added, but these changes take place over a time-scale of decades or centuries.

The taller vegetation types, dependent mainly on a groundwater supply, are known as fens. Rich-fens are wetlands on fertile sites, with a high water table and a relatively high pH. In the uplands such sites are only found in river valleys where flooding enriches the soil, in small drainage basins on calcareous bedrock or in areas where the ground water is enriched by agricultural run-off. Management is an important factor in determining the dominant vegetation. Grazing or mowing produce vegetation with a range of grasses, sedges and rushes. In the absence of management, taller plants usually take over, such as bottle sedge, common reed or reed sweet-grass. Where the fens have been drained, purple moor-grass or bog-myrtle may become dominant. On more acid sites with lower pH, poor-fens develop. These are much commoner and often occur on marginal agricultural land. *Sphagnum* mosses usually share dominance with sedges, black bog-rush or bog asphodel. Examples of poor-fens occur in many upland areas but they are usually of fairly limited extent and interspersed with other wetland habitats.

Plants growing in both poor-fens and rich-fens need to be adapted to waterlogged soils. Some can produce adventitious roots just above the surface, which ensure a physiological supply of oxygen even when the normal roots are flooded. Other plants have very porous root tissue and pass oxygen from their shoots down into the pores in their roots. Fen plants also have to be tolerant of high levels of some dissolved nutrients, such as iron or manganese. The animal life is also limited by the waterlogging. Some species usually associated with open water habitats are also found in fens, for instance, marsh snails and mites. The insect life includes mosquitoes and the larvae of many beetles, butterflies and moths. Occasionally, eels find their way into fens, where they can survive for some time by 'breathing' through their skin. Frogs and toads are common and find the shallow water of fens ideal breeding habitat. The mammal fauna is similar to that associated with open water, with the addition of shrews and the harvest mouse, which attaches its nest to reeds or tall grasses. The fens also provide cover for many breeding bird species, especially reed warbler, sedge warbler and reed bunting.

Peat bogs develop in three main situations[6]. Some develop in hollows or valleys, like poor-fens; some develop adjacent to these and spread outwards as blanket peat; and others develop on flat or gently sloping land in areas of high rainfall. A minimum of 1000 mm of rainfall a year seems to be necessary for these bogs to develop and there are usually at least 160 days with over 1 mm of rain. They include the extensive bogs of northern and western Scotland and also 'raised bogs', which are formed from other types of bog when the growth of peat raises the surface of the bog above the ground water table and the bog becomes dependent on rainwater alone.

The most important plants involved in peat growth are the *Sphagnum* mosses. The surface of their leaves is porous, giving them a water-holding capacity of more than twenty times their own weight. They also make the peat very acid, and the combined waterlogging and acidity limit the soil organisms and make it very difficult for plant remains to be decomposed. It is usually the central parts of the bog which are wettest and it is there that peat accumulates fastest. This means that peat bogs tend to develop a convex or domed shape. Surface drainage runs off from the centre of the bog and may collect in channels around the edge of the dome. The peat may also develop its own surface topography of hummocks and pools, as different species of *Sphagnum* prefer drier or wetter sites. Sometimes the hummocks and pools are arranged in distinct patterns, such as concentric crescent-shaped pools or pools aligned along the contours. There are some excellent examples of patterned bogs in the uplands, such as the Silver Flowe in Galloway, Muckle Moss in Northumbria, Claish Moss in western Scotland and Tregaron Bog in mid-Wales.

Many other plants accompany the *Sphagnum* mosses, including hair-moss, bog asphodel, cranberry, bog-rosemary and many sedges. Deeper pools may have bladderworts, bogbean and pondweeds. The drier hummocks or ridges are often dominated by heather, bilberry or bog-myrtle. Cottongrasses are also very common, especially in the Pennine bogs. In Scotland, deergrass is widespread and woolly fringe-moss colonises drier hummocks. These plants all face various problems growing in such a wet, acid habitat, such as the low level of oxygen available to their roots and the shortage of plant nutrients, particularly nitrogen. Some species, including sundews and butterworts, overcome this problem by supplementing their diet with insects trapped on sticky leaves. Bog-myrtle has nodules on its roots containing bacteria which fix atmospheric nitrogen for the plant. Other plants seem to be able to accumulate certain nutrients, such as phosphorus and potassium, which are in short supply on peats.

The invertebrate life of peat bogs is severely limited by the wetness and acidity of the habitat. Certain specialised water beetles can survive, and some beetle and hover-fly larvae live beneath the *Sphagnum* and tap oxygen direct from the roots of the bog plants. Some dragonfly larvae live in peat pools and adult dragonflies may be

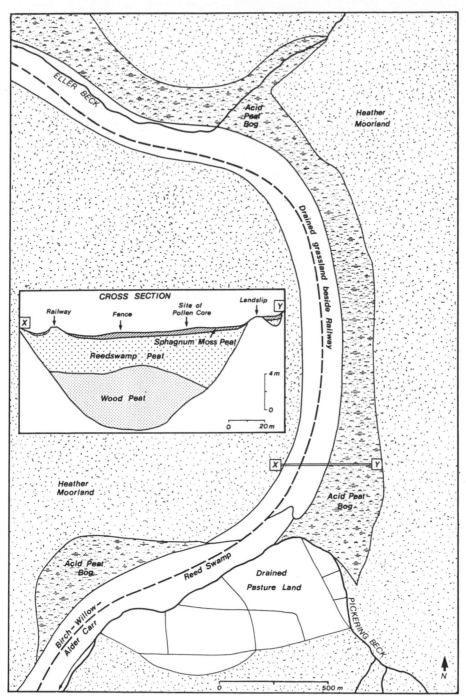

FIGURE 13 Fen Bog, North York Moors, showing surface vegetation and land use. (The stratigraphic cross-section is based on borings through the peat. The pollen diagram (Figure 5) is from this site; Colour plate 1 shows a view of the site from the north)

seen hunting over bogs in the summer. Butterflies are scarce but the large heath is of special interest, feeding on the leaves of the white beak-sedge. Frogs and toads use the pools in peat bogs, while common lizards may be found on the drier parts. Many moorland mammals cross peat bogs in their territories but few of them deliberately exploit the habitat in preference to others. Most bogs are grazed by sheep and grouse, although both prefer moorlands. There are several bird species which feed or nest on blanket bogs, such as snipe and golden plover. Some peat bogs are the sites of large gull colonies. For instance, on the Isle of Lewis there are colonies of great and lesser black-backed gulls. There were large gull colonies on the Pennines in the past but they have declined because of gamekeeping[7].

History of the peat bogs

The formation of peat is a slow but variable process. Rates of peat accumulation typically vary from about 20 cm to 1 metre in 1000 years, but there may be periods when growth stops altogether and others when it speeds up. Although the *Sphagnum* mosses are the most important peat formers, other plants are also involved, including common reed and cottongrasses. In pools, where the water table is at or above the surface, plant remains undergo virtually no decomposition and *Sphagnum* may look almost the same after several thousand years. However, in most peats the water table fluctuates through the top 10 to 50 cm during the year. In this top zone of peat, some decomposition of plant remains is possible in drier periods. The roots of the surface vegetation lie within this zone and it is the actively growing part of the bog. Below this is the permanently waterlogged zone, where hardly any decomposition is possible and no living roots are found.

As well as plant remains, animal and human remains are sometimes found in peat bogs, although mainly in lowland bogs. A recent example was the human corpse found in Lindow Moss, Cheshire. By examining the composition of the different peat layers, it is possible to trace the historical development of any peat bog. Figure 13 summarises the development of the peat bog at Fen Bog in the North York Moors, from which the pollen diagram (Figure 5) was presented in chapter 2 (Colour plate 1). As in many other valley bogs on the North York Moors, the vegetation in the early Post-glacial was a carr woodland, similar to that which occupies the southern end of the site today. This was replaced by a reedswamp or poor-fen vegetation, which dominated the site until the last few centuries. Remnants of this vegetation type survive in the drainage channels beside the modern railway line. Within the top metre of peat, a change occurs from reedswamp to acid bog peat, dependent on rain water rather than ground water. The name 'Fen Bog' is an appropriate one for this site, which has undergone a change from poor-fen to bog vegetation in the recent past.

At some sites, changes in stratigraphy seem to be related to climatic change and not merely to changes in the local drainage. At Bolton Fell Moss in Cumbria, changes in the particular species of *Sphagnum* suggest relatively wet conditions in the first millennium BC, followed by alternating drier/warmer and wetter/colder periods until the present day[8]. Many of these periods link with known climatic trends; for instance, during the warm early Medieval period there were apparently no pools or wet *Sphagnum* lawns on the bog, but during the Little Ice Age (AD 1550–1850) there was a marked increase in pools and *Sphagnum* growth. Such sites may provide a very important record of past climatic change.

Conservation

There are approximately 1.58 million ha of peat bogs in Britain, most of them in the uplands. This represents over 10 per cent of the total world resource and makes Britain one of the most important countries for conservation of these habitats. Blanket bogs cover large areas of western and northern Scotland and the Outer Hebrides, with other sites in the Southern Uplands, the Cheviots, the Pennines and Wales, and on the highest parts of the moorlands of south-west England. Many peat bogs on the Pennines have been badly affected by pollution since the Industrial Revolution. This has led to the elimination of *Sphagnum* mosses and their replacement by cottongrasses at many sites. Over-grazing and severe burning have led to drying out of the surface layers of many bogs. Once peat becomes dehydrated, it shrinks and loses its structure and is very difficult to re-wet. Being very light, it is easily eroded by rain or wind. Many Pennine bogs are in an advanced state of erosion, with bare peat 'haggs' dissected by gullies. These features are well illustrated on Kinder Scout and Bleaklow in the Peak District and at Moor House and Cross Fell on the northern Pennines. Once initiated, the process of peat erosion is almost impossible to reverse.

Peat bogs have many uses to humans. *Sphagnum* mosses were used as dressings for wounds in the first World War and they are used nowadays in hanging baskets. Some bog plants and animals were a source of food in the past, examples being cranberries and wildfowl. Peat has been used as a traditional fuel in most parts of the uplands and has been exploited commercially in a few cases. Peat cutting is still practised for domestic use in many parts of Scotland and the Scottish Isles. Peat is also a very valuable soil improver in horticulture and has been compressed into fibre board to make peat pots and containers. Public pressure has been mounting to stop some of these horticultural uses and conservation organisations have been in conflict with major firms for many years. Recently, several large chain stores have restricted sales of peat from Sites of Special Scientific Interest.

A further problem is that many peat bogs have been afforested with coniferous trees over the past few decades, leading to rapid drainage and shrinkage of the peat. Even where the bogs themselves are not planted up, afforestation of surrounding areas may lead to a lowering of the water table, as at Coom Rigg Moss in the Kielder forest district. Afforestation has also led to a major controversy in the Flow Country of northern Scotland.

PLATE 24 Open water dominating the scene in the Flow Country

The Flow Country

No part of Britain exemplifies the richness of wetland habitats and the problems of their survival better than the Flow Country of Caithness and Sutherland (Colour plate 9). North-east of a line from Loch Eriboll to the Dornock Firth, the mountains of the Highlands give way to a landscape of blanket bogs and lochans, with isolated hills, such as Ben Hope, Ben Hulig and Ben Loyal, rising steeply from a carpet of water and peat (Plate 24). The solid geology consists of metamorphic rocks and Devonian sandstone, overlain by glacial drift. The contours of the drift cover slope gently towards the coastal plains to the north and east. This relatively flat topography was ideal for the development of blanket peat. Another important physical factor is the climate. Rainfall ranges from 2500 mm on higher ground in western Sutherland to 700 mm on the north-east tip of Caithness. It is spread fairly evenly throughout the year and the area has at least 160 wet days (days when at least 1 mm of rain falls). Evaporation is low because of the northerly location, and winds are strong, averaging 30 kph, with frequent gales. This combination of acid rocks, low relief and a cool, wet, windy climate allowed blanket peat to spread gradually to cover over half of the landscape, to a depth of up to 5 metres. There are also substantial areas of open water, with 350 lochs or lochans and hundreds of streams (Figure 14).

There are records of tree trunks being dug up in the peat from the eighteenth century onwards, which show that woodland once grew in parts of the Flow Country. For example, a report on Cannisbay parish in Caithness in 1726 states that 'roots

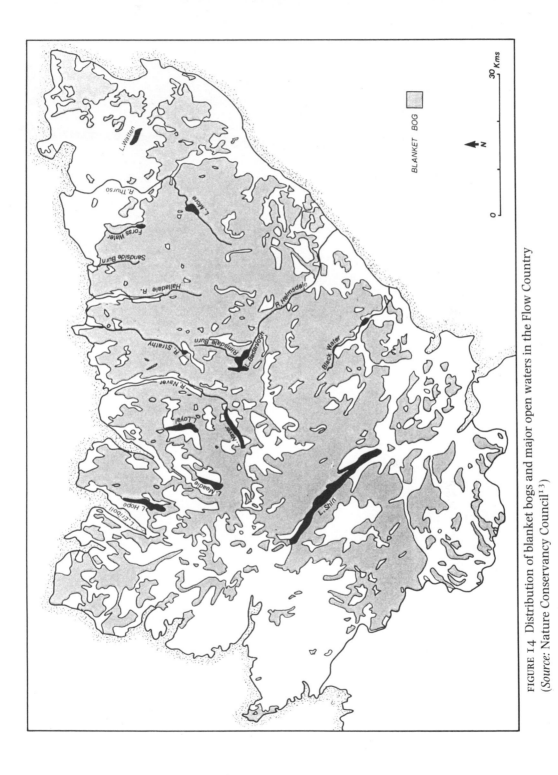

FIGURE 14 Distribution of blanket bogs and major open waters in the Flow Country
(*Source:* Nature Conservancy Council[13])

PLATE 25 The traditional landscape of the Flow Country: patterned mire near Loch Badanloch. The white fruiting heads of the cottongrasses and the large hummocks of woolly fringe-moss are conspicuous in the foreground

PLATE 26 The new landscape of the Flow Country: Sitka spruce and lodgepole pine planted on former blanket bog, east of Forsinard. Raindrops on the foliage in the foreground testify to the very wet climate

of firrs [pines], oaks and birch are digged up almost in all our mosses [bogs]', and other references to large oak or fir [pine] trunks in Caithness were made by Robertson in 1767[9]. Pollen analysis shows that the middle Post-glacial woodland in the west of the area was dominated by birch, with oak, pine and other trees[10]. The oaks now growing there are the most northerly natural oaks in Britain and are stunted by the strong wind, but they still regenerate freely. The pine stumps found in the peat are generally small and stunted, suggesting that this tree also was near its natural limit. Where the stumps have been dated, they are usually 4000 to 4800 years old, dating from a relatively dry period[11]. Further east in Caithness, the woodland thinned out; fewer tree remains have been found in the peat and those which have been recorded are mostly of birch[12]. Scrub woodland of birch, rowan, hazel, willows and alder occurred only in sheltered valleys.

The replacement of woodland or scrub by blanket bog was a largely natural process in the Flow Country, brought about by a gradual waterlogging of the acid soils. This can be seen in the peat stratigraphy, as fen peat with birch remains started to be replaced by acid bog peat with *Sphagnum* about 7000 years ago. Moorland and blanket bog increased in extent about 3000 years ago and the present pattern of pools and ridges was established within the last 1000 years.

Wildlife of the Flow Country

The Flow Country contains superb patterned mires and pool systems, including some types not found elsewhere in Britain. The vegetation of the drier areas of thin peat, ridges and higher hummocks is dominated by heath rush, heather, cross-leaved heath, crowberry or cottongrasses. Other common plants include cowberry, deer-grass, purple moor-grass, cranberry, bog asphodel, round-leaved sundew and bell heather. There are many types of *Sphagnum* and other mosses and lichens. Woolly fringe-moss often forms conspicuous hummocks (Plate 25, but compare with Plate 26). Lower ridges and hummocks are dominated by *Sphagnum* mosses, the particular species depending on the precise drainage conditions and height above the water table. Other bog plants grow amongst them, two very local species being bearberry and dwarf birch. Both species are members of the montane flora but in northern Scotland they also grow on blanket bog.

Hollows and pools within the blanket bog have their own special flora, dominated by different species of *Sphagnum*, which form carpets on the surface. The great sundew is characteristic of these *Sphagnum* carpets and forms conspicuous rosettes from which delicate white flowers appear on long stalks. Even the deeper pools may have a floating mat of *Sphagnum* or submerged plants of bladderwort. Other areas have fen communities, where *Sphagnum* mosses are less important. Purple moor-grass and bog-myrtle grow on the ridges, whilst sedges dominate the hollows. The rivers and lochs tend to be nutrient-poor except for a few sites in the extreme north-east. The plant life includes pondweeds, bulbous rush, shoreweed, water lobelia and water-milfoil. There are some rarities, such as the bog orchid, pillwort and the least water-lily.

The Flow Country is as important for its animal life as its plantlife. Mammals, such as red deer, roe deer, mountain hare and wild cat frequent the area, and the otter is still relatively common on the coast. Adders, frogs, toads and newts occur. The invertebrate life is less rich than that of areas further south but contains several interesting arctic alpine species of caddis fly and beetles. The fresh-water pearl mussel is a particularly important rare mollusc species. The crayfish has its only Scottish site in a loch near Durness. Another rare species is the blue hawker dragonfly. The rivers of the Flow Country used to be important for fish, especially salmon, but they have become less rich in recent years.

The area has an extraordinary diversity of birdlife compared to most moorland or blanket bog habitats. Fifty-five species have been recorded, at least 15 of which breed there. The commonest waders are golden plover, dunlin, greenshank and curlew, whilst rarities include the wood sandpiper, red-necked phalarope, ruff and Temminck's stint. Waterfowl are plentiful on the many rivers and lochs and the area is a stronghold for the red-throated diver and the very rare black-throated diver. Mallard, teal and many other ducks are widespread and numerous. Red-breasted mergansers frequent the larger rivers and lochs and occasionally goosanders are seen. There are native stocks of greylag geese nesting on islands in the lochs, and white-fronted geese (Greenland race) are winter visitors, along with whooper swan and goldeneye. Arctic skuas nest amongst the small lochans, although their numbers have decreased owing to persecution in the past by gamekeepers. The main game bird is the red grouse but population numbers have decreased over recent years. There is a good range of other typical moorland birds, whilst birds of prey include peregrine falcons, merlins, golden eagles, hen harriers, short-eared owls and kestrels. Most of the birds leave the area in winter, except the red grouse and some waterfowl.

Uses and abuses of the Flow Country

Prehistoric activity was limited and farming was concentrated on the better soils of the coastal plains. During historic times, human impact was relatively light until the nineteenth century. The north of Scotland was a stronghold of the crofting system, so cruelly disrupted by the Highland clearances. Black cattle were the main livestock and they were grazed on the better-drained ground, while crops were grown in small fields near the settlements and fish were caught in the rivers. The blanket bogs were not ideal for such farming but could be improved by drainage, a process known as 'moor-gripping'. This affected mainly the top layer of peat, which dried out and could then support more grass or heath plants. Drainage increased from the mid-nineteenth century on, when sheep replaced the traditional black cattle. As the peat dried out, it shrank, cracked and eventually decomposed, but drainage channels were widely spaced, so the effects were localised and not too serious.

When grouse-shooting and deer stalking developed in the nineteenth century, there was pressure to 'improve' the blanket bogs, not only by more drainage but also by burning. It has been estimated that about one third of the total peat has been

PLATE 27 Traditional peat cutting in the Flow Country, which did little damage to the ecology

PLATE 28 Modern commercial peat extraction, which has a devastating effect upon the landscape and wildlife

burned[13]. Burning leads to a reduction of the importance of *Sphagnum* mosses and the spread of heather, deergrass or purple moor-grass. The combined effects of burning and drainage can be serious and sometimes lead to erosion of the peat. Where the surface has been disturbed, for instance by trampling, heavy rain can occasionally lead to the mass of peat becoming liquid and flowing in a bog burst. Up to half the peat has been affected by some sort of erosion[14].

The signs of former peat-cutting are evident all over the Flows and the practice continues in some parts today (Plate 27). Squarish blocks of peat are removed from small sections of bog and stacked in beehive-shaped piles to dry. Most cutting was close to the settlements and therefore concentrated in the valleys. Because of the abundance of peat, the cuttings were fairly low in density and shallow in depth. Even areas which had been completely cut over would regenerate in time and the cuttings provided new pool areas. In the 1950s, an experimental peat-fired power station was set up in Caithness and, although short-lived, it drew attention to the large quantity of peat available for some sort of commercial exploitation. Present operations are limited to an area near Halsary, where the Highland Peat Company uses machinery to strip bare the bog surface and produce little sausage-shaped peat blocks. The result is the total destruction of the local blanket bog and its wildlife (Plate 28).

Forestry

Forestry in the Flows began soon after the Forestry Commission was established in 1919, but the technology to exploit the deep peat areas did not exist until recent decades. There were some experimental plots in the late 1950s, but it was not until the early 1970s that commercial plantations began to be established at the rate of 300 to 400 ha a year[15]. The main species used initially was lodgepole pine, which gave a relatively poor yield. Sitka spruce was the other main contender for planting but it needed large amounts of nitrogen fertiliser. Insect pests, especially the pine beauty moth and the pine sawfly, also caused problems. Several hundred hectares of trees were killed in the 1970s, especially on the deeper peats, where trees were more stressed and therefore susceptible to insect attack.

In the late 1970s, it was discovered that mixtures of lodgepole pine and sitka spruce produced better results than single species plantations (Plate 26). Insecticides controlled the insect pests and new machines enabled easier ploughing and draining of the deep peats. A private firm, Fountain Forestry, bought up land from 1979 onwards and began planting it at rates of up to 4000 ha per year. Tax exemptions encouraged many individuals, including some well-known public figures, to invest in forestry in the area. By 1988, a total of 61,000 ha had been planted up, with approval given for a further 15,040 ha, about half of this being Forestry Commission land and the other half private[16]. Plantations were scattered over a wide area but the greatest concentration was in the heart of the peatland complex, in the area around Forsinard and Westerdale (Figure 15).

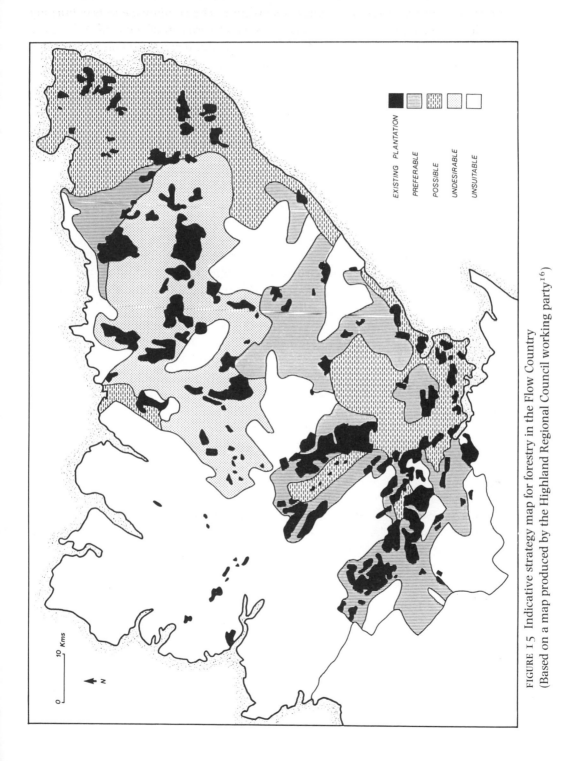

FIGURE 15 Indicative strategy map for forestry in the Flow Country
(Based on a map produced by the Highland Regional Council working party[16])

Modern forestry involves several operations which are detrimental to the blanket bog habitat. First and foremost of these is drainage, which is deeper and therefore more harmful than the traditional moor-gripping. Drains usually penetrate deep into the peat, speeding up the drying out process. Shrinkage is substantial, even in the rides between forestry blocks, as these are rarely wide enough to buffer the peat from the effects of the surrounding drains. Water which would once have soaked into the bog and sustained the pool systems flows along the forestry drains in torrents after rainstorms, carrying with it small amounts of peat in suspension. On the drier, shrinking peat surface, bog plants are replaced by dwarf shrubs, grasses and even rosebay willowherb.

The closely spaced trees cast a dense shade within 10 or 15 years. This suppresses the growth of plants beneath them and also has some effect on the vegetation in the rides between the blocks of trees. The combination of drainage and shade is usually sufficient to eliminate most of the original plant species and to upset the patterning of the bogs. The drainage associated with forestry also increases the amount of run-off entering the river systems initially. Later, there is a 20 to 30 per cent reduction, as the trees transpire water to the atmosphere. Such changes in run-off cause alterations to the stream velocity, which affect invertebrates and fish. The water draining off forested areas also carries more suspended material in it, which is damaging to many forms of aquatic wildlife, especially the rare pearl mussel.

The shading effect of the trees reduces the light for the plants growing at the stream margin. The presence of the forest may also reduce the temperature range, which can affect the growth rates of some fish. Fertilisers and insecticides used on the young trees can lead to enrichment of the waters, especially with phosphorus, potassium or nitrogen. The oxidation of the drying peat also releases nutrients which may get washed into the water bodies and cause algal blooms. Lastly, the water draining through the fallen needles on the forest floor is more acid than formerly, leading to a slight drop in pH and the release of heavy metals from the peat.

Bird species differ in their initial response to forestry. For instance, dunlin and arctic skua disappear within the first few years, whereas short-eared owl and hen harrier benefit from the increased number of small mammals associated with the early stages of afforestation. After 10 or 15 years, most of the original bird species will have moved out, to be replaced by woodland species. The areas of unplanted blanket bog surrounding the forestry plantations have a limited capacity to absorb more birds. The situation is more serious if the surrounding areas have themselves suffered from other impacts, such as drainage or burning, which will have reduced their carrying capacity for wetland birds. Perhaps the worst affected in the long run are the birds of prey, which require large territories to sustain them. A pair of golden eagles, for instance, may need up to 10,000 ha of hunting territory, so the fragmentation of habitat caused by afforestation is a further problem for such species. Estimates have been made of the losses of population due to afforestation for the three commonest bird species in the Flows. It is calculated that 19 per cent of the golden plover, 17 per cent of the dunlin and 17 per cent of the greenshank populations have already been lost[14].

The case for conservation

The Flow Country was not well known to most ecologists until recent years and so the full evidence for the richness and uniqueness of this area was not assembled until the late 1980s[13,14]. By the time the case for conservation had been established, several key areas of blanket bog had been destroyed, 15 per cent of the peatland area had been planted up and another 4 per cent was scheduled for afforestation. A major confrontation between conservationists and foresters was inevitable. Key elements in the conservation case are the patterned bogs, the rare plant communities and the diversity of breeding bird species. The blanket bogs are not only the largest area of such habitat in Britain but are also considered to be of international importance, as some of the bog types are known from nowhere else in Europe. The plant communities of the bogs are unique in their composition and include many rare species, whilst the open water areas hold ten nationally rare plant species and 21 rare invertebrate species.

The area is also of international or national importance for many species of bird. It is estimated to hold 18 per cent of the British breeding population of golden plover, 39 per cent of the population of dunlin and 66 per cent of the population of greenshank. It also holds significant proportions of the breeding populations of other birds, and for eleven species, the area contains a significant proportion of the European population as well. 'All the available evidence shows that the Flow Country is of unique importance on the British mainland for moorland birds, and that therefore forestry in this area is possibly more damaging to the conservation of birds of the open uplands than if it happened anywhere else in Britain'[15]. It has been suggested that the loss of habitat in the Flow Country to forestry represents the single most significant loss of wildlife habitat in Britain since the second world war[7].

As the conservation value of the area became apparent, the Nature Conservancy Council (NCC), which was then the national conservation body covering the whole of Great Britain, sought to schedule more and more Sites of Special Scientific Interest (SSSIs). By 1988, 98,800 ha of land in Caithness and Sutherland had been notified, including about 20 open water SSSIs and over 39,000 ha of blanket bog. A further 24,000 ha had been provisionally identified in 1984, and the NCC proposed to notify an additional 179,500 ha in two stages, making a potential total of 300,300 ha of SSSIs. This would have included about two thirds of the unafforested peatland – a figure thought to be excessive by other interests in the region and by the Secretary of State for Scotland, who had suggested in January 1988 that about half the unafforested peatland should be scheduled. A working party was convened by the Highland Regional Council to try to resolve the conflict of interests in the area[16].

The case for forestry was based chiefly on the employment opportunities which it would bring. In order to provide continuity of employment and a sustainable forestry industry in the region, a total area of 100,000 ha of forest was thought desirable. This would mean an additional 39,000 ha should be planted up over the following 20 years, a rate of about 2000 ha per year. Approval had already been given for some more land to be planted, so a relatively small additional area was required. However, trees in some of the earlier plantations were showing obvious signs of stress and yields were likely to be low, because the plantations had been made on land which was really unsuitable for forestry. The Forestry Commission has the authority to grant planting licences for both public and private afforestation and in 1987 the Scottish Office directed the Forestry Commission to consult the NCC over all new plantings. In 1988, budgetary changes meant that the planting of coniferous trees by private individuals no longer qualified for tax exemption. In the same year the Forestry Commission reviewed its planting policy in the Flow Country and published an 'indicative strategy' for the future.

The area was divided into four categories of land: 'unsuitable' for forestry (284,000 ha), 'undesirable' (150,600 ha), 'possible' (155,700 ha) and 'preferable' (123,800 ha) (Figure 15). Most of the western and central parts were considered unsuitable or undesirable for forestry. This area includes most of the area of high conservation value. The areas mapped as preferable or possible for forestry do include some areas which are of high conservation value but it is unlikely that more than a small percentage of this land will actually be afforested. In all the land categories, the presumtpion is in favour of small-scale plantations and a range of forestry rather than large, monotonous forestry blocks.

The Highland Regional Council working party's report now forms a blueprint for future planning in the region[16]. The case for some further afforestation was accepted, which will bring the total forested area to 100,000 ha by the year 2010. However, the new plantings will be confined to the preferable or possible categories (Figure 15) and will have to conform to set guidelines. The price to be paid on the conservation side was a restriction of consultation to those sites scheduled or proposed as SSSIs, thus precluding the opportunity for the input of conservation advice on other sites.

Although these recommendations are a compromise which will not completely satisfy either the foresters or the conservationists, there is no doubt that they go a long way towards halting the destruction of habitat in the Flow Country. Arguably, much of the damage has already been done, with key areas drained and the expanse of blanket bog interrupted by a plethora of forestry blocks (Figure 15). The characteristic landscape of much of the area has been changed and it will change further over the next few decades, as the trees mature. However, substantial areas of blanket bog remain and the tide of public opinion continues to flow towards conservation. Although there have been casualties, it looks as though this is one area of upland Britain where the battle for conservation has been won.

References

1   Smith, I and Lyle, A, *Distribution of freshwaters in Great Britain*. Institute of Terrestrial Ecology, Cambridge, 1979.
2   Pearsall, W H and Pennington, W, *The Lake District*. Collins New Naturalist Series, London, 1973.

3 Freethy, R, *The natural history of rivers*. Terence Dalton Ltd, Lavenham, Suffolk, 1986.

4 Macan, T T and Worthington, E B, *Life in lakes and rivers*. Collins New Naturalist Series, revised edition. London, 1972.

5 Fry, G L A and Cooke, A S, Acid deposition and its implications for nature conservation in Britain. *Nature Conservancy Council report No 7*. Nature Conservancy Council, Peterborough, 1987.

6 Moore, P D and Bellamy, D J, *Peatlands*. Elek Science, London, 1973.

7 Ratcliffe, D A, *Bird life of mountain and upland*. Cambridge University Press, Cambridge, 1990.

8 Barber, K E, Peat-bog stratigraphy as a proxy climate record. In Harding, A F (ed), *Climatic change in late prehistory*, pp 103–12. Edinburgh University Press, Edinburgh, 1982.

9 Anderson, M L, *History of Scottish forestry*. vol 1. Thomas Nelson and Sons Ltd, London and Edinburgh, 1967.

10 Moar, N T, A radiocarbon-dated pollen diagram from north-west Scotland. *New Phytologist*, 68, pp 209–14, 1969.

11 Birks, H H, Studies in the vegetational history of Scotland IV Pine stumps in Scottish blanket peats. *Philosophical Transactions of the Royal Society B*, 270, pp 181–226, 1975.

12 Peglar, S, A radiocarbon-dated pollen diagram from Loch of Winless, Caithness, north-east Scotland. *New Phytologist*, 82, pp 245–63, 1979.

13 Nature Conservancy Council, *Birds, bogs and forestry*. Nature Conservancy Council, Peterborough, 1987.

14 Nature Conservancy Council, *The Flow Country*. Nature Conservancy Council, Peterborough, 1988.

15 Avery, M and Leslie, R, *Birds and forestry*. T and A D Poyser London, 1990.

16 Highland Regional Council, Caithness and Sutherland Highland Regional Council Working Party Report, 1989.

8

Forestry plantations

The hills of Britain, owing to an ancient and varied geological history, are exceptionally varied and subtly modelled, and their whole character can be effaced by unsympathetic planting. Yet the character of these hills can even be accentuated when plantations complement the land-form, running up the sheltered valleys and down from exposed hill breasts, and incorporating sufficient variety in species and spacing to allow the forest to inflect to the character and contours of the land.

Dame Sylvia Crowe

History of forestry

Forestry plantations have a much shorter history than most other upland habitats. The beginnings of modern forestry can be traced back only as far as the early seventeenth century, and the vast majority of plantations date from the twentieth century. Nearly all of them occupy land which was originally wooded but much of it lost its woodland cover hundreds or thousands of years ago and was converted to open moorland or grassland. The recent afforestation of these open upland landscapes has given rise to much controversy.

As we saw in chapter 2, the first forestry plantations were made by private landowners, inspired by the writings of such men as Arthur Standish and John Evelyn in the seventeenth century[1]. The motive force behind their writing was the decreasing amount of woodland in Britain and the perceived demand for more timber, but many of the early plantings had more to do with ornament and fashion than with timber production. Trees from many parts of the world were introduced and used in landscaping schemes. European trees were the first to be used. Norway spruce and sycamore had been introduced in the sixteenth century, European silver-fir and European larch in the early seventeenth and Corsican pine in the eighteenth. Nineteenth century introductions included several species from North America, such as Douglas fir, Sitka spruce, western hemlock-spruce and lodgepole pine. The native Scots pine was also used, along with broad-leaved species such as oak, ash and beech.

In the eighteenth and nineteenth centuries, Parliamentary Acts for the enclosure of common lands and the disafforestation of the former Royal Forests provided further opportunities for planting. However, the opening up of the colonies and burgeoning world trade meant that many timber needs could be met by imports rather than relying on British woodlands. The potential danger of this situation

gradually became clear. There was increasing interest in forestry in the late nineteenth and early twentieth centuries but progress was slow and piecemeal and still in
the hands of private landowners. Between 1850 and 1914, six royal commissions,
select committees or departmental committees of the House of Commons produced
reports, many of them arguing that there was a need to stimulate home production
by state involvement in forestry. However, it was the First World War which finally
persuaded the government to act. Imports were cut off, so British timber had to be
used, especially for pit-props in the coal mines. During and immediately after the war,
182,000 ha out of an estimated total of 1.2 million ha of woodland were felled,
reducing Britain's woodland cover to less than five per cent of the land surface.
Following the Acland Report in 1917, the Forestry Commission was established by
Act of Parliament in 1919.

The main aim of the Forestry Commission was to provide a strategic reserve of
timber in time of war. A target was set of 80,000 ha of new plantations within ten
years, with the eventual aim of achieving 715,000 ha by the end of the century. A
subsidiary aim, which grew in importance during the economic depression of the
1930s, was to provide new employment opportunities in areas of rural depopulation.
Forest villages were built to house the work-force and within twenty years
240,000 ha had been planted, mostly in the uplands, where land was easier and
cheaper to acquire and less valuable for food production. The remaining Crown
forests were transferred to the Forestry Commission in 1923. As well as acquiring
land and growing timber, the Forestry Commission had another role: to give advice
on management techniques and tree health to private woodland owners. During the
inter-war period, 51,000 ha of new planting was carried out on private estates, as
neglected woodlands were re-stocked.

The Second World War was a severe blow to the developing forestry industry.
Most of the Forestry Commission plantations were too young to contribute to the war
needs and only 12,000 ha were used. The burden fell on private woodlands, nearly
200,000 ha of which were felled. During the war, plans were being made for the
future, and a white paper published in 1943 set a target for a national forest estate of
2 million ha within 50 years. After the war, Acts of Parliament introduced financial
grants for private woodland owners who managed their woodlands in ways
approved by the Forestry Commission. It was envisaged that private planting would
average about 10,000 ha a year but this figure was more than doubled in succeeding
decades. However, the main aim remained the same as in 1919 – to provide a
strategic timber reserve – and little attention was paid to other aspects of forestry.

Since 1945, the emphasis has changed several times. The importance of
timber for shipping and mining has declined and the nature of modern warfare has
changed. In 1957, the idea of providing a strategic timber reserve was abandoned in
favour of economic and social objectives. Timber production was still seen as the
main business of both the Forestry Commission and private woodland owners but the
main concern now was to reduce Britain's dependence on imports. Rural employment was still an important issue and more villages for forestry workers were estab-

lished. The policy in the early days had been to keep public access to a minimum, partly because of the perceived fire risk. However, the increasing demand for recreational facilities and greater mobility of the population eventually brought about a change of heart. In the 1967 and 1968 Countryside Acts, the provision of recreation facilities and amenity were added to the Forestry Commission's remit and this recreational role has gained in importance ever since.

The Forestry Commission redefined its objectives in 1974 to include the provision of recreational facilities and the protection of the environment. Government policy continued to favour the expansion of forestry, both by enlarging the Forestry Commission estate and by new grant schemes for private owners. However, there was also growing criticism amongst the general public of the intensive nature of much forestry and of the 'blanket' afforestation of large areas of the uplands. This criticism, together with the difficulty of acquiring more land, led to a re-appraisal of the Commission's role in the 1980s. It was felt that the bulk of new planting should be carried out by private landowners in future and the Forestry Commission was required in 1980 to rationalise its estate and reduce its call on government funds by disposing of some of its land.

New policies were introduced for broad-leaved trees and the preservation of semi-natural woods. The Wildlife and Countryside (Amendment) Act of 1985 required the Forestry Commission to endeavour to achieve a reasonable balance between the interests of forestry and those of the environment. Since 1988, applicants for grant aid have had to prepare detailed plans and make a statement about the environmental effects of their planting schemes. In the 1990s, the government policy is for multi-purpose use of forests for timber production, nature conservation, recreation and amenity. The Forestry Commission has been reorganised internally into two separate parts: the Forest Enterprise, concerned with timber production, and the Forestry Authority, involved with granting licences for planting and felling.

Today woodland covers about 11 per cent of Britain and about 23 per cent of the uplands. Many forests, especially in Scotland and south Wales, are less than 20 years old and the majority of them are coniferous. The shortest time required before the trees can be profitably felled is about 45 years and many trees reach a much greater age, so there is a time-lag of several decades before the effects of new planting strategies become evident in the forest landscape. In most upland areas today, we are seeing the results of planting policies of the 1940s and 1950s, and the full effects of the present multi-purpose forestry policies will not be seen until well into the twenty-first century.

Wildlife of forestry plantations

Trees grown in forestry plantations provide a habitat for wildlife which is quite different from that of semi-natural woodlands. This is because of the species of tree used, the age structure of the plantations and the methods of management employed. Most commercial forestry involves stands of one or two tree species and, in the

PLATE 29 Production forestry, Clocaenog, North Wales

uplands, conifers are dominant. The trees are planted at the same time and arranged in regularly spaced rows. This encourages the trees to grow straight and have small branches, thus producing good timber, and facilitates weeding and thinning. There is economy of scale in felling the whole stand of trees at the same time (Plate 29). However, the system poses certain problems for other wildlife.

The even-aged structure of the plantation means that all the trees will go through their life-cycles together. In the first few years after planting or restocking, the preceding vegetation of the site will remain dominant, but the absence of grazing may mean that grasses and other herbaceous plants grow tall and coarse, crowding out low-growing plants. This stage provides ideal conditions for many small mammal species, such as field voles, which often increase in number in the early stages of a plantation. They may, in turn, attract birds of prey, such as hen harrier, kestrel or short-eared owl, or mammal predators, such as stoat, weasel or fox. Deer also use the young plantations, which are rich in food plants. In Snowdonia, the polecat survives in forestry plantations, whilst in Scottish forests the pine marten and occasionally the wild cat may be found. Songbirds are attracted to the young plantations, especially stonechat, whinchat, common whitethroat, goldcrest, willow warbler and sometimes grasshopper warbler. In Scotland and north-east England, nightjars breed in young plantations, whilst the black grouse has adapted to open plantations bordering moorland in Scotland, Wales and the Cheviots.

Within six or seven years, the branches of the young trees usually start to touch and by 10 to 15 years they form a complete canopy, casting a dense shade on the ground below. This is known as the thicket stage and it has drastic effects on the ground flora[2]. Under many conifers, the original ground flora decreases by about half when the thicket stage is reached and continues to decrease during the next few years. Most plants cannot tolerate the dense shade and the only species to survive are often a few mosses or ferns. In pine plantations, the shade is not quite so dense and a few grasses or bilberry plants may survive. In Scottish pine plantations which are adjacent to native pinewood sites, some of the interesting plants from the pinewood ground flora find their way into the plantations, such as one-flowered wintergreen and creeping lady's-tresses. Larch, being a deciduous conifer, allows more light to reach the ground and may support a patchy flora of wavy hair-grass and bilberry. The rest of the ground flora species either die out in the thicket stage or survive as buried seeds in the litter layer. Species with good seed dispersal, such as rosebay willowherb, move to rides, edges or newly felled areas in other parts of the forest, whilst bracken moves by spreading vegetatively.

The diminished ground flora leads to a corresponding decrease in the mammal and insect populations. Birds fare better and some species nest or feed in the canopy, including coal tit, willow warbler, chaffinch, robin, wren, song thrush and blackbird. Wood pigeons also use the thicket-stage plantations and sometimes provide food for birds of prey, such as peregrine falcons or goshawks, which hunt along rides through the forest. As the trees reach the fruiting stage, seed-eating birds are attracted. Sitka spruce produces cones after about 20 years and provides food for common crossbills and siskins, whilst pine seeds are eaten by Scottish crossbills.

Most plantations are thinned at least once from 20 years onwards, although in very windy sites they may be left unthinned to prevent loss of trees during storms. Thinned plantations allow more light to reach the ground, so a continuous ground cover may be re-established at this stage, the plants growing from buried seed or colonising from other parts of the forest. Native broad-leaved shrubs and trees often become established under larch or pine, providing more layers for animal life to utilise. Several bird species use the thinned plantations, such as woodcock, tawny owl, sparrowhawk, treecreeper, blackcap, spotted flycatcher and common redstart. If some dead wood is left standing, great spotted or green woodpeckers may use the plantations for nesting.

Mammal life also increases during the mature, thinned stage of coniferous plantations. Bats may be found in some plantations, especially species which use holes in trees for roosting or hibernating, such as pipistrelle, noctule or common long-eared bat. Red squirrels are attracted to plantations in the Lake District, Wales, Northumberland and parts of Scotland, particularly where the scarcity of broad-leaved trees with large seeds reduces competition from the introduced American grey squirrel. The latter is becoming common in some parts of the uplands and is culled as a pest species by foresters, as it can cause considerable damage to trees. Other unwelcome mammals from the forester's point of view are the deer, which have increased in numbers tremendously as the area of plantations has grown. In Scotland, red deer are the major problem; in most other areas except Wales it is roe deer. Active culling of deer is carried out in most forests. Sika deer live wild in north and west Scotland and on the Pennines and are spreading into other areas. Fallow and muntjac deer also occur in plantations occasionally, but their numbers are not yet large enough to cause major damage. In parts of Wales and Kielder Forest, feral goats occasionally visit the plantations from higher ground.

The invertebrate life of forestry plantations has been studied in a few areas. On Rhum, over 130 species of butterfly and moth have colonised plantations[3]. In Hamsterley Forest, there are records of seven dragonfly, six social wasp, three hoverfly, seven sawfly, two rare ground beetle and nine rare moth species. The diversity of invertebrates depends on the diversity of plants, as many insects are specific to individual plant species, an example being the sawfly specific to spruce. There is a smaller number of insect species associated with most conifers than with most broad-leaved trees, partly because most conifers are not native to Britain, but the number is likely to increase through time as new species are introduced or find their way to Britain. Species particularly associated with conifers include the spruce budworm, a species of lacewing and the bordered white moth. 'Woolly bear' caterpillars of several other moths are also common, such as the white ermine, fox and northern eggar.

The list of insect species includes some notable pests, which can cause defoliation of the trees. The pines suffer most, as Scots pine is a native species and therefore has its own suite of insects, many of which can also attack introduced pines, such as the lodgepole pine. They include the pine beauty moth, the pine weevil, the pine shoot moth and the pine sawfly. Other conifers are sometimes attacked by these species but also suffer from introduced pests, a recent example being the great spruce bark beetle. The fact that the trees are grown in single-species stands makes it easier for the pest species to build up their numbers, sometimes necessitating the use of chemical sprays or biological control. Dead timber attracts bark-boring beetles and longhorn beetles, whilst ground beetles forage in the conifer litter.

The mature stages of plantations offer many opportunities for fungi to colonise dead wood or litter on the forest floor. There is a great range of species involved, some of them colourful and abundant, and many are confined to conifer woods and plantations. Amongst the larger, more conspicuous species are the false chanterelle, the saffron milk cap, the red milk cap, the club foot, the sickener, the deceiver and the wood woolly-foot. In most plantations there is relatively little dead wood, as the trees are felled before they reach the stage of senescence, but occasional dead standing timber provides habitats for bracket fungi characteristic of coniferous woods, such as conifer heartrot. Some fungi are relatively recent introductions, such as *Calocera palido-spathulata*, which was introduced from New Zealand in the 1970s and is now widespread in conifer plantations in northern England. Other fungi are rare, an example being *Tremiscus helvelloides* (Colour plate 11).

When the plantations are felled, the rotation is complete and plants and animals can begin to colonise the site again before the next generation of trees is planted. If the cut stumps, branches and other debris from the crop of trees are removed, the ground may be green again in a matter of weeks or months, although the soil will not be replenished with nutrients. If the woody litter is left on the site, it may retard the re-vegetation of the site but provide cover for small mammals or birds. Pioneer plant and animal species can colonise such re-stocking sites quickly from surrounding areas, but the survival of species which are poor colonists will depend on their ability to tolerate the shade of later stages in the cycle. The shorter the length of the rotation, the greater their chances of survival. On the other hand, longer rotations give more scope for plants and animals to re-establish themselves from surrounding areas during the thinned stage of the cycle.

Sycamore, beech and oak are the commonest broad-leaved species grown in plantations. Sycamore, as an introduced species, has a more limited range of wildlife associated with it than beech or oak but all three species add diversity to forestry plantations and provide habitats for additional species of plant and animal. As they are grown under plantation conditions, they go through a series of marked changes similar to those described above for conifers. Many of the same problems for wildlife occur, such as lack of light in the thicket stage or lack of old and decaying wood in the later stages. Broad-leaved trees grown for timber tend to be grown on longer rotations than most coniferous species, which provides more time for other wildlife to colonise during the mature stage. However, shorter rotations may be grown for firewood or charcoal production and in some parts of Britain coppice systems are being re-introduced, which resemble traditional woodland management practices, an example being in Grizedale Forest in the Lake District. Coppice systems are unusual in the uplands at present but they may well become more widespread in the future, as markets for wood products increase.

Thus, although their wildlife is generally less rich than that of semi-natural woodlands, forestry plantations do have a good range of plant and animal species, including some uncommon ones. The structure of the plantations imposes limitations on the range of species present and there are marked changes during the rotation cycle. However, within any large, well-established forest area, different stands will be at different stages in the cycle, allowing rapidly dispersed plants and mobile animals to move between stands. Slow colonists and less mobile species are the ones least likely to survive. Natural regeneration of native broad-leaved trees and shrubs, particularly in the early and mature stages, leads to greater diversity within stands, providing food and shelter for species not able to utilise the planted trees. Increasingly, volunteer conifers, self-seeded from plantations, are becoming another source of diversity, both within forests and outside them. Finally, it should be remembered that there is a minimum of about 5 per cent of other land within forests, such as rides, roads, water bodies, rock outcrops and other unplantable land. Such areas increase the plantation edge and provide opportunities for the survival of species other than those adapted to plantation life.

Conservation problems

Despite their variety of wildlife, plantations, especially coniferous ones, have met with much opposition from conservationists over the years. One of the main ecological arguments against afforestation concerns the loss of the other habitats which the plantations replace. In some cases, semi-natural woodlands have been converted to plantations. For example, Kirkdale on the North York Moors has lost most of its broad-leaved woodland cover since the Second World War and has been replanted with conifers. Surviving fragments of the semi-natural woodland cover have three times as many ground flora species as adjacent plantations of Scots pine at the thicket stage, including typical old woodland species, such as early-purple orchid, lily-of-the-valley and toothwort. The poor powers of dispersal of many woodland herbs prevent them from moving between stands to avoid the dense shade of the thicket stage. It is not yet possible to tell how many rotations woodland plants will be able to tolerate as buried seeds but it seems probable that a progressive impoverishment of the ground flora will take place on sites where conifers replace old deciduous woodland. At least 48 plant species have decreased nationally as a result of afforestation and many other species are still common but have suffered some reduction in range[4].

In other parts of the uplands, coniferous plantations have replaced open communities such as heather moorland, blanket bog or grassland. Although not usually the natural vegetation cover, these plant communities had acquired both interest and stability over the years and many of them supported characteristic assemblages of animal species. It is the loss of these open communities and the traditional upland landscapes to which they gave rise which has particularly incensed many of the critics of forestry. There is a powerful argument that open communities of the uplands are difficult or impossible to re-create once lost, whereas forestry plantations can easily be replicated.

> The new forests are quite different from the heaths, grasslands, peat bogs and sand dune communities which they replace. However good they may become as wildlife habitats in their own right, these forests are not and never can be a compensatory substitute for such open ground ecosystems, which are highly valued in their existing condition[5].

The loss of moorland and rough pasture has been proportionately greater than the loss of other habitats because these areas were easiest for foresters to acquire. For some upland bird species there is good evidence of a decrease in population due to forestry, for example for ravens in the Southern Uplands and Cheviots and for buzzards in Galloway[6]. The decreases in greenshank, golden plover and dunlin populations in northern Scotland have already been discussed (chapter 7). Other bird species at risk include the ring ouzel, black-throated diver, common scoter and red grouse[7]. All moorland species have been affected to some extent by afforestation but in many cases detailed evidence is lacking.

It is often claimed that afforestation replaces rich and interesting moorland bird communities with an assemblage of common songbirds, dominated by species, such as willow warbler and chaffinch, which are abundant in other habitats. On the other hand, some formerly uncommon bird species have definitely benefited from afforestation of open land and have spread. They include the siskin, common cross-bill and redpoll. In Kielder Forest, merlins have successfully adapted to nesting in old crows' nests in trees as plantations have replaced their traditional moorland nest sites. Other moorland species, such as nightjar and black grouse, have colonised restocked or open areas within forests, where there is often less disturbance and more shelter from predators than on open moorlands, although populations of both species are declining in Britain. It should also be noted that not all moorland areas are rich in their birdlife. On intensively managed grouse moors, for instance, many birds of prey continue to suffer (illegal) persecution and there is often a limited range of other birds, the most abundant being common species such as skylark or meadow pipit. Some birds of the native pinewoods, such as the Scottish crossbill and capercaillie, have also been able to extend their range into adjacent pine planta-tions.

Unfortunately, there have been some cases in the past where afforestation schemes have had disastrous impacts on particularly valuable upland sites. Before the Wildlife and Countryside Act (1981) safeguarded Sites of Special Scientific Interest (SSSIs), afforestation went ahead on sites such as the Northern Mountains of Arran. Even after the Act, other sites were damaged, such as Strathy Bogs in north-ern Scotland, and the full force of the law had to be brought to prevent a private company from planting Creag Meagaidh in 1983. The general principle has now been accepted that afforestation is inappropriate on most SSSIs, but these examples have served to get forestry a bad press and have fuelled the public antipathy towards the afforestation of open land.

As well as objecting to the direct loss of the pre-existing habitats of the uplands, conservationists have also criticised forestry plantations for their indirect effects on soils and drainage systems. The ploughing and draining of deep peats, leading to the drying out of blanket bogs, was discussed in chapter 7. The effects on non-peat soils are not so dramatic but ploughing may still lead to a fall in the local water table and an increased rate of drainage through the soil. However, this is not necessarily a disadvantage. For instance, where ploughing breaks up an iron-pan in the soil, it usually leads to a marked improvement in the drainage and aeration of the top-soil. If fertilisers are used to boost the growth of the young trees, they may raise the nutrient status of the soil, allowing a greater range of herbaceous plants to grow.

Needles shed by the conifers contribute to the build up of an acid litter layer at the surface of the soil. This may lead to surface waterlogging and create conditions inimical to many soil micro-organisms. The effects of these trends are not very marked on brown earths or calcareous soils, but where the soil was already showing signs of podzolisation or gleying, these trends are exacerbated[8]. In mixed plantations or those with significant natural regeneration of broad-leaved trees, the effects of acidification will be less than in pure conifer stands. Conifers also contribute to soil acidity by scavenging pollutants from the rain, so the water flowing through the canopy and down the trunks contributes to the acid deposition on the soil.

The deserted Loch Dubh Hotel, surrounded by water and blanket bog in the Flow Country

Sensitive planting producing an attractive forestry landscape in mid-Wales

Tremiscus helvelloides: a colourful and rare fungus of conifer plantations in northern England

Unplanted heather moorland areas in Llanrwst Forest, North Wales, provide a habitat for black grouse

A traditional, colourful upland hay meadow in Snowdonia, photographed in the 1960s, when such fields were common throughout the uplands

Limestone pavement on the Pennines, parts of which retain a soil and vegetation cover

Rosebay willowherb provides a splash of brilliant colour beside the Esk Valley railway line

The traditional farmed landscape of the uplands. Changes in agricultural prosperity or price support systems could have far-reaching effects on the appearance and wildlife of areas such as the North York Moors

Forests and people

Not all the arguments about forestry are ecological ones. There are also aesthetic and landscape considerations, as well as questions of recreation and public access. Many of the early plantations, established for strategic purposes with timber production as the sole aim, had a devastating impact on the upland landscape. Square blocks of exotic tree species, with straight edges, criss-crossed by rectilinear drainage lines and fire-breaks, were both incongruous and unattractive. Not surprisingly, they triggered an adverse reaction in the general public. Two early examples will suffice to illustrate the point. In 1936, Symonds wrote of Whinlatter and Ennerdale forests in the Lake District: 'What is seen is the rigid and monotonous ranks of spruce, dark green to blackish, goose-stepping on the fellsides.' In 1945, Dower wrote of 'large-scale afforestation, blanketing the varied colours and subtle moulding of the hillsides with monotonous sharp-edged conifer plantations'[9].

In many cases, it was not just the appearance of the coniferous plantations themselves but also the loss of much-loved traditional upland landscapes that upset the general public. After many adverse reactions to the early plantings, and vociferous opposition from conservation bodies, agreement was reached to limit further forestry in the central Lake District fells. More recently, the government has confirmed its intention to halt afforestation in other national parks in England and to limit it in national scenic areas in Scotland. The sheer scale of afforestation in some areas has given cause for concern, particularly in the Scottish borders and Southern Uplands. Some Scottish islands have also seen a substantial proportion of their land surfaces planted up, for instance Mull, Islay and Skye. 'The devastating impact on landscape and wildlife is steadily compounded by the tendency of plantations to link up and cover great tracts of hill land'[10]. In other areas, such as parts of Wales, forestry has been carried out on a smaller scale and has been better integrated into the farmed landscape, producing a patchwork which is more pleasing to the eye (Colour plate 10).

Modern forestry has overcome many of the early problems of the appearance and scale of plantations[11]. Nowadays, the edges of plantations are shaped to fit in with the contours, rising up valleys and depressions and falling from spurs and high ground. Larger blocks are appropriate on open plateau tops, whereas the scale of plantations needs to be smaller in valleys. Different tree species are used to vary the colour and texture of plantations, the larches being particularly useful in this respect with their seasonal colour changes. Broad-leaved trees intermixed with conifers are also useful, especially near water courses and to soften the edges of plantations. Bare rock outcrops, open spaces and water features add interest to the landscape, so trees are kept well back from them. Some of the unsightly scars caused by quarries or roads through the forests may be screened by trees of appropriate heights.

These and other measures are gradually transforming the forestry landscape but one or two problems remain. One is that not all private woodland owners are as sympathetic to landscape considerations as the Forestry Commission and there are only limited powers available at the moment to make them comply with the guidelines. A second problem is the long time-scale of changes in forestry, which means that examples of earlier unsympathetic planting will continue to disfigure the landscape for several decades to come.

Public access and the commercial nature of forestry plantations are also important issues. The following description is of Glen Ample in the Scottish Highlands: 'In fifteen years this stretch of wild, open, freely accessible moor will have become a dark and forbidding timber factory'[12]. It is true that in many parts of the uplands, especially in Scotland, there is *de facto* public access to open moorland, but in other areas, such as grouse moors, access is restricted to rights of way. Privately owned deciduous woodlands and farmland also have limited access. Since the 1960s, the Forestry Commission has had a very good record on public access, welcoming people on foot almost anywhere, allowing vehicular access on specified routes, and encouraging a range of recreational activities, including horse-riding, orienteering, picnicking and even, on occasions, allowing car and motor-cycle rallying. Private woodland owners have a generally much more constrained attitude to public access, although the situation varies from forest to forest. The provision of recreation facilities is considered inadequate by Tompkins, who considers the coniferous plantations uninviting and regrets the loss of open views as the trees grow up. He also criticises the production element of the plantations: 'Vast acreages of alien conifers have all the uniformity and mass production efficiency of a field of wheat... The purpose of modern plantations is to maximise the financial return from the forest. It requires the production of the maximum volume of timber in the shortest possible time'[10]. Prince Charles echoed this theme: 'The majority of [the Forestry Commission's] plantations are nothing more than industrial, cellulose factories, with minimal recreational opportunities'[13].

Opponents of modern forestry often draw attention to the similarities between 'tree farming' and intensive agriculture. Many of the objections to forestry plantations are reminiscent of those to modern arable fields: for instance, the idea of private individuals or public bodies putting financial return as the top priority, whatever the cost to the environment. The economics of forestry are complicated by the long-term nature of the investment and the impossibility of predicting markets several decades ahead. As we saw above, the aims and objectives of forestry have changed several times during the twentieth century, and trees planted for one purpose have often been harvested or managed for a quite different purpose. For example, many of the plantations being harvested today were planted as potential pit-props for use in coal mines but will end up as chipboard or as pulp for paper. Short-term markets for firewood or charcoal may be relatively easy to predict but the likely future demand for hardwoods for furniture in 80 or 100 years' time is a matter for speculation.

One of the arguments in favour of the further expansion of forestry is that it will reduce the imports bill. Britain met 13 per cent of its requirements for wood products from home-grown timber in 1990, including about 17 per cent of the sawn softwood, 28 per cent of the newsprint and 49 per cent of the particleboard (for furniture, etc). It was originally envisaged that the Forestry Commission would become self-financing, but this has not yet happened and public money has continued to subsidise the forestry industry, to the tune of £58.2 million in 1989–90[14]. Just over half of this grant-in-aid was used to provide grants to private woodland owners and to carry out the other tasks of the forestry authority, the remainder being used by the Forestry Commission in its timber production. A notional 3 per cent net return on investment is expected on forestry, a figure which is seen as unrealistic in some parts of the uplands. Windthrow is a particular problem in some areas, causing the premature felling of plantations and a consequent reduction in profit.

Even more contentious than the public subsidy to the Forestry Commission was the exploitation of loopholes in the tax system prior to 1988, which enabled some wealthy private investors to off-set up to 70 per cent of the cost of afforestation through tax relief. The investment in the Flow Country was the best known example of this tax avoidance and resulted in a public outcry (chapter 7). The forestry business had all the elements of a good political scandal, with absentee landlords, big forestry companies making large profits and the occasional enterprising smallholder making a quick fortune by selling at the right time[10]. Pension funds also invested heavily in forestry from the mid–1970s onwards, stimulating a rise in land prices in some parts of the uplands. Once the tax loopholes were closed in the 1988 budget, a system of grants was introduced which still enables woodland owners to recoup up to 60 per cent of the cost of new plantations, although stricter environmental and landscape guidelines are now imposed.

Another aspect of the economics of forestry is the employment opportunities which it offers. These are still a strong argument in its favour with local authorities, such as the Highland Regional Council. However, total employment in forestry has been falling since about 1960, owing to greater mechanisation, and was only about 40,000 in 1986–87. Direct employment by the Forestry Commission has also decreased to 8100 in 1986–87, owing to the increasing use of contract labour for tasks such as tree felling. Thus, it is difficult to sustain the argument that forestry makes a major contribution to overall employment, although it may be significant locally.

The forests of the future

The conflicting views about forestry are gradually being reconciled in the era of greater environmental consciousness in the 1990s. It has now been accepted by most foresters that the forests of the future will be multi-purpose forests. Timber and wood production will continue to be important but they will not be the top priority everywhere. In the lowlands, the concept of community forests is being developed, with recreation and amenity as key objectives. In the uplands, wildlife conservation and landscape considerations are becoming major elements of forestry policy. All the Forestry Commission's forest districts now have conservation plans, which fit in with policy guidelines published in 1990[15]. Furthermore, it is the Forestry Commission's stated aim that private woodland owners will only be supported if they agree to manage their plantations along similar lines. This new policy offers great scope for environmental improvement in the uplands.

One important feature is the conservation of sites of particular ecological value which lie within forestry estates. There are over 340 SSSIs on Forestry Commission land alone. There is a great range of habitat types represented on these SSSIs, including wetlands, woodlands, grasslands and moorlands. For instance, there are 1000 ha of wetland within Kielder Forest. Two examples from the North York Moors will serve as illustrations of the type of management involved. In Dalby Forest, a limestone bank is being managed specifically to benefit the rare Duke of Burgundy butterfly. Conifers which had been planted on the site have been felled and there will be no replanting. Instead, deciduous scrub has been allowed to develop, amongst which glades have been cleared mechanically to encourage primroses and cowslips, the caterpillar's food plants. At Rosekirkdale Fen, Norway spruce had been planted over an unusual fen vegetation dominated by the black bog-rush but with a variety of other fen plants. The trees have been felled and some of the drainage ditches blocked in order to preserve the unusual wetland plant community. Sites such as these form valuable conservation enclaves within the forestry estate.

In other cases, the trees themselves are the wildlife resource. There are special policies for ancient broad-leaved woodlands and native pinewoods. Opportunities will be taken to enlarge existing areas of ancient broad-leaved woodland by both planting and natural regeneration, with the aim of producing an uneven-aged structure. Attempts will also be made to increase the area of native pinewoods and to preserve their genetic integrity, for instance by using rooted cuttings from native stock. The Forestry Commission has declared 46 Forest Nature Reserves, 26 of which are in the uplands. They include five native pinewoods and 13 deciduous woodland sites. Many of them include coniferous or mixed plantations, but there are also lakes, bogs and moors. Where they do not cause undue disturbance to the wildlife, facilities are being developed to help visitors experience the plant and animal life at first hand. For instance, the otter haven at Kylerhea on Skye has a nature trail and hide, and interpretation facilities are provided in Grizedale Forest in the Lake District. The Forestry Commission has made several appointments of conservation staff in recent years.

Although the setting aside of these special areas for nature conservation is a very important gesture, more significant in the long run is the management of the bulk of the Forestry Commission estate and the private plantations to enhance their value for wildlife. Plantations now cover nearly 5 per cent of Great Britain and they could make a major contribution to conservation, if managed sympathetically. The Forestry Commission is implementing a major re-structuring of many coniferous plantations to make them more attractive habitats for plants and animals. This involves increasing the diversity of habitats present and improving the age structure of the plantations by felling off small stands within larger blocks, by taking advantage of windthrow to fell some stands sooner than planned or by staggering re-planting times. Some upland areas have very large areas of uniform age structure at the moment, but selective felling policies can create a more varied pattern (Figs 16A and 16B). The size of felling coupes can be altered in order to produce more visual variety in the landscape, and replanting with a greater variety of tree species, including larches and broad-leaves, will add to this aesthetic effect and will also be attractive to a greater range of wildlife. Leaving some older trees to grow on past their optimum harvesting date and tolerating some dead wood within the plantations will provide habitats for hole-nesting birds, bats and wood-boring insects. Encouraging the growth of shrub layers in thinned plantations will offer more food resources for birds and mammals. Plantation edges can be improved by allowing transitional scrub or verge zones to develop.

Within forests, the open spaces, such as deer glades, water-courses, rides and roadside verges, are also important wildlife habitats. Between 10 and 20 per cent of the total forest area should be composed of open habitats and these should be linked by open corridors, facilitating the movement of animal and plant species through the intervening plantation blocks. It is important that the plantation trees do not shade out the herbaceous vegetation of these open habitats when they reach their full height, so the width of verges should ideally be about 30 metres. Where this is not practical, scallops may be made on alternate sides of rides. Aquatic wildlife should also be protected by ensuring that the central part of the stream is open to full sunlight. To minimise soil erosion and acidification of water-courses, drains should stop at least 20 metres away from the streams and conifers should be planted well back from the stream edge. In some cases this is being achieved by removing conifers close to water-courses.

Habitats can also be created deliberately to enhance the wildlife value of forests. There are numerous examples of small fire reservoirs which have become sites for frogs, toads or newts. Larger lakes have also been created, for example at Staindale on the North York Moors, where species such as tufted duck and Canada goose may be seen. In Hamsterley Forest, two large artificial ponds have been allowed to colonise naturally with plants and animals from the surrounding forest. Dabchicks, black-headed gulls and greylag geese nest on islands in the Grizedale Tarns in the Lake District. Nest box schemes have enabled species such as pied flycatcher and common redstart to colonise plantations where natural nest-holes are scarce. Amongst the more unusual species to use nest boxes, are goldeneye, goosanders and barn owls. Artificial eyries have been provided for ospreys at some Scottish sites and for red kites in Wales. Bats have also benefitted from the provision of boxes, and in Dalby Forest a 'hibernaculum' has been built in which it is hoped bats will be able to over-winter for many centuries to come. Steps are being taken to protect roosts of the common long-eared bat in bridges in northern Scotland.

It is obvious that great strides are being made in the direction of conservation within existing forests, but so far the impact of the new policies has been uneven. There are show-piece forests, such as Hamsterley, Dalby, Grizedale and Coed-y-Brenin, where multi-purpose use is well established and the wildlife resources are

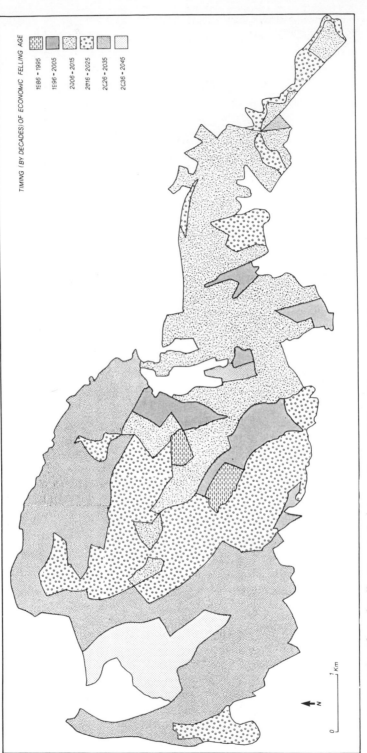

FIGURE 16A Plan of Dalby Forest, showing pattern of felling if trees were to be felled when they reached economic maturity, as originally envisaged when they were planted

(Reproduced by permission of the Forestry Commission, Pickering Office)

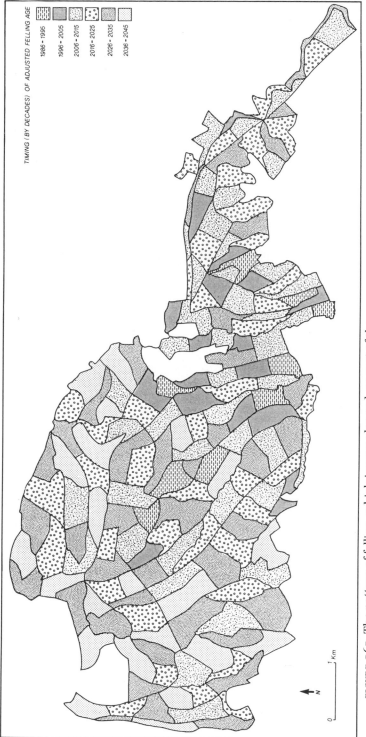

TIMING (BY DECADES) OF ADJUSTED FELLING AGE

1986 - 1995
1996 - 2005
2006 - 2015
2016 - 2025
2026 - 2035
2036 - 2045

FIGURE 16B The pattern of felling, which is now planned, as part of the re-structuring of the forest; this pattern will benefit the wildlife and have a less drastic impact on the landscape
(Reproduced by permission of the Forestry Commission, Pickering Office)

rich. However, there are far more forests where such measures have been minimal so far and which still qualify for their description as, 'vast rectangular blocks of gloomy conifers'[12]. Many plantations in the Southern Uplands, for instance, are monocultures of Sitka spruce, planted at a time when no consideration was given to matters other than timber production and where little effort has been made since then to diversify them and enhance their value for wildlife.

Privately owned plantations have tended to lag behind Forestry Commission estates as far as conservation and amenity measures go. There is less incentive for an individual than for a public body to respond to public opinion. The Woodland Grant Schemes[16] are supposed to ensure that private woods are managed to the same standards as Forestry Commission plantations but it remains to be seen whether the Forestry Commission will have the power to enforce this and bring all plantations up to the standard of the best Forestry Commission practice.

PLATE 30 Free-range turkeys in Over Silton Forest, North York Moors: an unusual example of diversification within forestry plantations

Despite many people's misgivings or even positive abhorrence of modern forestry, coniferous plantations are now established as part of the British landscape. Their area is likely to increase over the next century, particularly in Scotland, and some of the tree species from them will inevitably establish themselves in the wider landscape. Novel uses are being developed for some forests, such as free-range turkey production in Over Silton Forest on the North York Moors (Plate 30). There is undoubtedly a tremendous potential for real multiple use of the new forests, for timber production, recreation and wildlife conservation, but it is a challenge which will require foresters and conservationists to work together.

Forestry in Wales

The first plantations in Wales were made in the early seventeenth century, but were mainly for ornamental purposes and concentrated in the lowlands. Larger, commercial plantations date from the end of the seventeenth century onwards and mark the beginning of upland afforestation. In the mid–1770s, Wyndham remarked on the unusual planting of conifers on the Gogerddan estate in mid-Wales: 'a very extensive and flourishing plantation of firs, which covered the steep declivities of two hills . . . . in country where the soil and climate seem averse to the production of all other kinds of forest trees'. New trees were introduced on to estates in the eighteenth century by pioneers such as Thomas Johnes, and the first tree nurseries were established in Wales at the end of the century. Eighteen species of conifer and 24 species of broad-leaved tree are known to have been planted on Welsh estates between 1750 and 1825[17].

The shallow, stony upland soils were being planted up in areas thought to be useless for agricultural improvement. In 1810, the Revd Walter Davies urged land-owners to undertake more planting in the uplands for economic reasons: 'While we have such extensive wastes, capable of bearing firs and pines without number, why must we be indebted annually to foreign nations? By planting extensively, the face of the country would, in a few years, be inconceivably improved and the present generation would thereby buy stock in the wooded funds of Cambria for the use of their posterity'. However, landscape considerations were already significant, as illustrated by Fenton's description of the landscape at Gwydyr as 'disfigured by a strait belt-planted line of grim fir trees'[17].

Wales had only 3 or 4 per cent woodland cover by the late nineteenth century and the rate of new planting (about 400 ha a year) hardly kept pace with the rate at which deciduous woods were falling into disuse and being grubbed up to make way for other land uses. Some people were arguing strongly for the development of commercial forestry. For instance, in 1885, Evan Powell claimed: 'there is probably a larger area of unplanted land in Wales that would pay for planting than in any other portion of the kingdom'[17].

During the First World War, nearly one quarter of the woodlands in Wales were felled. By the time the Forestry Commission began activities in Wales, there were more conifers than broad-leaved trees and forestry was well established as a large estate activity, often with absentee landlords. The Forestry Commission started with five forests in 1920: Gwydyr, Coed-y-Brenin, Margam, Ebbw and Llantrisant. As in other parts of Britain, it was land with the poorer soils which was most readily available for purchase, so the emphasis on conifers was maintained. The first attempts at diversification had just been made and the first forest parks set up, when the Second World War broke out. In the immediate post-war period, agriculture was the greater priority, so forestry was pushed 'up the hill' on to the higher ground. Most new planting was carried out by the Forestry Commission until the mid–1950s,

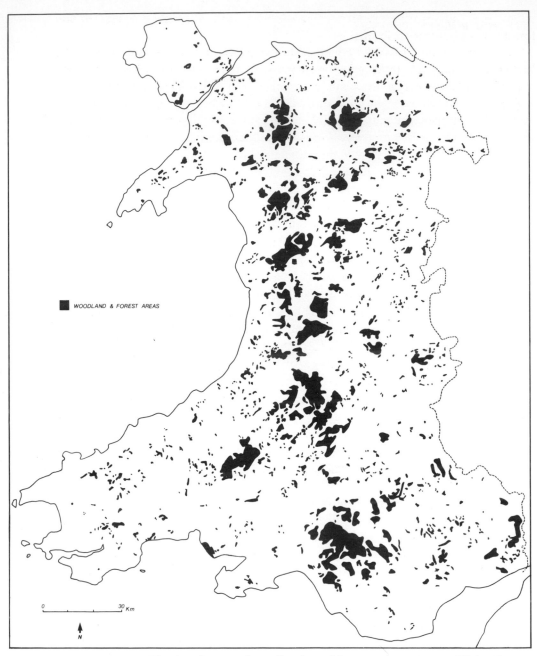

WOODLAND & FOREST AREAS

0   30 Km

N

FIGURE 17 The distribution of woodlands and forestry plantations in Wales. Large blocks of forestry dominate the landscape in parts of south and central Wales, but many small patches of woodland are scattered over the rest of the agricultural landscape (Reproduced by permission of the Forestry Commission, Aberystwyth Office)

when grant aid encouraged private woodland owners to plant their estates and forestry companies were formed.

Afforestation gathered momentum in the 1960s and 1970s, especially on the higher ground. Large blocks of the uplands were afforested in many parts of Wales, such as near Llandovery in the south, near Dolgellau in mid-Wales, and near Betwys-y-Coed in the north. Nearly 13 per cent of the land surface of Wales is now wooded and 70 per cent of the woodland is coniferous (Figure 17). Most of the broad-leaved woodland is on private estates, where it forms 55 per cent of the total area of 117,000 ha, often in small farm woodland blocks. Of the 131,000 ha of Forestry Commission estates, 95 per cent is coniferous, with spruces making up 55 per cent of the total.

This great expansion of forestry in Wales has not been without its problems, such as changes to the soils, especially peat soils, which have suffered considerable shrinkage and structural damage[18]. There have also been changes in the run-off from the afforested land, which have led to changes in acidity and turbidity of the streams[19]. These have led to decreases of wildlife; for instance, dippers have suffered because their invertebrate food supply has decreased. In some specific cases, afforestation has damaged sites of high wildlife interest. Two well-documented examples are the afforestation of one of the largest and most important blanket bog areas in Wales, at Migneint, and the planting of Llanbrynmair Moors, which was part of a large moorland area of great importance to upland birds. Following these controversial issues, Welsh forestry is moving towards multi-purpose woodland management in the 1990s. Indeed, this is the first priority in the Forestry Commission's corporate plan for 1992. There are still plenty of examples of older plantations with straight edges and uniform species and age structures, which are limited in both their wildlife value and their aesthetic appeal. However, alongside these production forests are others where recreation or conservation have a high priority.

A large area of forestry in north Wales has been designated as the Snowdonia Forest Park and specified forests have been targeted for the development of recreation facilities. The most important of these are Gwydyr, Beddgelert and Coed-y-Brenin forests and those on popular tourist routes or close to population centres, such as Clocaenog, Rheidol or Rhonnda. There were four visitor centres, one forest drive, one camp-site, over 100 picnic sites and about 160 forest walks or nature trails on Forestry Commission land in Wales by 1986. Despite these developments, some people feel that more could be done by way of providing more specialised facilities, such as adventure playgrounds, bird feeding stations or open spaces for events such as barbecues[20]. The principles of landscape design were incorporated in a project in Beddgelert Forest in the early 1980s[21], and all other Forestry Commission forests are currently subject to re-design. There are over 70 SSSIs and 11 nature reserves on Forestry Commission land in Wales. Some of these are managed by the Commission as Forest Nature Reserves, such as Coed-y-Rhaiadr woodland near Aberdare or Dyffryn Crawnon near Brecon, while others are leased to conservation bodies. There are agreements between the Forestry Commission and other bodies over the management of particular sites or species, a good example being the agreement with the Countryside Council for Wales in the Hafod area over the red kite, which nests in broad-leaved trees and larch within coniferous forest.

Two areas where multi-purpose forestry is well established will serve to illustrate the potential for wildlife conservation within Welsh plantations in the future. Llanrwst Forest, near Betwys-y-Coed, has over 100 conservation sites and a proposed Forest Nature Reserve within it. The conservation sites include both plantations and other habitats, such as grasslands and water bodies. There are ancient woodland sites, which have been partly planted up with beech, sycamore and conifers and invaded by Rhododendron. Management policy is to remove the non-native species and restore the sites to naturally regenerating broad-leaved woodland. Planted broad-leaved trees are also being managed to produce an uneven-aged structure and encourage a more vigorous ground flora. An area of rich marshy grassland is grazed by cattle and horses and will be maintained as unimproved meadow land. Here natural regeneration of broad-leaves is not wanted and will be suppressed by felling or the use of chemicals. Lesser horse-shoe bats roost in an old barn on the site, which will be maintained. An upland heather moor surrounded by conifer plantations is important as a site for black grouse, almost the entire Welsh population of which is now found on Forestry Commission land (Colour plate 12). A fire in the early 1980s killed many of the trees on the higher ground. Sitka spruce and lodgepole pine will be removed from other parts to create large habitat islands of moorland as black grouse habitat.

In Coed-y-Brenin Forest, near Dolgellau, over-mature Douglas fir trees are to be retained because of their high landscape value in the valleys of the rivers Mawddach and Wen. Goshawks nest in this forest and the flora includes the rare filmy-ferns. The rocks in the area are rich in minerals and both copper and gold mining occurred in the past. In the middle of the forest is a remarkable bog, with water rich in copper and other minerals. Its flora includes an extraordinary combination of species, with thrift, spring sandwort, sea campion and adder's-tongue growing alongside acid bog plants such as cross-leaved heath, bog asphodel, purple moor-grass and round-leaved sundew. On the drier surrounds grow lesser butterfly-orchid, northern marsh-orchid and broad-leaved helleborine. This forest also has upland sites important for black grouse and other birdlife, where clear-felled areas are being allowed to regenerate with broad-leaved scrub woodland and western gorse over heather moorland. These sites not only form important wildlife enclaves within the forest but also provide spectacular views towards Cadair Idris in the heart of the Cambrian mountains.

These two Forestry Commission areas show how production forestry can be reconciled with conservation and amenity objectives. At the same time, they serve as a standard against which forestry in other parts of Wales may be measured. The comparison is an unfavourable one, not only for some of the other Forestry Commission forests but especially for many of the large private plantations. Conservation measures and the provision of recreation facilities can be costly undertakings and rarely bring in much by way of income. If we wish to invest in multi-purpose forestry in the future, it will need to be on a different financial basis from that of the past; but, with over 170,000 ha of coniferous plantations in Wales, the rewards for wildlife and public enjoyment could be enormous.

References

1 James, N D G, *A History of English forestry*. Blackwell, Oxford, 1981.
2 Hill, M O, Ground flora and succession in commercial forests. In Jenkins, D (ed), *Trees and wildlife in the Scottish uplands*, pp 71–8. Institute of Terrestrial Ecology, Abbots Ripton, Hunts, 1986.
3 Young, M R, The effects of commercial forestry on woodland Lepidoptera. In Jenkins, D (ed), *Trees and wildlife in the Scottish uplands*, pp 88–94, 1986.
4 Ratcliffe, D A, The effects of afforestation on the wildlife of open habitats. In Jenkins, D (ed), *Trees and wildlife in the Scottish uplands*, pp 46–54, 1986.
5 Nature Conservancy Council, *Nature conservation and afforestation in Britain*. Nature Conservancy Council, Peterborough, 1986.
6 Ratcliffe, D A, *Bird life of mountain and upland*. Cambridge University Press, Cambridge, 1990.
7 Avery, M and Leslie, R, *Birds and forestry*. T and A D Poyser, London, 1990.
8 Miles, J, What are the effects of trees on soils? In Jenkins, D (ed), *Trees and wildlife in the Scottish uplands*, pp 55–62, 1986.
9 Fishwick, A, Woodland management and recreation in the Lake District. In Adamson, J K (ed), *Cumbrian woodlands – past, present and future*, pp 43–53. Institute of Terrestrial Ecology, HMSO, London, 1989.
10 Tompkins, S, *Forestry in crisis*. Christopher Helm, London, 1989.
11 Crowe, S, *The landscape of forests and woods*. Forestry Commission booklet No 44, HMSO, London, 1978.
12 Shoard, M, *This land is our land*. Paladin, London, 1987.
13 Prince Charles quoted in Tompkins, *Forestry in crisis*.
14 Forestry Commission, *Annual report, 1989–90*, 1990.
15 Forestry Commission, *Forest nature conservation guidelines*. HMSO, London, 1990.
16 Forestry Commission, *Woodland grant scheme*. Forestry Commission, Edinburgh, 1991.
17 Linnard, W, *Welsh woods and forests: History and utilization*. National Museum of Wales, Cardiff, 1982.
18 Hornung, M et al, The effects of forestry on soils, soil water and surface water chemistry. In Good, J E G (ed), *Environmental aspects of plantation forestry in Wales*, pp 25–36. Institute of Terrestrial Ecology, Grange over Sands, 1987.
19 Ormerod, S J et al, The influence of forest on aquatic fauna. In Good, J E G (ed), *Environmental aspects of plantation forestry in Wales*, pp 37–49, 1987.
20 Baylis, D O, Recreation potential of Welsh forests. In Good, J E G (ed), *Environmental aspects of plantation forestry in Wales*, pp 50–6, 1987.
21 Lucas, O W R, Landscape design of forestry. In Good, J E G (ed), *Environmental aspects of plantation forestry in Wales*, pp 57–63, 1987.

9

Grasslands

Now daisies pied, and violets blue,
And lady-smocks all silver white,
And cuckoo-buds of yellow hue
Do paint the meadows with delight.
William Shakespeare, *Love's Labours Lost*

Grasslands form one of the most widespread and extensive habitats in all upland regions from south-west England to the Northern Isles. A few grasslands are found above the potential limit of tree growth or on steep cliffs, where exposure prevents tree growth, but the vast majority occur in areas which were once wooded. They owe their existence to management such as grazing or mowing, which prevents trees or shrubs from becoming established. Most have been derived from natural vegetation and consist of wild plants, but some have been planted.

History of the grasslands

The development of grasslands below the potential tree limit went hand in hand with the human exploitation of the uplands. Their spread can be traced on pollen diagrams by the records for grasses and typical grassland herbs, such as plantains, buttercups and daisies. The first grasslands were merely extensions of natural glades within the woods, kept grassy by the grazing of wild animals and burning by Mesolithic hunters. In the Neolithic and Bronze Age periods, domestic animals were grazed in the woods and this made it difficult for trees to regenerate. Gaps began to appear in the woodland cover, recorded on the pollen diagrams as small temporary expansions of grasses and weeds. The pollen or seeds of at least 25 grassland plant species have been recorded in Britain from these periods[1]. Arable farming was also practised and this involved periods of fallow, during which the fields were grazed. Arable and pastoral farming were more closely integrated in prehistoric times than they are today, so the distinction between them was less clear.

The first major increase in grassland came in the Iron Age in most areas from North Yorkshire and Cumbria southwards. In Northumberland, Durham and southern Scotland, it was delayed until the Roman period, and in the north of Scotland it was even later. It is likely that this extensive clearance phase coincided with the development of regular grass cutting for hay, as scythes and other relevant agricultural tools are known from Roman times onwards. Several grassland weeds are first recorded in Iron Age or Roman times, including cat's-ear, oxeye daisy and yarrow, and there are records for 50 grassland plant species in Britain[1]. Hay was a very important agricultural commodity, as its supply determined the number of animals which could be kept over the winter period.

Domesday Book shows that meadowland and pasture were widespread in England by 1086 and that both grassland types were more valuable than arable land. By medieval times, large hay meadows were associated with many settlements. Situated in the valleys, they had communal or shared ownership and their own laws and traditions[2]. On the higher ground, vast areas were managed as sheep walks by the monastic houses, resulting in another major expansion of grassland. By now the traditional pattern of upland farming was established, with enclosed arable and hay fields near the farms in the valleys, enclosed permanent pasture for cattle or sheep on the valley sides, and unenclosed rough grazing on the higher ground. The price of wool was high in the Tudor and Stuart periods, so many landowners turned some of their arable land over to grassland. In other areas, rabbit warrens were established. They reached their peak of popularity in the eighteenth and nineteenth centuries, when they were often the most profitable use of poorer agricultural land. Fluctuations in the economy led to expansion or contraction in the amount of enclosed farmland in the uplands in the nineteenth and twentieth centuries. For instance, during the Napoleonic Wars and the two World Wars, more arable land was required, so grassland was ploughed up. Some of this land was later put back to hay production or permanent pasture. In times of agricultural depression, as in the 1870s, some pastures were allowed to revert to rough grazing land.

Since the mid-twentieth century, there has been increased mechanisation of farming and greater use of inorganic fertilisers, herbicides and pesticides. The majority of enclosed permanent pastures in the uplands have been improved by the addition of fertilisers and slurry and many are now ploughed up and re-seeded every few years. This has led to a great increase in the number of livestock per hectare. Former hay meadows have mostly been converted to silage production. This involves fertilising and re-seeding to produce a quick-growing grass crop, which can be cut several times a year while it is still green. Those hay fields which remain in an unimproved state under traditional management are usually found towards the heads of the valleys and on steeper land, often in the ownership or tenancy of elderly, conservative farmers. However, the unenclosed rough pastures have remained much the same as in previous centuries, except for changes in the numbers of sheep grazed on them.

Management techniques

Variations in intensity and type of management result in different kinds of grassland. In all of them, grasses are an essential and often dominant component of the vegetation. They are particularly adapted to withstand grazing or mowing because of the way they grow. Their main growing point lies at the base of the shoot, close to the ground surface. When the upper part of the shoot is removed by grazing or cutting, the grass plant shoots again from lateral buds at the growth point – a process known as tillering. The more the upper shoot is removed, the more the grass tillers, to produce a close network of shoots spreading out in several directions.

Heavy grazing pressure produces a turf type of grassland, dominated by short grasses, amongst which are other plants which can withstand grazing by having a prostrate growth form or a basal rosette of leaves, such as creeping buttercup or mouse-ear-hawkweeds. This type of grassland is particularly associated with sheep grazing, as sheep feed by eating the uppermost parts of the plants across the whole field, producing a fairly even reduction in height of the sward. Rabbits also produce a close grazed turf but tend to be more concentrated in their feeding areas, which can result in locally overgrazed and bare areas. Cattle (Plate 31) and horses feed by curling their tongues around the plants and tearing rather than biting them. They graze less closely to the ground than sheep and produce larger quantities of dung, producing an uneven sward. With horses this effect is exacerbated by the fact that the animals keep their feeding areas quite distinct from the areas on which they deposit their dung, so pasture that is grazed by cattle or horses tends to be more variable and to include areas of coarser grasses alongside more intensively grazed patches. If the grazing pressure is low, the coarser grasses may dominate the pasture, growing in large tussocks, with dead leaves and stems at the base.

Where grazing is absent during the main growing season, a meadow type of grassland develops (Colour plate 13). The grasses and other plants grow taller, competing for light, so that the shorter plants are shaded out, but there may be a large number of species present. One major difference from the other grassland types is that most species can flower and set seed in the meadow before it is cut for hay in late summer. This means that the main method of reproduction for the plants is by seed, in contrast to the vegetative spread which is more important in grazed grasslands. Some hay meadows lie on land which was prone to winter flooding in the past, the silt providing a source of mineral nutrients. In Exmoor, there was formerly a variation of the lowland water meadows, known as catch meadows. In spring, water was led on to the meadows via special channels. The water warmed up the soil and encouraged an early growth of grass, before being drained away again a few weeks later. Modern silage production is a variant of the meadow type of grassland, in which the high doses of fertiliser give a competitive advantage to a few grass species. The early and repeated cutting in this case prevents the plants from flowering and setting seed, so their reproduction is by vegetative means or by artificial re-seeding.

Burning is sometimes used to remove coarser grasses, whilst drainage may improve the soil in wet sites. Combinations of all these management techniques and variations in the intensity or frequency with which they are used lead to a complex array of different grassland types. It is relatively easy to alter the characteristics of a grassland by changing the management regime, so grasslands are constantly

PLATE 31 Highland cattle grazing in an upland pasture

responding to changing farming methods, as hay meadows are turned into silage fields or sheep replace cattle in pastures. Whenever management slackens off, the grassland starts to develop towards scrub or woodland, with hawthorn, gorse or trees invading, reminding us that nearly all grasslands are the products of human intervention.

Grassland plantlife

The plant species to be found in grasslands vary greatly according to the underlying soils and geology. A basic division may be made into acidic, neutral and limestone grasslands[3,4]. Acidic grasslands are the most widespread type, occurring from near sea level to 900 metres altitude on non-calcareous rocks throughout the uplands. Most have been managed by a system of rough grazing which has probably altered little since prehistoric times. Sheep are easily the most important grazing animals today but cattle, horses and formerly pigs have also played their parts and continue to do so in some areas, such as Dartmoor and Exmoor. The soils are acid, partly as a result of the underlying rock type and partly because of the many centuries of leaching in the cool, wet upland climate. Only recently have some of these grasslands been treated with fertilisers; most of them have never had any replacement for the nutrients lost when leaching occurs or the carcasses of grazing animals are removed. Consequently, the grasslands have a limited range of plant species, except where springs or outcrops of calcareous soil introduce some variety. They are dominated by a few common grasses, interspersed with other herbaceous plants, including sedges, rushes and ferns.

The best agricultural fields amongst the acidic grasslands are the bent–fescue pastures of the foothills of areas such as the Southern Uplands, central Highlands, Wales and the Pennines. They are generally confined to land below 300 metres altitude, and they overlie well-drained brown earth soils. They are sometimes treated with fertilisers or farmyard manure. The dominant grasses are common bent, velvet bent and sheep's-fescue, but others include crested dog's-tail, sweet vernal-grass and wavy hair-grass. Other plant life is usually limited to mosses and a few plants found also on moorland, such as heath bedstraw or tormentil. However, sometimes woodland species like bluebell or wood-sorrel survive as relics of the deciduous woodland cover which the grassland has replaced. Where grazing pressure is greater or where soils are less well drained, mat-grass replaces the bent–fescue pastures. It is not a woodland grass and is found on areas above 300 metres, which have been open land for many centuries. It is common in the Cheviots, the northern Pennines, Wales and the Highlands, where it gives the hillsides a whitish appearance. It may be accompanied by bilberry or by heath rush, as well as some of the species from the bent–fescue grasslands. An increase in rainfall and less good drainage favour purple moor-grass, which grows in large tussocks, often with deergrass, covering large areas of western Scotland. In other areas, tufted hair-grass is dominant, especially where soils are gleyed.

Neutral grasslands are found on the heavier clay soils of upland valleys and are usually enclosed and more intensively managed than the acidic grasslands. Leaching is counteracted by manuring or the addition of fertilisers. They have a wider range of grass species than the acidic grasslands: as well as the bents and fescues, there are meadow foxtail, sweet vernal-grass, false oat-grass, crested dog's-tail, Yorkshire-fog, cock's-foot and species of meadow-grass. However, where they have been fertilised and improved for agriculture, they are dominated by perennial rye-grass or timothy and diversity is low. There are two main land uses: pasture and hay meadows. In the unimproved grazed pastures, the long list of wild flowers may include burnt orchid, greater butterfly-orchid, saw-wort, grass-of-parnassus or red bartsia. Many of these pastures were formerly used as arable fields and some still retain the old 'rigg and furrow' pattern of the former ploughed strips.

Traditional upland hay meadows are varied and colourful, with a wide range of grasses and other flowering plants (Colour plate 13). As well as the ubiquitous buttercups and daisies, there are common knapweed, hogweed, lady's-mantles and many more. Regional variations reflect differences in soils and management practices. Where drainage is poor, wetland species, such as marsh-marigold, meadow-sweet and rushes, grow alongside the typical meadow species, as in parts of the Cheviots and Southern Uplands. On the Shetlands there are some exceptionally rich wet meadows with conspicuous yellow iris and ragged-robin. Other rich hay meadow communities are found in the Pennines, Dartmoor, the Lake District and north Wales. In general, the more traditional the farming methods, the greater the variety of hay meadow plants. The most diverse meadows receive no inorganic fertiliser and only small amounts of farmyard manure; grazing is excluded for several months and they are cut late in the season.

There are many calcareous rocks in the uplands, on which limestone grass-lands occur. They include the Carboniferous limestone of the Pennines, southern Lake District and south Wales; the Jurassic limestone of the North York Moors; the Durness and Dalradian limestones of Scotland, and the shelly sands of the Outer Hebrides. Most of the grasslands are unenclosed sheep pastures, in which the grazing pressure prevents any one species from becoming dominant, so they are often very rich in plant species. Soils are calcareous and usually thin, sometimes with the top-soil resting directly on weathered rock with no real sub-soil between them. All the soils are free-draining and drought can be a problem in summer. Some plants, like the fairy flax, have adapted by having shallow spreading root networks to catch as much rainfall as possible. Others, like lady's bedstraw or salad burnet, have very long tap-roots, which penetrate fissures in the rock to draw on deeper water reserves.

The main grass species vary from region to region. In Derbyshire and the southern North York Moors, fescues, meadow oat-grasses and quaking-grass are the most important species; whereas in the Lake District, Wales and many parts of Scotland, fescues and common bent predominate. On the Carboniferous limestone in a broad belt across Cumbria, Lancashire and Yorkshire, blue moor-grass assumes dominance. On the Uists in the Outer Hebrides, very unusual grasslands occur over shell sands near the coast. They include wetland species, such as amphibious bistort, common spike-rush and parsley water-dropwort, mixed with maritime ones, such as sea plantain and sea arrowgrass. Maritime species are also found intermixed with arctic-alpine plants and dwarf shrubs in the exceptionally rich coastal grasslands of north-west Scotland. At Durness and Bettyhill, the grasslands are adorned with a colourful carpet of thrift, mountain avens, common bird's-foot-trefoil, mountain everlasting, Scottish primrose, field gentian, wild thyme and many more. The addition of inorganic fertilisers can alter the unique characteristics of such habitats, allowing a few species to out-compete the rest and dominate the sward. Agricultural improvement has led to the replacement of many of the more interesting limestone grasslands with less diverse but more productive agricultural swards.

Animal life

Because most grasslands are part of the agricultural system, their animal life is controlled by humans to a greater or lesser extent. The greatest variety of animals is found on those grasslands under traditional management regimes. Unenclosed rough grazing land supports a richer animal life than the more intensively managed enclosed fields, although both are characterised by an absence of large predators which might attack the domestic livestock. As the grasslands considered in this chapter have been derived from woodland, they had no original fauna with which to compare their present animal life. Some of the woodland creatures, such as small mammals, managed to adapt to grasslands, whilst others, such as butterflies or lizards, spread from other habitats to colonise the new meadows and pastures.

Deer, foxes, badgers and wild goats may include grasslands within their territories. Hares and the introduced rabbit are the most conspicuous wild mammal species and their grazing can determine the type of grassland produced, as described above. The rabbit, being a colonial species, has a greater effect than the hares, and rabbit burrows are thick on the ground in many grassland areas. Weasels and stoats are attracted to grasslands because of the rabbits and other small mammals, particularly field voles, bank voles and mice. Shrews are insectivorous predators, which feed on invertebrates in the grass or litter layer. There are also moles, especially in limestone or neutral grasslands, where there is a plentiful food supply of earthworms. The presence of mole-hills in a grassland is a good indicator of a fertile soil, rich in earthworms and other soil organisms which break down organic matter and mix it into the top-soil. All burrowing animals play an important part in the drainage and aeration of grassland soils and their absence from many of the acidic grasslands increases the contrast between these and the other grassland types. Bare ground caused by trampling, heavy rabbit grazing or mole hills may provide a habitat for annual plant species and for some invertebrates, such as mining bees and wasps.

The invertebrate life of grasslands is rich and varied, reflecting the diversity of plant species. Sawflies, beetles, leaf hoppers, grass hoppers, woodlice, weevils, bees and spiders may all be found, feeding on the vegetation or in the litter layer. The meadow ant builds large ant-hills, which increase in size each year, providing a clue to the age of the pasture. Most invertebrates are commonest in sites with little grazing, so areas of coarser grassland, which tend to be of little botanical interest, may turn out to have a rich invertebrate fauna. The addition of farmyard manure and inorganic fertilisers leads to a decrease in the range of species but an increase in the numbers of those which remain.

PLATE 32 The small pearl-bordered fritillary, a frequent butterfly on calcareous grasslands

Perhaps the most attractive and noticeable invertebrates are the butterflies and moths, which are a particularly conspicuous feature of many of the limestone grasslands. Butterflies include the common blue, dingy skipper, wall, meadow brown, small tortoiseshell, peacock, red admiral, small copper, large white, ringlet, Scotch argus, brown argus and the fritillaries (for example, the small pearl-bordered fritillary, Plate 32). Amongst the equally numerous moths, the day-flying species most likely to be seen are the burnet moths, with their bright red spots. Other grassland moths include the common rustic, dark arches, cloud-bordered brindle and Mother Shipton, but most of these fly by night.

The insects provide food for songbirds, such as the meadow pipit and skylark, which may nest in the grasslands. Lapwings are also ground nesters and used to be common in grasslands and arable fields, but their population has been decreasing over the past few decades. Many other birds use grasslands as part of their feeding territories but nest elsewhere, including the common whitethroat, whinchat, stonechat and curlew. Numbers of such birds are highest where there is some scrub invasion or where grasslands form a mosaic with woodlands, moorlands or hedgerows. Birds of prey, such as kestrel and short-eared owl, also feed in the grasslands, preying on small mammals. In parts of Scotland the golden eagle feeds on rabbits or hares as well as sheep carrion. Grasslands are good places to catch a glimpse of reptiles, particularly common lizards and adders, which may be seen sunning themselves on summer days.

Conservation

The conservation interest of grasslands centres on their botanical composition and their invertebrate life. The acidic grasslands are of relatively little interest to conservationists, as they have a low diversity of species. Hill farming is not a very profitable enterprise and at present is heavily subsidised. Many farmers have reduced or sold off their upland sheep flocks in recent years, thus reducing the grazing pressure on the grasslands. This leads to scrub invasion or conversion to moorland – trends which could dramatically alter the characteristic landscape of areas such as the Lake District fells or the Southern Uplands.

Traditional hay meadows have been described as 'the most threatened of all British habitats with high nature conservation interest'[5]. Being inherently more fertile and therefore more likely to repay investment than acidic grasslands, many of them have been converted to short-term leys or silage and are heavily fertilised. The effect on their wildlife is drastic. The rich fauna of butterflies, birds and other animals, which depended on the meadow flowers, is eliminated in a very short time and the use of insecticides limits the colonisation of any species which could utilise the seeded grasses. More intensive management and earlier mowing prevents the successful nesting of bird species and disturbs small mammals and reptiles, so the whole diverse community of animals and plants is destroyed. The loss of traditional hay meadows within the past few decades has been striking and the richest remaining region is now the Yorkshire Dales. The pace of change is such that, even on the remoter Scottish isles, few traditional hay meadows are likely to survive into the twenty-first century, except those which are specifically designated as conservation sites or where financial assistance is given to support traditional farming methods.

The limestone grasslands have also seen great changes since the Second World War. The pastures with greatest potential for agricultural improvement have been ploughed up and re-seeded with commercial grass mixtures to support larger numbers of livestock, or converted to arable fields. Those sites which retain their traditional character tend to be found on steep slopes or overlying very stony soils which are difficult to plough. Their distribution has thus become fragmented and many sites are very small. This may pose problems for the future survival of some of the species. Although many of these sites now contain populations of rare species, they may be expected to lose some of these over the next few decades, as local populations die out and cannot be replaced from adjacent sites. This is a problem even where the sites are protected as nature reserves, and artificial methods of cross-fertilisation or introduction may be necessary to retain the species richness. The fortunes of grasslands are inextricably bound up with those of upland farming and their survival may depend on the extent to which we are prepared to subsidise it. The Yorkshire Dales National Park provides an interesting demonstration of the issues involved in grassland conservation.

PLATE 33 A spectacular display of common rock-rose in a traditional pasture in Wharfedale

The Yorkshire Dales

The Yorkshire Dales National Park covers the central part of the Pennines and contains rich examples of several different grassland types (Plate 33). Carboniferous limestone dominates the scenery of the Craven district, giving way further north to the sandstones, shales and limestones of the Yoredale rocks. On the east and west sides the limestone is overlain by Millstone Grit, which also caps some of the higher limestone hills, such as Pen-y-ghent and Whernside. Glacial drift forms thick deposits in the dales, thinning out on the higher ground. It is still a matter of dispute whether or not the higher limestone areas formerly had a drift cover.

As in most other parts of the uplands, the grasslands are largely man-made. The vegetation cover which developed in early and middle Post-glacial times was composed of woodlands dominated by broad-leaved deciduous trees. Pine was also common, along with hazel, which may have formed pure hazel woods on some of the limestone areas. The first grasslands may have been created as a result of Mesolithic activities on the higher ground[6]. The development of farming in the Neolithic and Bronze Age led to the formation of small grassy clearings in the woodlands. Pollen of typical limestone grassland plants, such as Jacob's-ladder, rock-rose and salad burnet, has been recorded at some sites from Bronze Age times onwards.

In the Iron Age, grass pollen increased markedly and pastoralism was probably the most important activity on the higher ground, with arable farming in the dales. This agricultural impact was sustained through the Roman period, when exports of wool show that sheep farming was important on the Pennines. There are some excellent examples of ancient field systems in the Malham and upper Wharfe-dale areas, some of which are believed to date from the Iron Age or Roman period. Three types of field may be recognised:-small 'garden' plots, squarish arable fields up to half an acre in size, and larger pastoral fields with double-banked entrances[7]. Some of these fields directly overlie limestone pavement, which suggests that there was formerly a soil cover, which has been lost by erosion. Some of this erosion may have been due to the effect of water draining through the soil and enlarging the joints in the limestone by solution to form deep grikes. Soil could then gradually be lost down the grikes, exposing the bare limestone clints. But it is also possible that the removal of the tree cover and cultivation of the soil speeded up the process of erosion, so early farming activities may be responsible for the emergence of large areas of limestone pavement on the Pennines (Colour plate 14).

By the time the Romans left Britain in the early fifth century, much of the grassland on the Pennines was probably already in existence. Continued grazing pressure on the uplands in the Anglo-Saxon and Viking periods maintained the open character of these areas. Grasslands expanded further in the early medieval period, especially in the areas controlled by the large monastic houses, such as Fountains Abbey and Bolton Priory. These areas remained as common pastures in the centuries that followed. In the late eighteenth or early nineteenth century, some of them were divided up into large fields, the boundaries of which were marked by limestone walls. However, substantial areas of the higher land remain to this day as unenclosed commons, with a mixture of heather moorland and grass-heath vegetation. In the dales the story is different. Many fields have been ploughed up and improved for agriculture, so that semi-natural grasslands remain only on the steep slopes at the heads of some dales or on farms where change has been resisted.

The grasslands of the Pennines today reflect this long and chequered history of exploitation. There is a wide variety of grassland types in the area, corresponding with the variety of soil types. Acidic grasslands are characteristic of Millstone Grit areas, where they are intermixed with moorland vegetation over brown earths or podzolic soils. However, they also occur over limestone on upland plateaux, where there was formerly a drift cover and leaching occurred. Acidic grasslands cover nearly a quarter of the Yorkshire Dales National Park. Being poor in species, they are not considered of high conservation interest but they play a major role in the traditional scenery of many parts of the area.

Neutral grasslands are more commonly associated with the enclosed fields in the lower parts of the dales. Some are grazed while others are mown for hay or silage. The more intensively managed grasslands have only half the number of species found in the traditionally managed grasslands. Hay meadows are a special feature of the Yorkshire Dales National Park, where about 30 per cent of the enclosed fields are cut for hay. The traditional meadows have a range of grasses, mixed with a colourful array of other flowers. Rarities include globeflower, melancholy thistle, green-winged orchid and meadow saffron. The richest sites have up to 85 plant species and receive no artificial fertilisers. They occur in dales such as Wharfedale, Wensleydale and Swaledale, but comprise less than 1 per cent of the hay meadows in the Yorkshire Dales National Park. Teesdale also has some very rich hay meadows, with woodland relic species, like wood anemone and wood crane's-bill, growing alongside the typical hay meadow plants. On the flood-plains of the Pennine dales, tall herbs, such as betony and meadowsweet, compete with grasses to produce rich wet meadows. The addition of artificial fertilisers can turn any of these neutral grasslands into less diverse swards. Improved fields are dominated by grasses, with few of the colourful flowers of the hay meadows. They are similar to the perennial rye-grass leys found in other parts of the uplands and are of little conservation interest.

Where limestone rock is close to the surface and exerts a strong influence on the soil, limestone grasslands are found. The Yorkshire Dales National Park has some magnificent examples, dominated by the blue moor-grass. The upper valley sides are closely grazed and grassland is interspersed with limestone screes and scars (Plate 34). On these dry sunny slopes grows a profusion of common rock-rose, wild thyme, fairy flax, salad burnet, bloody crane's-bill and northern bedstraw. Particular rarities include dark-red helleborine, bird's-eye primrose, fragrant orchid and dwarf milk-wort. Rarest of all, the spectacular lady's-slipper survives in just one native site, guarded day and night in the flowering season to deter theft (see back cover). It was

PLATE 34 Grasslands in Upper Wharfedale. Limestone walls enclose pastures and hay meadows on the valley floor and rough grazing land on the plateau top

once a common sight in the Pennines and bunches of its gorgeous blooms were sold in Skipton market in the early twentieth century. It has the sad distinction of being one of the few British plants which has been brought to the verge of extinction by being picked.

Limestone pavements have their own special grassland flora. Excellent examples occur in the Malham area, in upper Wharfedale and on the Ingleborough massif (Colour plate 14). On the bare limestone clints, only a few mosses and lichens grow, but the grikes provide a moister, sheltered environment. Wall-rue and maidenhair spleenwort grow near the top of the grikes, with Hutchinsia and wall lettuce, while the lower sides have brittle bladder-fern and green spleenwort. In the deeper shade near the bottom grow hart's-tongue, holly-fern and several woodland flowers, including bluebell, wood-sorrel, ramsons, dog's mercury, sanicle and baneberry. These provide clues to the former woodland cover of the pavements, remnants of which can be seen at Colt Park Wood and Scar Close on the Ingleborough massif and at Long Ashes in Wharfedale. The trees and shrubs include ash, sycamore, bird cherry, hawthorn and spindle.

The limestone grasslands, limestone pavement and hay meadows of the Pennines are of very high botanical interest. They are all scarce habitats in upland Britain and vulnerable to changes in farming practice. For these reasons they are considered to be a high priority for conservation. There are several National Nature Reserves, such as those at Ingleborough and in Upper Teesdale. Other nature reserves are managed by county wildlife trusts, such as two limestone pavements in the Ingleborough area managed by the Yorkshire Wildlife Trust. Management of these grassland sites depends on the cooperation of farmers, as a proper grazing regime is essential.

For the hay meadows, a different approach has been taken in the Pennine Dales Environmentally Sensitive Area[8]. Here the sites are managed by the farmers under a voluntary agreement by which they are paid to maintain traditional management practices. Such a scheme has been in operation for many years in Upper Teesdale but in 1986 it was extended to eight blocks of land in the central and northern Pennines. The traditional management involves the use of minimum amounts of fertilisers and only light dressings of farmyard manure, a long spring 'shut up' period without grazing, and a delay in cutting the hay until July. If such schemes can be introduced in other areas and extended to include limestone grasslands, we may be able to save some of upland Britain's rarest and most threatened habitats at the eleventh hour. The number of semi-natural grassland sites of high interest which remain is very small indeed. Any which can be maintained now will represent just a tiny sample of the sites which existed before the Second World War, but they might be enough to offer succeeding generations a glimpse of the rich natural heritage of the traditional farmed landscape of the uplands.

References

1 Greig, J, Some evidence of the development of grassland plant communities. In Jones, M (ed), *Archaeology and the flora of the British Isles*, pp 39–54. Oxford University Committee for Archaeology, Oxford, 1988.

2 Hughes, J and Huntley, B, Upland hay meadows in Britain – their vegetation, management and future. In Birks, H H et al (eds), *The cultural landscape – past, present and future*, pp 91–109. Cambridge University Press, Cambridge, 1988.

3 Ratcliffe, D A, *A nature conservation review*. Cambridge University Press, Cambridge, 1977.

4 Rodwell, J S (ed), *British plant communities: vol 3, Grasslands and montane communities*. Cambridge University Press, Cambridge, 1992.

5 Wells, D A, In Ratcliffe, D A, *A nature conservation review*, 1977.

6 Smith, R T, Aspects of the soil and vegetation history of the Craven District of Yorkshire. In Manby, T G and Turnbull, P (eds), *Archaeology in the Pennines*, pp 3–28. British Archaeological Reports, British Series 158. Oxford, 1986.

7 King, A, Early agriculture in Craven, North Yorkshire. In Bowen, H C and Fowler, P J (eds), *Early land allotment in the British Isles*, pp 109–14. British Archaeological Reports, 48. Oxford, 1978.
   King, A, Prehistoric settlement and land use in Craven, North Yorkshire. In Spratt, D A and Burgess, C (eds), *Upland settlement in Britain*, pp 117–34. British Archaeological Reports, British Series 143. Oxford, 1985.

8 Smith, R S, Farming and the conservation of traditional meadowland in the Pennine Dales Environmentally Sensitive Area. In Usher, M B and Thompson, D B A (eds), *Ecological change in the uplands*, pp 183–99. Blackwell, Oxford, 1988.

Boundaries and highways

Of their kind there are few things more beautiful than the field-walls in a stony country ... for innumerable plants take root in the earthy crevices and enrich the lovely grey stonework with a natural ornament that is entirely pleasing.

O G S Crawford

Interspersed amongst the woodlands, moorlands, wetlands and grasslands are minor habitats associated with boundaries and lines of communication. Hedgerows, walls, waysides and verges act as corridors for wildlife and play an important role in conservation.

Boundaries

People have been erecting boundaries in the countryside since prehistoric times, in response to changes in land organisation and ownership, the reclamation of new farmland and changes in agricultural practices. Boundaries are least common in the Scottish Highlands, where vast areas of moorland, mountain and blanket bog remain unenclosed and are most common on the flanks of the uplands and in the valleys, where farming is most intensive. In general, stone walls are more characteristic of the higher ground and hedges or fences are associated with lower land, but there is much regional variation. For example, in Caithness there are walls formed from vertically placed flagstones; in Exmoor beech hedges grow on top of stone walls or banks; in Wales, traditional Celtic banks were made of stone cobbles and earth; and limestone walls are conspicuous on the Pennines.

The choice of material was largely a question of local availability. Hedges were commonest in areas where woodland was plentiful, although 'dead' hedges, made of cut stakes, were often used in preference to 'live' hedges. Walls were found where stone was plentiful and banks where the soil was relatively easy to dig. Another factor was the availability of labour to maintain the boundaries, as hedges required more regular attention than walls or banks. Boundaries also tended to change with time, as trees or shrubs established themselves on top of banks or alongside dead hedges or walls, and fences replaced neglected hedges or tumbled walls as a cheaper, less labour-intensive alternative.

Early historical evidence for boundaries is often scarce. Walls and banks are longer-lasting features than hedges or fences so they more often occur in archaeo-logical contexts. Early examples are the low banks of ancient field systems on the Pennines or the walls around Bronze Age enclosures on Dartmoor. Dating of these boundaries is usually by association with related features, such as burial mounds or hut circles, although occasionally artefacts such as pottery or coins are found buried under or within them. Sometimes the boundaries are better drained than the sur-rounding soils and are conspicuous by having a slightly different flora. At archaeo-logical sites, changes in soil coloration can occasionally reveal the former presence of fence posts or hedgerow trees.

The first documentary evidence comes from the Anglo-Saxon period. Unfortu-nately, there is very little evidence for the uplands, as most of the Anglo-Saxon charters refer to lowland England, but there are examples in the Peak District and South Yorkshire[1]. Medieval evidence is more plentiful, although the term 'hedge' tends to be used for any sort of boundary. The large open fields which occurred in some parts of the English uplands probably had dead hedges around them, separating them from the meadow or pasture. There are also records of the court rolls, where offences such as stealing wood from hedges or allowing hedgerow trees to obstruct the highway, show that live hedges were common in some areas.

In upland parts of Scotland and Wales, the medieval farming system often involved the infield–outfield system, where the infield was in more or less permanent cultivation or fallow but the outfield was usually grazing land and only brought into cultivation occasionally. There may have been banks, walls or hedges separating the infield from the outfield or subdividing parts of the infield, but the documents tell us very little about them. The old medieval farming systems gradually changed from Tudor times onwards. In many parts of the uplands, communally–managed land was enclosed by agreement and the new fields were bounded by hedges or walls. Changes in the type of farming over the years sometimes led to larger fields being subdivided or smaller ones amalgamated, so the boundaries were by no means static.

From the seventeenth century onwards, the Enclosure Movement gathered momentum and was reinforced by Acts of Parliament where agreement could not be reached locally. These Acts were accompanied by detailed maps, on which we can see the precise boundaries of the fields. The majority of Enclosure Acts refer to the lowlands and were passed between AD 1750 and 1850, but a few concern foothills or valley lands in upland areas where open fields persisted. In the rest of the uplands, it was more often the common pastures which were enclosed. For instance, on the Pennines the Enclosure Act for Burnsall and Threshfield involved 1690 acres (676 ha) of common pasture but only 70 acres (28 ha) of open fields, whilst the Act for Applewick enclosed 6330 acres (2532 ha) of upland moors but only 9 acres (3.6 ha) of open fields[2].

The boundaries of the enclosed pastures were straight and the fields were large, as seen in the geometric wall patterns of areas such as Nidderdale and Craven. Enclosure roads were laid out between the fields, edged by their own stone walls.

Enclosures went on right through the nineteenth century, some areas not being enclosed until comparatively late; for example a large area of common grazing at Oare on Exmoor was enclosed in 1863[2]. Changes in agriculture in the twentieth century have caused modifications in field boundaries, particularly after the second World War. Rackham[3] claims that almost every hedge recorded in 1870 was still there in 1950, and the same probably applies to the stone walls. The dramatic loss of hedges seen in the lowlands since 1950 has been far less marked in the uplands, where there is greater emphasis on pastoral farming and stockproof boundaries are still important. The removal of a stone wall is a more costly undertaking than grubbing out a hedge, so boundaries formed by walls have tended to be more permanent features in the landscape. However, even if most boundaries have remained in place in the uplands, many of them have fallen into disrepair over the past few decades. Stones have fallen or have been knocked out of drystone walls; hedges have been badly trimmed by flail cutters and have become gappy. The skills of drystone walling and hedge laying have declined, so walls and hedges have been repaired by short lengths of wire fencing.

Flora and fauna of boundaries

Walls and hedges have been colonised by many plants and animals over the years. Walls share some characteristics with limestone pavements and natural cliffs, whereas hedges are linear extensions of the woodland habitat. As a general rule, the longer the wall or hedge has been established, the more opportunity there will have been for colonisation and the richer the wildlife. The colonisation of stone walls provides a good example of plant succession in operation (Plate 35). The stone blocks are an inhospitable environment to most plants, but lichens manage to anchor themselves to the stone surface. They are tolerant of a large temperature range and need little water; and they extract the nutrients they require from the surface of the rock, helping to weather it. In areas without significant air pollution, there may be several different species of lichens, distinguishable by their range of colours – grey, orange, yellow and black. They grow slowly but increase regularly with time, the diameter of the plants giving an approximate clue to the age of the wall. As the stones become encrusted with lichens, mosses may colonise on top of them or in the damp, shady crevices between the stones. They, too, can survive with relatively little water and soil, as they are able to dry out from time to time without permanent damage to their tissues. The cover of lichens and mosses retains more water than the bare stone surface and their dead tissues provide organic matter, gradually making the environment less hostile for other plantlife.

Ferns are other early colonisers of upland walls, anchoring themselves firmly between the stones. Commonest are those species which can tolerate dry environments, particularly the spleenworts and wall-rue. Brittle bladder-fern and polypody are also typical, while hart's-tongue, male-fern and other larger species often grow rooted in the soil at the base of the wall. Amongst flowering plants, there are a few

PLATE 35 A Lake District wall, richly encrusted with lichens, colonised by mosses, ferns, grasses and navelwort, and overhung with ivy

species particularly well adapted to grow on walls, including navelwort, wall lettuce and ivy-leaved toadflax. On older walls, as the plant material builds up and a thin soil cover is trapped between the stones, grasses and many other flowering plants begin to colonise. If the wall is not repaired or rebuilt, colonisation can continue until practically the whole surface of the wall is covered with vegetation and a thin veneer of soil. The plant cover will eventually come to reflect the surrounding vegetation, be it heather moorland, woodland or grassland. The wall resembles an earth bank and it may be difficult to make out the original structure.

The plantlife of hedges is closely related to that of deciduous woodland. Indeed, in some cases the hedges originated as uncleared strips of woodland between fields. In other cases, the hedges grew up naturally along unmanaged boundaries, sometimes in the shelter of a fence or wall. Such hedges are likely to be rich in species and are usually ancient. Others were deliberately planted, including those established as part of Enclosure Acts. They were usually of hawthorn, although mixed hedges were sometimes planted, and they have more or less straight lines. The original hawthorn or other hedging shrubs were gradually joined by other species, as the wind spread seeds of ash or field maple, birds scattered elderberries or sloes and small mammals moved hazelnuts.

The number of tree and shrub species provides an approximate method of dating a hedge, as an average of one new species per century will colonise a length of about 30 metres[4]. For example, the richest hedges in the Yorkshire Dales National Park have 9 or 10 species, suggesting that they originated in the tenth or eleventh century[5]. The species composition of the hedge may also give some useful information. Elder is the fastest coloniser but a relatively short-lived tree, so its presence tells us little about the age of the hedge. Field maple is slower to become established and is seldom found in hedges less than 300 or 400 years old, whilst hazel is commonest in hedges at least 500 years old. Small-leaved lime is hardly ever found as a hedge coloniser and is more or less confined to hedges which are relics of woodland[3].

Shade-tolerant herbs spread along the hedge bottom, those which reproduce freely from seed being the fastest colonists and those which spread vegetatively taking longest to become established. Characteristic species often have appropriate names, for example upright hedge-parsley or hedge woundwort. There are also climbers, rooted in the soil at the bottom of the hedge but using the shrubs or trees for support. Finally, there may be hedgerow trees, such as oak or ash, allowed to grow to maturity to provide shelter and shade for livestock and, formerly, a supply of timber for the farmer. Altogether, nearly 600 plants have been recorded in hedges in Britain[4].

Many animal species have colonised boundary walls and hedges, spreading, like the plants, from adjacent habitats. For the larger creatures, hedges are generally more attractive than walls, but reptiles and amphibians are the exception here. The cool, damp, cave-like recesses at the base of stone walls form good hibernating or resting sites for the common lizard, slow-worm, adder, frog and toad. On sunny days, the stones warm up fast and provide ideal basking habitats for the reptiles. Walls are also good hunting grounds for many spiders, which can lurk in the crevices and spin their webs amongst the stones and vegetation. Some small birds, such as the wren and wheatear, will use holes in walls for nesting sites, raising their broods in the protection of the stones.

Both walls and hedges offer shelter to small mammals, some of which are agile climbers. Voles, mice, shrews, hedgehogs, stoats and weasels are all common. Some of these species are very localised; for instance, bank voles usually stay within 5 metres of the hedge[6]. Others show marked seasonal fluctuations in response to food supplies, especially those which feed on ripening crops in the adjacent fields. Hedges also provide habitats for the mole and the rabbit, and the latter became a major pest at the period of Parliamentary Enclosures, as the new hedges were ideal for it. Larger mammals, such as foxes and badgers, use the hedges, too, and sometimes make their dens or setts there.

Other predators include birds of prey, particularly owls and the kestrel, and opportunists, such as crows and magpies. There is a long list of other birds which feed in hedges[4,6]. Some utilise the hedgerow trees and shrubs for nesting in; some feed on the trees, whilst others feed on the seeds of the ground flora or in the hedge bottom. Twenty-three species nest regularly in hedges, the commonest being the blackbird, wren, chaffinch, dunnock, song thrush, yellowhammer and robin. In summer they are joined by migrants, especially the common whitethroat, chiffchaff and willow warbler. Hedges provide an excellent habitat for many of these birds, being an extension of the woodland edge, with easy access to the open fields. Perhaps the most successful species are those like the blackbird, which exploit a range of habitats and food sources at different times of year.

Hedges are also rich in invertebrates of many different kinds, including aphids, beetles, flies, millipedes, woodlice, ladybirds and bugs. Some are specific to particular hedge plants, such as a sap-sucking bug which lives on hawthorn or a gall wasp which causes robin's pincushions on rose. Spiders spread their gossamer webs across the hedges, sparkling in the morning dew, whilst snails scavenge in the hedge bottom. There are a few butterfly species especially characteristic of hedges, particularly the gatekeeper, meadow brown, ringlet and wall. Moths are numerous, the caterpillars of over 100 species feeding on hawthorn alone.

Thus, hedges and walls have evolved over the years into a fascinating range of habitats, providing refuges for a large number of plant and animal species. Management is an integral part of these habitats but changes in management technique can easily decrease their value for wildlife. Without any management, walls and hedges would eventually become overgrown and indistinguishable from their surroundings. On the other hand, too intensive a management regime can easily disturb the wildlife and prevent some of the more interesting species from becoming established. The richest boundaries for wildlife are, therefore, in a delicate state of balance. They represent some of the most easily destroyed habitats in the uplands but they also have a great potential contribution to make to the conservation of the flora and fauna.

Roadside verges

The roadside verge is a very widespread habitat. Even the most minor roads usually have a narrow strip of verge and in some cases the verge is wider than the road itself. The verge has several important functions. It gives structural support to the road and receives drainage water from it. It ensures good visibility for drivers, especially around bends and at junctions and sometimes acts as an informal parking area. It is a convenient location for services such as drains, pipes and power lines and for storing equipment or materials. It gives safe passage to horses and pedestrians and allows public access to parts of the countryside. Last but not least, it offers a relatively safe haven to many plants and animals and functions as a sort of linear nature reserve.

Although there were undoubtedly many prehistoric tracks, the first roads with an artificial surface probably date from the Iron Age, when wheels with iron-shod tyres were invented[3]. Techniques of road building developed further in the Roman period, when at least three different classes of roads were used. The main military roads were usually raised up on an embankment about 15 metres wide, known as an agger, partly surfaced with gravel, stone or slag, and flanked by side ditches about 30 metres apart. Woodland or other dense vegetation was cleared for some distance beside the road to prevent the ambush of troops on the march. This may have been the first formalised road verge habitat and the vegetation would have been cleared regularly while the road was in military use.

The Roman road building standard was not equalled until the Industrial Revolution. In medieval times, bulky items, such as timber, grain or building stone, were transported by water wherever possible, while carts and large four-wheeled wagons transported other goods. Much of the traffic consisted of pedestrians and horse-riders, so security was still important and clearings or 'trenches' continued to be made alongside roads through woodland until about AD 1300. As the volume of traffic increased, the condition of the roads deteriorated and the primitive verges gradually became incorporated in the road itself. In 1555, the Highways Act made parishes responsible for the maintenance of roads but there was little improvement in their quality. New roads were built deliberately wide enough to allow for the traffic to make detours around bad patches in poor weather. Documentary references are full of the complaints of travellers about the poor state of the roads.

From the sixteenth century on, cattle were driven to markets in the south and east of England from Scotland, Wales and northern England along special drove roads. They were wide enough to allow the cattle to graze during their journey and were often flanked by stone walls. Their routes were punctuated by inns, fairs and markets. Some of these drove roads have become modern metalled roads but others fell into disuse when droving declined in the nineteenth century and are now green lanes. The Cheviots are criss-crossed with drovers roads, many of which had been used previously by Border cattle raiders[7].

The first significant improvements to the state of the roads came with the establishment of turnpike trusts from the late seventeenth century onwards. In the uplands, most turnpike roads date from the late eighteenth or early nineteenth centuries, examples being the Richmond to Lancaster turnpike over the Pennines, built in 1751, or the Holyhead to Betwys-y-coed turnpike in north Wales, built in 1815. The turnpike trusts exacted tolls from travellers to pay for road building and repair, and the opportunity was taken to upgrade some existing routes into turnpikes. Some improvements were noted by travellers, although roads were still constructed from loose material and liable to erode in bad weather. The nineteenth century enclosure roads had a standard width of 40 feet (about 12 metres), to allow for detours in bad weather and to enable flocks of sheep or herds of cattle to be driven along them. In Scotland, there were some 400 km of new roads built in the early eighteenth century by General Wade and his soldiers as part of the military campaign to suppress the Jacobite rebellions. Wade also built the military road which follows the course of Hadrian's Wall, in order to move his troops westwards towards Carlisle. This is an example which has been incorporated into a later route but others have fallen into disrepair.

In the late eighteenth and nineteenth centuries, solid foundations were introduced by pioneers such as John Metcalfe, Thomas Telford and J L McAdam. The new road-making techniques provided a firm, all-weather surface for the first time. This meant that roads did not need to be so wide. The new techniques were also expensive, so most roads were only tarred in the centre, leaving the remainder of the roads as permanent verges. The vegetation was kept short by hand-scything by men known as lengthsmen, who were responsible for particular stretches of the highway. The tradition of leaving a substantial verge either side of the road has been maintained down to the present day, when we have found many additional uses for the verge, as described above.

The number of roads has increased in the twentieth century and motorways and dual carriageways have been built. Motorways involve much larger areas of land than other roads, especially at intersections, and often have unusually wide verges. They sometimes cross high ground in cuttings, with rock outcrops providing cliff-like niches for plant growth, as on the highest parts of the M62 across the Pennines. In other cases, embankments have been constructed and the soil material is often brought from elsewhere. Along parts of the M62, colliery waste was used as the verge material. Unlike the verges of other roads, where plants are usually allowed to seed themselves naturally, motorway and dual carriageway verges are often planted with a standard seed mixture, dominated by perennial rye-grass with other grasses and white clover. Many other roads have been widened, straightened or re-routed, and the verge habitat has continued to expand throughout the twentieth century. It has never been more extensive than it is today and it is one of the few habitats for wildlife which is likely to expand rather than contract in the future, giving it enormous conservation potential.

Wildlife of road verges

The roadside verge is not a single habitat but in reality a whole series of microhabitats. Up to seven distinct zones may be recognised, if hedges and ditches are included (Figure 18). The road surface itself is generally inhospitable to wildlife, although the inkcap fungus can grow through concrete or asphalt[8]. Many animals cross the tarmac as part of their territorial movements and there are numerous casualties amongst toads, rabbits, hedgehogs, foxes and badgers, not to mention insects and birds which are hit by moving cars. Crows, gulls and other scavengers wait near the roadside to pick the bones.

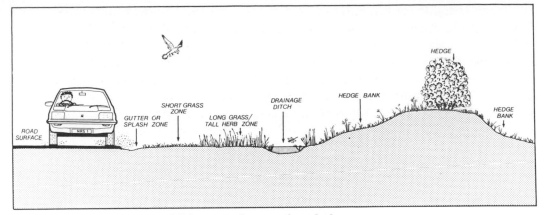

FIGURE 18 Wildlife zones of a typical roadside verge

The gutter or splash zone adjacent to the road surface is the first one which is colonised by plants. It consists of species which are resistant to being trampled or run over by vehicles and tolerant of being sprayed with mud and salt from the road and pollutants from vehicle exhausts. Only the toughest plants can survive; common species are greater plantain, knotgrass and pineappleweed. The last species obviously thrives in such conditions, as it had a very restricted distribution before AD 1900 but has now spread along roads throughout Britain[8]. The concentrations of salt may sometimes build up beside major roads to such an extent that saltmarsh plants are able to compete. Reflexed saltmarsh-grass is the commonest and it has spread alongside many of the major roads. The effects of salt are usually confined to the metre nearest to the road surface, although vehicles can spray it further on occasions.

Beyond the splash zone is the short grass zone, where the herbage is usually mown several times a year to maintain visibility for drivers and provide easy walking for pedestrians or horses. This zone also provides emergency parking and a location for the storage of equipment or materials such as salt, so parts of it may resemble the splash zone. However, it mostly consists of a close turf of fine-leaved grasses, interspersed with short or rosette herbs, such as speedwells or mouse-ear-hawkweeds. Its precise botanical composition depends on the underlying soil: sometimes a limestone grassland results and sometimes a neutral or acidic one.

Behind the short grass zone there is usually a zone of longer grassland, cut only once a year. This is dominated by coarser grasses, like false oat-grass or cock's-foot, or by tall herbs, such as cow parsley, hogweed or bracken. Here the finer-leaved grasses and shorter herbs are out-competed but the less frequent cutting may allow species like common spotted-orchid or meadow crane's-bill to survive. It is also a good zone for invertebrates, such as grasshoppers and butterflies, and for small mammals. Kestrels patrol many road verges, preying on voles and mice in the long grass.

If the verge is wide, the tall grass zone may be backed by a drainage ditch. If the ditch is deep enough not to dry out in summer, it forms a linear aquatic habitat, with plants such as water-cress, brooklime or crowfoots and animals such as frogs, newts and dragonflies. Where the water is only seasonal, a marshy flora develops, with marsh-marigold, meadowsweet or common valerian. If the ditch is not cleared out regularly, a proper hydrosere may develop. Beyond the ditch there may be a bank topped by a hedge. The bank flora will vary according to aspect, especially if the bank runs east–west, with shade-loving plants on north-facing banks and sun-lovers on the south side. Many of the plants and animals described above for the hedge habitat will be found here, in close proximity to the verge, and there is much interchange of organisms between the different zones. Although not all zones may be found on every roadside, even the most insignificant minor road usually supports several of the zones and thus forms a series of habitats for wildlife.

Railway verges

Unlike road verges, railway verges have a relatively short history, the oldest dating from the nineteenth century. The first railways were industrial tramways, designed to move mineral ores or building stone, and some of them linked to the canal network. At first the wagons were horse-drawn but in 1825 the first steam locomotives were introduced on the Stockton–Darlington tramway in north-east England. Within ten years, there were 430 km of railways, including some in the uplands, such as the Whitby–Pickering line on the North York Moors and the line from Wadebridge to Bodmin in Cornwall. In the Peak District, there was a 53 km rail link across the limestone plateau between the Cromford and Peak Forest canals. Particularly steep gradients were overcome by the use of inclines, where trains were hauled up by metal ropes and counter-balances.

The major cross-country routes were established in the 1840s but most of the lines in the uplands date from the latter half of the nineteenth century. The Settle–Carlisle line was the last English main line to be built, opening in 1876. Wales was well served with railway links, including attractive routes through mountain valleys, such as the Rheidol valley. There were three major routes through Scotland, parts of which involved crossing extensive areas of blanket bog. For instance, the line north of Inverness crossed part of the Flow Country, whilst the West Highland Line crossed the bleak expanse of Rannoch Moor. Only the highest mountain areas and the Scottish islands were untouched by the railway age.

A strip either side of the new railway lines was required for servicing and maintenance purposes. In the days of steam trains, there were frequent fires started by sparks from the engines, so lineside vegetation was burned regularly to reduce the risk of serious damage. More recently, chemical weedkillers have been used to restrict the growth of lineside vegetation within 3 metres of the track. Because of the need for gentle gradients, railways are often situated on embankments or in deep cuttings. Walls and tunnels are also a feature of railway architecture, each providing a differ-

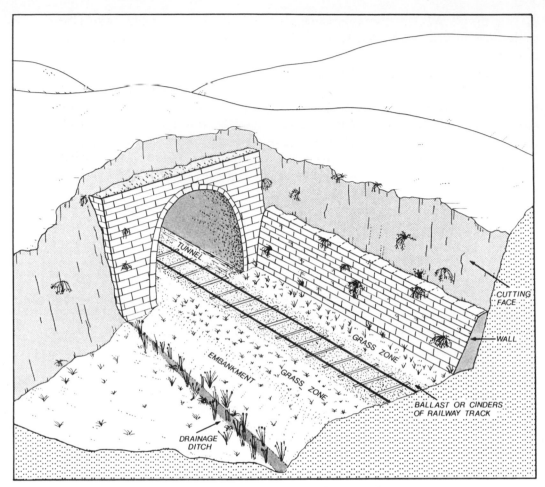

FIGURE 19 Wildlife habitats associated with railway lines

ent habitat for wildlife. Up to seven zones may be distinguished in the vicinity of railway lines (Figure 19).

Underneath the track itself and extending for a metre or so either side is the 'cess' zone of ballast or cinders, which is generally inhospitable to plant and animal life[9]. If weedkillers are not used or used only sparingly, a few pioneer plants may be able to grow in this zone, such as stonecrops or field bindweed. Further out, a richer grassy vegetation grows on the flat verge, resembling the tall grass zone of the roadside verge. This zone may be backed by a drainage ditch, with aquatic plants and animals. On embankments, particularly sunny south-facing slopes, the vegetation is similar to that found on hedgebanks, although it may be growing on introduced material, including spent ballast. In cuttings, there are opportunities for plants to colonise cliff faces of natural rock, and often there are retaining walls at the base of the cutting, where ferns, mosses and lichens can find a niche. Tunnels provide a dark, damp environment, which may be colonised by bats, especially on disused railway lines.

Many railway lines have been abandoned in the second half of the twentieth century. Their verges are rapidly colonised by scrub woodland and have become a haven for small birds, mammals and insects. Some of the former lines have been turned into footpaths or cycle tracks, so that the central part of the track is kept clear of scrub invasion. In some cases, abandoned railway lines have been managed as nature reserves, as in Derbyshire, where the Derbyshire Wildlife Trust has eight nature reserves on the Tissington and High Peak railway trails. They include several cuttings through Carboniferous limestone, marshy areas, woodland and scrub. They are managed by occasional burning or scrub clearance, imitating the techniques used when the railways were in use.

As a result of the railways, some plants have been able to extend their ranges dramatically. A well-known example is the rosebay willowherb, which is now common beside tracks throughout Britain (Colour plate 15). Others include small toadflax, annual wall-rocket, Oxford ragwort and sticky groundsel. Some rarities grow beside railway lines, such as fragrant orchid, frog orchid and globeflower on verges of the Settle–Carlisle railway. Introduced species and garden plants have escaped from stations and railway cottage gardens, including Londonpride, cotoneasters and dame's-violet in Derbyshire. Altogether nearly 2000 plant species have been recorded beside railways[9] and they have added colour and diversity to the upland scene.

The North York Moors

For a more detailed consideration of the vegetation of road and railway verges, we can look at the North York Moors. There are relics of roads from many periods, including the Roman road across Wheeldale Moor, hollow-ways and paved 'trods' used by packhorses in medieval times, eighteenth century 'lime' roads used for the transport of fertiliser, and 'turf' roads on which peat was moved on horse-drawn sleds[10]. Much of the present road system is based on medieval roads, one of which ran along the western escarpment and later became the Hambleton Drove Road. There are also Enclosure roads, seen particularly well in the south-west part of the area. In the eighteenth century, the major routes became turnpike roads. In the course of the nineteenth and twentieth centuries, some 888 km of the roads in the area have been tarred. There are also many new roads through Forestry Commission plantations, which are maintained to a reasonably high standard.

There are several factors which influence the type of plantlife to be found on road verges in the North York Moors, including the underlying rock type, the management regime and the use of the adjacent land[11]. Grasses and herbs like cow parsley, common nettle and ribwort plantain are widespread and abundant. However, there are some good limestone grassland verges, with quaking-grass, wild thyme, fairy flax and other typical limestone plants. On the higher parts of the moors, heather moorland extends over the verge and the grasses are replaced by heathers, crowberry, tormentil and heath bedstraw. These verges are a blaze of colour in late summer, when the heathers are in bloom (Colour plate 7).

Many of the verges are heavily grazed by sheep, which produces a very short turf in which it is impossible for most plants to flower and set seed. Sheep even graze some of the verges in the villages, so there is no need for any cutting of the verge vegetation. On the lower ground, minor road verges are cut by local farmers at irregular intervals. Along main roads, a tier system is used, with the front of the verge cut frequently but the vegetation at the back allowed to grow taller. This provides an opportunity for some of the more unusual species to survive, such as clustered bell-flower, pyramidal orchid and greater butterfly-orchid.

Where verges adjoin woodland, primroses, violets and dog's mercury spill over on to the verge. These sites are a delight to the eye in spring but by midsummer they are heavily shaded by the tree canopy. Ditches back many of the verges and support rushes, sedges and butterbur. Near to houses, plants often escape from the gardens and become naturalised on the verge. They include Welsh poppy, winter aconite and snow-in-summer. Along several main roads, where salt is used frequently in winter, the reflexed saltmarsh-grass has established itself, whilst alexanders is a feature of some verges near the sea.

Over 430 plant species occur on the verges, representing more than half the total flora of the North York Moors. The richest sites clearly make a major contribution to conservation, but they are very susceptible to changes in management. Since the 1950s, most ungrazed verges have been cut mechanically, and the timing and frequency of cutting are crucial to the survival of the interesting plants. Some minor road verges are still cut by hand and a few are cropped for hay – a use of verges which was undoubtedly more widespread in the past. In a few cases, herbicides are used, particularly near villages. These can wipe out the flora almost instantly and destroy the potential for other forms of wildlife. Where dairy cattle pass over the verges on their way to be milked twice a day, the verges tend to become seas of mud with hardly any vegetation.

The greatest threat to the verges comes from changes to the roads themselves. Road works can wreak havoc with the vegetation and may destroy colonies of rare plants. On the other hand, sensitive seeding of new verges can produce some rich plant communities, as on the verges near Hinderwell, where species such as wild carrot grow. The fencing of large areas of moorland adjacent to the main roads has eliminated grazing from many moorland verges over the past few years. As the fences tend to be sited well back from the roads, it is unlikely that more than a narrow strip of these verges will be cut in the future. The rest may eventually be colonised by scrub woodland and will provide an interesting study in succession over the next few decades.

Railways have also played a significant part in the ecological history. The first line ran from Whitby to Pickering, opened in 1836, and was originally horse-drawn.

PLATE 36 A steam train on the North Yorkshire Moors Railway

PLATE 37 Common spotted-orchid growing among the rich flora beside the Esk Valley railway line

It was a major engineering feat involving some steep gradients, particu-larly between Beck Hole and Goathland. Here an incline was used until 1865, when the present deviation line was built following a fatal accident. Further south, the deep peat bog of Fen Bog had to be crossed, which was achieved by sinking turfs, timber and sheep fleeces filled with heather to make a firm foundation for the embankment.

Other railways followed: from Scarborough to Whitby; from Scarborough to Pickering and Helmsley; from Whitby to Middlesbrough via the coast; and from Whitby through the Esk Valley to Stokesley. There was also a series of lines linking the Rosedale ironstone mines with Teesside via an incline near Ingleby Greenhow[10]. By 1885 the North York Moors was well served by railways and the pattern remained intact until 1928, when the Rosedale lines closed. In the 1950s, the Helmsley–Pickering line and part of the coastal line north of Whitby closed, followed by further closures in the mid–1960s. By 1970, only the Esk Valley line and the mineral line to the potash mine at Boulby were still operational. In 1973, the Whitby–Pickering line re-opened as a private venture, the North Yorkshire Moors Railway (Plate 36).

It would be difficult to find two more attractive routes than the Whitby–Pickering one through the dramatic glacial drainage channel of Newton Dale and the Whitby–Stokesley one through the picturesque valley of the River Esk. Both lines run through a variety of countryside, including deciduous woodland, arable land, pas-ture, open moorland and coniferous plantations. The lineside flora reflects these habitats (Plate 37), with woodland herbs in some sections changing to typical grass-land and heather moorland species in others[12]. There are some very fine wetland areas, where rushes, reeds, meadowsweet, bog-myrtle, yellow iris, marsh-marigold and common valerian may be seen. One bank beside the Esk Valley line has a remark-able clump of greater butterfly-orchid.

However, it is the distinctive railway flora which is of especial interest, consist-ing of plants which are uncommon in other habitats. Several species have spread along the ballast or cinders, including common toadflax, purple toadflax, small toad-flax, Oxford ragwort, fox-and-cubs, common centaury, American willowherb and lesser swine-cress. The stonework of walls, bridges and station platforms provides a niche for biting stonecrop, English stonecrop, reflexed stonecrop, ivy-leaved toadflax, wall lettuce, weld, wild mignonette, yellow corydalis, hart's-tongue, wall-rue and maidenhair spleenwort. Many garden flowers have escaped in the vicinity of stations, including opium poppy, lupins, aubretia, cornflower, snapdragons, horse-radish and green alkanet, together with shrubs such as privet, butterfly-bush, snowberry, Duke of Argyll's teaplant, lilac, Japanese knotweed and many more. Although most of these plants are still found close to the stations, many of them appear to be thriving and may be able to extend their ranges in the future. In this way, the railways have introduced new and unexpected elements into the flora of the North York Moors. The colourful displays of these newcomers must have brightened up many a traveller's journey and hopefully they will continue to delight both locals and tourists for many years to come.

References

1 Spratt, D A, Recent British research on prehistoric territorial boundaries. *Journal of World Prehistory*, 5, pp 439–80, 1991.

2 Hoskins, W G, *The making of the English landscape* (edited by C Taylor). Hodder and Stoughton, Sevenoaks, Kent, 1988.

3 Rackham, O, *The history of the countryside*. Dent, London, 1986.

4 Pollard, E, Hooper, M D and Moore, N W, *Hedges*. Collins, New Naturalist Series, London, 1974.

5 Information from an unpublished botanical survey of the Yorkshire Dales National Park by the Nature Conservancy Council, edited by A Stewart and A Drewitt, 1989.

6 Dowdeswell, W H, *Hedgerows and verges*. Allen and Unwin, London, 1987.

7 Wright, G N, *The Northumbrian uplands*. David and Charles, Newton Abbot, Devon, 1989.

8 Mabey, R, *The roadside wildlife book*. David and Charles, Newton Abbot, Devon, 1974.

9 Sargent, C, *Britain's railway vegetation*. Institute of Terrestrial Ecology, Cambridge, 1984.

10 McDonnell, J and Spratt, D A, Communications. In Spratt, D A and Harrison, B J D (eds), *North York Moors: Landscape heritage*, pp 184–98. David and Charles, Newton Abbot, Devon, 1989.

11 Atherden, M A and Sykes, N, *Roadside verges of the North York Moors*. North York Moors National Park, 1985.

12 Information from an unpublished survey by M A Atherden and N Sykes, 1990.

II

Conservation and the future

We trained hard, but it seemed that every time we were beginning to form into teams we would be reorganised. I was to learn later in life that we tend to meet any new situation by reorganisation; and a wonderful method it can be for creating the illusion of progress while producing confusion, inefficiency and demoralisation.

Caius Petronius, AD 66

The need for conservation has been a recurrent theme throughout this book. A study of the ecological history of the uplands leads to an awareness not only of the fascinating complexity of upland habitats but also of their vulnerability. Human impact over the millennia has created and maintained many of the wildlife communities which we value today, examples being heather moorlands and limestone grasslands; but it has also led to the destruction or reduction of others, such as woodlands and wetlands. The pace of change has quickened dramatically in the second half of the twentieth century, so that upland wildlife is under greater threat today than ever before. At the same time, public appreciation of our ecological heritage has grown, and concern for its future has evolved into a powerful movement for conservation. In this chapter we shall trace the development of the conservation movement, consider its achievements in the uplands and assess the priorities for the future.

The history of the conservation movement

The first conservation organisations were established in Victorian times, in response to public concern over cruelty to animals (Table 9). They were 'voluntary' bodies, being supported by public subscriptions and independent of government. An early example was the East Riding Association for the Protection of Sea Birds, set up following public outcry over the shooting of birds for sport on the Yorkshire cliffs. Other issues included the use of skins or feathers in the fashion trade and the over-zealous keepering of woods and moorlands used for shooting[1]. Another element of the early conservation movement was the demand for public access to open countryside, in the face of expanding towns and the enclosure of former common lands. Natural history became a very popular pastime, as is reflected in the large number of local natural history societies established in the late nineteenth century. This in itself

TABLE 9 The development of the nature conservation movement in Britain

Date	Development
C17th–C18th	First societies concerned with natural history, eg Royal Society, Society of Apothecaries, Society of Aurelians.
	Early naturalists, eg Gilbert White of Selborne.
C19th	Writers, eg Wordsworth, start to popularise uplands.
	Public outcry over cruelty to animals:
1824–	Royal Society for the Prevention of Cruelty to Animals.
1868	East Riding Association for the Protection of Seabirds.
1869	SEABIRDS PROTECTION ACT.
	Pressure grows for access to countryside:
1865	Commons, Open Spaces and Footpaths Preservation Society (now the Open Spaces Society).
1880	WILD BIRDS PROTECTION ACT (updated many times since).
C19th	Many natural history societies founded, eg Botanical Society of Edinburgh; Natural History Society of Glasgow; Manchester Field-Naturalists' Society; Yorkshire Naturalists' Union.
1889	Royal Society for the Protection of Birds founded (received royal charter in 1904).
1895	Establishment of National Trust.
1908	Wildfowlers' Association of Great Britain and Ireland (later the British Association for Shooting and Conservation).
1912	Society for the Promotion of Nature Reserves (now the Royal Society for Nature Conservation).
	Growth of science of ecology:
1913	British Ecological Society founded.
1926 on	Establishment of County Trusts, eg Yorkshire Naturalists' Trust, 1946 (now the Yorkshire Wildlife Trust); Scottish Wildlife Trust, 1964.
1926	Council for the Preservation of Rural England (now the Council for the Protection of Rural England). Council for the Preservation of Rural Scotland (now the Association for the Protection of Rural Scotland).
1928	Council for the Preservation of Rural Wales (Now the Campaign for the Protection of Rural Wales).
1931	National Trust for Scotland established.
1935	The Ramblers' Association founded.
World War II	Nature Reserves Investigation Committee, 1942.
	Scott Report on rural land use, 1942.
	Dower Report on National Parks, 1945
	Hobhouse Report on National Parks, 1945.
1946	Wildfowl Trust established (now the Wildfowl and Wetlands Trust).
1947	Huxley Report listed 73 potential National Nature Reserves in England and Wales.
1949	Ritchie Report listed 50 potential National Nature Reserves in Scotland.
	NATIONAL PARKS AND ACCESS TO THE COUNTRYSIDE ACT.
	Establishment of 10 National Parks and the Nature Conservancy.
1954	PROTECTION OF BIRDS ACT (amended several times since).

Date	Development
1959	Conservation Corps founded to carry out practical work (later the British Trust for Conservation Volunteers).
1961	World Wildlife Fund founded (now the World Wide Fund for Nature).
1968	COUNTRYSIDE ACT. Countryside Commissions established.
1969	Farming and Wildlife Group set up (now the Farming and Wildlife Trust).
1971	Friends of the Earth established.
1972	Woodland Trust established.
1973	Formation of the Ecology Party (now the Green Party). Nature Conservancy divided into the Nature Conservancy Council and the Institute of Terrestrial Ecology.
1975	CONSERVATION OF WILD CREATURES AND WILD PLANTS ACT.
1981	WILDLIFE AND COUNTRYSIDE ACT (amended 1985).
1990	ENVIRONMENTAL PROTECTION ACT.
1991–2	Reorganisation of Nature Conservancy Council and Countryside Commissions: England – English Nature, Countryside Commission. Wales – Countryside Council for Wales. Scotland – Scottish Natural Heritage.

posed problems, as the collecting of specimens brought some plant and animal species to the verge of extinction.

These various aspects of conservation led to the establishment of a multiplicity of voluntary organisations – a trend which has continued throughout the twentieth century. Some, such as the Royal Society for the Protection of Birds (RSPB), were concerned with particular groups of species; others, such as the Woodland Trust or the Wildfowl and Wetlands Trust, concentrated on particular habitats. Other bodies were primarily interested in the appearance of the landscape and rights of access, examples being the Councils for the Protection of Rural England, Wales and Scotland. County Trusts have been established covering all parts of Britain, the first one in the uplands being the Yorkshire Naturalists' Trust in 1946 (now the Yorkshire Wildlife Trust). Changing priorities and approaches led to many reorganisations and changes of names over the years, which consumed much time and energy and led to confusion in the minds of the general public. For instance, the Royal Society for Nature Conservation, which acts as the umbrella body for all the County Trusts, has changed its name twice.

Pressure from the voluntary organisations and increasing public interest in conservation issues eventually led to the enactment of legislation and the involvement of the government – the 'official' side of the conservation movement (Table 9). The 1949 National Parks and Access to the Countryside Act established the first ten national parks in England and Wales, all except the Pembrokeshire Coast within the uplands (Figure 20). It also led to the establishment of the Nature Conservancy (later

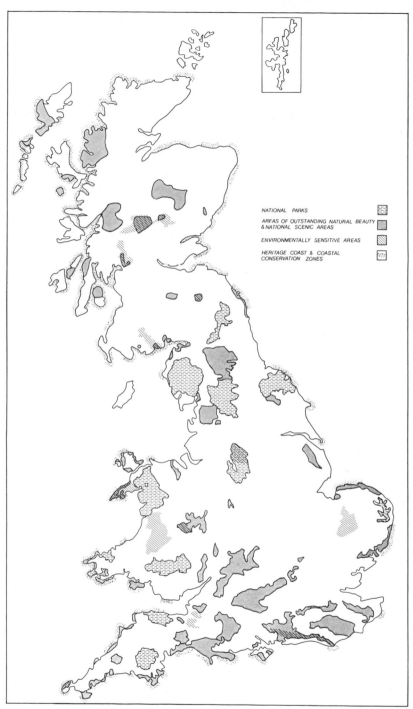

FIGURE 20 Protected areas in Britain, 1991 (Note: it has not been possible to show the Pennine Dales ESA, which covers 8 separate blocks within the Yorkshire Dales National Park. ESAs due to be declared in 1992 are not shown)

the Nature Conservancy Council), which was concerned with the scientific conservation of plants and animals. The Countryside Commission, set up in 1968, took on overall responsibility for countryside issues and coordinated the work of the National Park Authorities. In 1991, a major reorganisation took place. In England, the body responsible for nature conservation is now English Nature, whilst the Countryside Commission continues to deal with broader countryside issues. In Scotland and Wales there are now unitary organisations, with responsibilities for both nature conservation and countryside matters, known as Scottish Natural Heritage and the Countryside Council for Wales.

There have been several important pieces of legislation since 1949, including a whole string of Acts concerned with the Protection of Birds. All birds and their nests are now protected, except for certain listed pest species, such as the carrion crow, and especial protection is given to birds of prey and other particularly vulnerable species. The 1975 Conservation of Wild Creatures and Wild Plants Act gave legal protection to a range of other species for the first time. A milestone was the 1981 Wildlife and Countryside Act (amended in 1985), which extended legal protection to a wider range of species and introduced safeguards for Sites of Special Scientific Interest. Under the Act, the management of these Sites must be in accordance with specified principles and, in some cases, financial compensation is paid as a result of these restrictions.

Conservation has assumed a high priority in domestic politics in recent years, with most political parties embracing 'green' issues and the emergence of the Green Party (formerly the Ecology Party). Britain is also subject to European Directives and International Conventions, such as the Directive on the Conservation of Wild Birds and the Ramsar Convention on Wetlands of International Importance. International voluntary bodies, such as the World Wide Fund for Nature and Greenpeace, have also played their part in the protection of British wildlife and the stimulation of public interest in conservation.

Nature reserves in the uplands

The official and voluntary conservation bodies manage and protect an enormous number of sites in upland Britain. The most important sites are designated National Nature Reserves (NNRs) and are managed by English Nature, the Countryside Council for Wales or Scottish Natural Heritage. In March 1991 there were 242 of these reserves, 95 of them within the uplands. They include the first National Nature Reserve to be declared, Beinn Eighe in north-west Scotland, and several other montane areas, such as Snowdon, Cadair Idris, Ben Lawers and the Cairngorms (Plate 38). Moorland and upland grassland reserves include Moor House and Upper Teesdale on the Pennines, Rhinog in Wales and Cairnsmore of Fleet in the Southern Uplands. Deciduous woodlands are well represented, especially in Wales, where there are 18 reserves. There is also a reasonable number of peat and blanket bog sites, 7 in England and Wales and 11 in Scotland.

PLATE 38 Winter scene in the Cairngorms National Nature Reserve, viewed from Loch Morlich

The National Nature Reserves together cover over 100,000 ha in upland Britain. This is not a large area and regional variations are marked. The biggest NNRs are in Scotland, where Cairngorms NNR covers 25,949 ha and Inverpolly and Rhum NNRs cover well over 10,000 ha each. Some parts of the uplands are not represented at all, such as Exmoor. There are few sites on the southern Pennines and only one on the North York Moors. The larger Scottish islands also have relatively few reserves, although some of the smaller islands, such as those in the St Kilda group, are NNRs. North Wales and the southern Lake District, on the other hand, have a high density of reserves. The tenure and, therefore, to some extent the security of these reserves varies, with only 29 per cent of their area in Britain being owned by the three official national bodies.

By 31 March 1991, there were 5671 Sites of Special Scientific Interest (SSSIs) in Britain, covering 1.8 million ha. Lists are not published for these sites and the majority of them are on private land, although some are NNRs and others are nature reserves managed by county trusts or other voluntary bodies. Conservation is not necessarily the first priority on SSSIs but designation does pose restraints on land use and future development. There is no intention that most of these sites should become nature reserves or be open to public access, but their importance to the nation is reflected in the financial grants and compensatory payments available under the Wildlife and Countryside Act.

Although SSSIs have been designated from the early 1950s onwards, it was not until 1977 that the rationale for their selection was made public[2] and the criteria for their selection were listed (Table 10). It was intended that these criteria should be applied in combination by experienced ecologists, but they have attracted many criticisms over the years[3]. Firmer guidelines for applying the criteria were published in 1982 and minimum viable sizes were given for specific habitats (Table 10). The number of sites scheduled depends on the rarity and fragility of the habitat, and detailed guidelines for their selection are now published[4]. The aim in scheduling SSSIs is to safeguard as many as possible of the key wildlife habitats in Britain, but notification tends to be a lengthy and complex process, so progress has been slow. Many conservationists have criticised the official conservation bodies for failing to protect all important sites by SSSI designation, whilst planners and landowners have often tended to assume that sites which are not SSSIs are not worthy of conservation[5].

TABLE 10 Criteria for the selection of Sites of Special Scientific Interest

| Criteria for the selection of key sites (SSSIs) | Refinements of the selection criteria | | | |
	Principal criteria	Ancillary criteria	Criteria for choosing number of sites	minimum sizes for sites (ha)
Size	Typicalness	Recorded	Rarity	Open water	0.5
Diversity	Naturalness	history	Fragility	Peatland	1.0
Naturalness	Diversity	Position in		Woodland	5.0
Rarity	Size	ecological or		Lowland grassland	10.0
Fragility		geographical		Heathland	10.0
Typicalness		unit		Upland grassland/	50.0
Recorded history		Potential value		heath	
Position in ecological/		Intrinsic appeal			
geographical unit					
Potential value					
Intrinsic appeal					

There are other forms of official designation, stemming from the international conventions signed by Britain. The Ramsar Convention protects 44 wetlands of international importance, 16 of them in upland Britain. Forty Special Protection Areas (SPAs) are designated under the European Directive on the Conservation of Wild Birds, ten in the uplands, and some sites enjoy dual designation as Ramsar sites and SPAs. Most of these sites are also SSSIs and some are NNRs, so there is a degree of over-designation of the best sites. For example, Loch Druidibeg on South Uist is a Ramsar site, an SPA and an NNR. Thus, government legislation protects the key representative sites in Britain but the official conservation bodies have few powers to conserve the rest of the uplands.

Complementary to the NNRs are the reserves managed by the voluntary conservation bodies. There are 47 county trusts in Britain, which are members of the

Royal Society for Nature Conservation Wildlife Trusts Partnership. Between them they manage more than 2000 nature reserves, some of them in the uplands. The best of these are SSSIs and of national interest but others are of only regional or local importance. In some cases, minor habitats are protected, for example the North Wales Trust has several roadside verge sites and the Derbyshire Trust has a reserve in old brickyards. The criteria for the selection of these sites vary. They include the sort of scientific criteria employed for SSSIs, together with others, such as availability, cost, degree of public access and educational potential. The overall distribution of county trust reserves, in contrast to that of the National Nature Reserves, is heavily concentrated in the lowlands of England and Wales. There is a dearth of sites in the Scottish Highlands and Islands, reflecting the difficulties for voluntary bodies of raising funds and management expertise in areas of low population density. Most of the reserves are small, too, as the county trusts rely largely on volunteers and are not well equipped to manage large land holdings with agricultural or forestry involvement. Thus, the contribution which the county trusts make towards the direct conservation of land in the uplands is limited, but their combined membership of over 250,000 people plays a significant role in raising public awareness of nature conservation.

The RSPB, with an adult membership of over 870,000, has an even greater potential influence on public opinion. It has over 100 reserves, 45 of them in upland Britain, of which 30 are island or coastal sites. The emphasis is firmly on marine or freshwater sites, with only six sites in the uplands designated primarily for their dryland habitats. However, some of the wetland sites also include other habitats, such as pinewoods at Loch Garten or oakwood at Haweswater. This emphasis reflects the greater diversity of birds in wetland habitats and also the public interest in bird-watching, which is most easily satisfied at such sites. Most of the non-wetland reserves are woodlands: for example, Killiecrankie in Scotland and Geltsdale on the northern Pennines. Unlike the county trusts, the RSPB has pursued a policy of acquiring a relatively small number of high profile reserves, managed by professional wardens and open to the public. Although the reserves are important assets, the RSPB puts a great deal of emphasis on other activities, such as lobbying for changes in legislation or prosecuting offenders.

The Woodland Trust is the other major conservation body with significant land holdings in the uplands. It manages 65 woods in the uplands, covering about 1190 ha, but average size is only about 18 ha and many are of only local importance. The criteria for acquisition are not published and the Trust has tended to acquire as many sites as it could afford, putting the emphasis on quantity rather than quality. There are some important sites amongst the Woodland Trust holdings, such as Coed y Foel, which is a good example of a Welsh upland oak coppice; Coed Lletywalter, which is also an NNR; and a juniper wood on the Pennines. However, there is only one Scottish pinewood reserve, near Carrbridge. Many woods include planted trees, such as Wood Hill Wood on the Ochil Hills, which is a good example of early formal planting in Scotland. Some sites are totally planted and the Trust sometimes acquires open land suitable for future planting. As their number grows, these woodland reserves may play a significant part in conservation[6].

Other bodies also manage nature reserves, notably the Forestry Commission, with its Forest Nature Reserves (chapter 8), and some local authorities. The National Trust and National Trust for Scotland are also involved in managing land for conservation purposes. Amongst their properties are some superb areas of scenery and many habitats of high conservation value, such as the Sugar Loaf in the Brecon Beacons, Glen Coe in Scotland, Dunkery Beacon on Exmoor, Kinder Scout in the Peak District and many sites in the Lake District, where 25 per cent of the National Park is in National Trust ownership.

Other designated areas

There are many other parts of the uplands which enjoy a degree of protection whilst being managed primarily for other purposes. The National Parks cover a combined area of 1.2 million ha in the uplands (Figure 20). The 1949 Act gave them two main statutory duties: to preserve and enhance the natural beauty and to encourage and provide facilities for public open air enjoyment. Most National Park Authorities today put conservation as a high priority and also aim to support the rural communities living within the Parks, but these objectives have sometimes proved difficult to reconcile[7]. Most of the powers which the National Park Authorities have are those of planning authorities, controlling developments such as housing and industry. There have been problems where national and local interests conflict, such as with mineral exploitation in the Yorkshire Dales, with military training in Dartmoor, and with low-flying aircraft in Northumberland.

Farming and forestry are outside the normal planning system in Britain, which has caused major problems in some National Parks. The conversion of heather moorland to improved farmland was a major cause of contention in Exmoor, where 15 per cent of the moorland area was lost between 1957 and 1966. Other National Parks had similar problems and the Brecon Beacons, Dartmoor, the North York Moors and northern Snowdonia lost over 15,000 ha of moorland between them in their first 30 years of National Park designation. The issue led to the Porchester Report (1977), as a result of which changes were introduced to prevent grant aid being used for the destruction of core areas of moorland. Further restrictions and changes to the grant aid system since then have largely halted the process of moorland reclamation, and National Park Authorities are gradually exerting a greater influence over the management of land within their areas, despite the fact that they own only a tiny proportion of the land. Maps are now produced by all National Parks, showing key areas of moorland and other semi-natural habitats which are considered of top conservation priority. Plans to give the National Park Authorities more autonomy in the future should enable them to take a more positive attitude towards land management and conservation. Other designations, conferring a degree of protection from development, include Areas of Outstanding Natural Beauty, Heritage

Coasts, and National Scenic Areas (Figure 20). The last named operate in Scotland, where no National Parks have yet been declared.

Conservation in the wider countryside

A large part of upland Britain is now subject to some sort of conservation management, but we can never hope to designate the whole of the uplands as a conservation area. The preservation of the majority of habitats and the survival of their plants and animals will depend ultimately on the ways in which we manage the wider countryside. As we have seen in previous chapters, many of the interesting features of upland habitats have been produced by past management techniques. For instance, grasslands have a greater diversity of species when grazed and also supply grass or hay for domestic animals; heather moorlands which are burnt and grazed provide both sheep and game-birds for human consumption.

The continued interest of many upland habitats depends on the maintenance of farming and other land use practices and will not be achieved in the absence of management. Whilst the protection of sites of particularly high ecological interest may be secured by their designation as nature reserves, the survival of the flora and fauna of most of the uplands will be best achieved by sustainable, environmentally-friendly farming techniques. Farmers are usually more skilled at implementing such management techniques than conservationists, who often lack experience in land management (Plate 40). Britain is unusual amongst developed countries in having nearly 80 per cent of the land surface in some type of agricultural use. Most upland habitats apart from woodlands and plantations are farmed, with the emphasis being on grazing rather than arable cultivation. Approximately half the sheep and wool production and a quarter of the cattle production is from the uplands and the relative importance of sheep has increased in the twentieth century[8]. Parts of Wales and northern England are heavily stocked with sheep, which has led to a deterioration in the pastures and local soil erosion. High stocking rates are encouraged by a range of European Community subsidies, including some especially aimed at Less Favoured Areas (which include most of upland Britain). Without these subsidies, hill farming would hardly be viable, as sheep prices are low and demand is static[9]. Plans to reform the European Community's Common Agricultural Policy may result in major changes in the level of support for hill farming over the next few years. In other parts of the uplands, particularly northern Scotland, sheep farming has declined in recent years, allowing an increase in red deer numbers and leading to pressure for afforestation.

Where sheep grazing occurs, it is a major factor in determining the balance of the vegetation communities. With a decrease in grazing pressure, trees and shrubs begin to recolonise many areas which have been open for centuries, whilst increased pressure leads to the spread of rough pasture or grass-heaths at the expense of heather moorland. By ploughing, fertilising and re-seeding, agricultural improvements may be accomplished relatively quickly, but the reversion towards semi-natural vegetation following a decrease in grazing pressure takes much longer. Up to 10 years may be required for improved pasture to revert to rough pasture, 20 to 50 years for rough pasture to revert to grass-heath and up to 100 years for grass-heath to revert to heather moorland. 'Change is normal, but many of the changes in upland vegetation are detectable only over decades. The current vegetation may still be responding to adjustments in management which took place 50 or more years ago'[10].

Thus, changes in agricultural prosperity are likely to be reflected in major long-term changes in the ecology and landscape of the uplands. However, there is also great potential for deliberately manipulating grazing pressure to benefit certain vegetation types at the expense of others. We now have the knowledge, based on research into past management techniques, to use agriculture as a powerful tool for conservation, protecting the landscape and its wildlife at the same time as producing food. Aspirations such as these have been expressed since the 1960s but it is only within recent years that they have begun to be realised.

In 1987 and 1988, 19 Environmentally Sensitive Areas (ESAs) were declared, eight of them in the uplands (Table 11), where they cover nearly 440,000 ha. Twelve more areas will be declared in 1992, including four in the uplands, but this is less than half the number of areas originally proposed. In ESAs, farmers are eligible for grant aid to support traditional, environmentally-friendly farming methods. The total expenditure on ESAs in Britain in 1990–91 was £9.43 million and this is planned to increase to £64.5 million in 1994–95. The effectiveness of the ESA system has been reviewed by various official and voluntary organisations. Amongst criticisms of the system are the slow progress in designating new areas and the

TABLE 11   Environmentally Sensitive Areas (ESAs) in the uplands

ESAs in the uplands declared in 1987–88			ESAs in the uplands declared in 1992
Pennine Dales	15,960 ha	Hay meadows, pastures, woodland	Lake District South-west Peak
North Peak	50,250 ha	Heather moorland, blanket peat, grasslands	Exmoor Dartmoor
Cambrian Mountains	153,000 ha	Rough grazing, hay meadows, woodland	
Breadalbane	120,000 ha	Montane grasslands, open water, woodland	
Loch Lomond	42,000 ha	Heather moorland, blanket bog, open water	
Uists and Benbecula	7,500 ha	Machair, dunes	
Stewartry	42,000 ha	Wetland, rough grazing, woodland	
Whitlaw/Eildon	8,000 ha	Heather moorland, bogs, rough grazing	

conflict between the agricultural price support system and the grant system for ESAs. Although designation has halted the loss of habitat and deterioration of the environment, it has done little to restore or enhance the wildlife[11]. In parts of the North York Moors, a scheme similar to that in ESAs operates and has proved to be a great success (Colour plate 16). Ironically, this may have contributed to the area's failure to gain ESA status so far.

A great range of other grants is available to encourage farmers to care for the environment. The Countryside Stewardship Scheme gives grants for work which improves the habitat for wildlife or gives greater public access to the countryside. Money is available for capital works under the Farm and Conservation Grant scheme. The Set-Aside scheme, introduced in 1988, pays farmers to take a minimum of 20 per cent of their arable land out of production for five years. This is mainly designed to cut over-production and so far it has been of little direct benefit to conservation. However, in the long run it may provide an opportunity for the development of alternative land use practices on some of the enclosed land in the uplands. There is also a pilot scheme on Extensification, which encourages farmers to reduce their number of stock by between 20 and 70 per cent. Another initiative is English Nature's Wildlife Enhancement Scheme, which provides incentives for farmers to preserve and enhance the wildlife value of land within SSSIs. However, perhaps of greater significance than any of these schemes was the withdrawal in 1989 by the Ministry of Agriculture, Fisheries and Food of all grants for agricultural operations which are not environmentally desirable, ending several decades of public support for increasingly intensive farming methods.

Farm Diversification Scheme grants are intended to help farmers to invest in secondary sources of income, such as tourism or farm shops. There have also been several suggestions for alternative agricultural enterprises, such as rearing deer for venison or goats for cashmere. Another idea is the development of agroforestry, whereby grazing is combined with timber production from widely spaced, fast-growing trees. A different possibility is the exploitation of vegetation types currently regarded as weeds, such as bracken, gorse or rhododendron, for the production of biofuels[12]. However, it is important to assess the environmental as well as the economic implications of all these schemes, as they could have significant effects on other wildlife. The priority should be to establish farming schemes which are sustainable in the long term and which allow as much as possible of the native flora and fauna to coexist alongside them.

Although farming has been the traditional land use of most of Britain and may be manipulated for conservation ends, it is not necessarily desirable that it should continue to be practised in all upland areas. Forestry offers an equally attractive option for some areas, especially when designed for multi-purpose use rather than timber production alone. The tide of public opinion may have turned against large-scale conifer plantations but mixed and broad-leaved woods have much to recommend them to the conservationist, especially when compared with over-grazed rough pastures or intensively managed farmland. As woodland was the natural vegetation cover of most parts of the uplands below the montane zone, its partial reinstatement should be welcomed as offering the greatest potential productivity of plant and animal life.

There are several recent initiatives to protect existing woodlands and encourage the planting of others. A good example is the Coed Cymru scheme, introduced in Wales in 1985. It is a collaboration between conservationists and farmers to encourage the regeneration of derelict woods and develop markets for native hardwood products. Many woodlands are in poor condition as a result of grazing pressure and there have been calls for financial compensation for farmers who reduce flock sizes. The Forestry Commission's Woodland Grant Scheme gives greater support for the planting of broad-leaves rather than conifers, and small woods rather than large blocks. The Ministry of Agriculture, Fisheries and Food also has a Farm Woodland Scheme, which gives planting grants for woodlands over 3 ha in size on former arable land or improved pasture in Less Favoured Areas. The scheme includes woodland managed as coppices, and there is much interest in the re-establishment of this traditional form of woodland management. In National Parks, similarly, the emphasis is on small woodland blocks rather than large forestry plantations[7].

Access to the countryside

Alongside the primary uses of the countryside for farming and forestry, there is the increasing secondary use for recreation. The shorter working week, greater mobility of the population and growing number of people not in full-time employment have led to a vast increase in the demand for access to upland areas. The trend is also towards active participation in sports such as horse riding, orienteering, cross-country skiing and mountain bike riding, rather than more passive pastimes like picnicking. Large areas of the uplands of England and Wales are common land, registered under the 1965 Commons Registration Act. Although this strictly means that certain common-right holders have rights to graze specified numbers of animals or carry out activities such as the collection of turves, in practice there has been *de facto* access for the general public to much common land. Organisations such as the Ramblers' Association have been prominent in campaigning for legal rights of access to all common land and have organised mass trespasses on various occasions from the 1930s onwards[13]. In 1991, there were 40 mass trespasses, such as the one on Thurlstone Moor in Derbyshire, where access is restricted because of the leasing of land by Yorkshire Water to a shooting syndicate.

In 1986, a wide range of conservation bodies established the Common Land Forum, with the aim of securing access agreements over all common land. The sticking point proved to be the heather moorlands managed for grouse shooting. One hundred and fifty landowners, who controlled 90 per cent of the heather moorland in England and Wales, formed the Moorland Association to defend their rights of ownership and exclusive access, arguing that walkers not restricted to rights of way, especially those accompanied by dogs, would cause undue disturbance to nesting

PLATE 39 Recreational impacts in the Cairngorms: chair-lifts, visitor centre and car park create ugly scars on the landscape of one of Britain's top conservation sites

game-birds or disruption to shooting parties. Some landowners have taken a more positive approach, such as the Duke of Devonshire, who has signed an access agreement for the whole of his 520 ha Chatsworth Estate. In Scotland, where there has been a tradition of access to most open land, recent attempts by new landowners to restrict access, for instance on the Letterewe Estate in the north-western Highlands, have met with fierce opposition from the general public.

Some forms of recreation do pose serious threats to the conservation of wildlife, an example being winter sports. There is relatively little land suitable for skiing in Britain and, unfortunately, it is also of very high ecological value (chapter 3). Recreation developments may also have undesirable knock-on effects, as when chair-lifts enable summer visitors to penetrate formerly undisturbed mountain tops (Plate 39) or when tracks constructed for deer-stalking or shooting give access for motor-cycles. However, such impacts are far more localised than the impacts of grazing pressure, moorland burning or afforestation, and it is easy to over-emphasise their significance. Arguably, access to larger areas of countryside would spread the impact of recreation more thinly, alleviating the problems of the most popular areas.

Priorities for the future

Having traced the historical development of the wildlife habitats over the past 15,000 years and examined some of the present trends and conflicts in land use, it is appropriate to close by setting out priorities for the future. Such an approach is necessarily a personal one, depending on an individual assessment of the most valuable wildlife features and the most desirable balance of habitats. It is to be hoped that, from the amassing of the views of many individuals with a concern for the countryside and its wildlife, a consensus may emerge on how we may most effectively manage the uplands in the twenty-first century.

The first priority must be to give better protection to sites of high ecological value. The criteria used so far to identify SSSIs and nature reserves are not necessarily the most appropriate ones to apply to wildlife sites in general. The SSSI system was designed to identify and protect Britain's most important wildlife communities, but this has resulted in greater vulnerability for sites which have not been scheduled. This in turn has led to the fragmentation of habitats and a reduction in the genetic diversity of the plants and animals. There is a pressing need to replace the SSSI system with one which protects all sites which satisfy specified minimum criteria. Such criteria could be defined relatively easily for most habitats and could be applied quickly in the field, without the need for a comprehensive survey of every site. Following publication of the National Vegetation Classification, work is now taking place on the mapping of habitat distributions, using satellite imagery to help identify vegetation types and computers to store the data. Within a few years it should be possible to map all areas of semi-natural vegetation and assess their level of interest as international, national, regional or local.

Conservationists have tended to be rather parochial in outlook, placing great emphasis on species or habitats which are rare locally, even if they are of little significance at a national or international level. Top priority should be given to those habitats and species for which Britain has a significant proportion of the world population. On this basis, the most important upland habitats are the blanket bogs of northern Scotland and the high montane habitats of the Cairngorms, both of which have come under intensive pressure in recent years. In a European context, ash woods with bluebell-dominated ground floras and wet heaths are of especial significance and should be conserved. Individual bird species of importance include the greenshank and golden plover, whilst plant species include gorse, cross-leaved heath and bog asphodel. By protecting these species we would be making a greater contribution to international conservation than by concentrating our efforts on organisms which are at the limits of their distribution in Britain, such as the lady's-slipper.

As well as protecting the most important conservation sites, another priority is to develop a positive land use strategy for the rest of the countryside. Despite a long tradition of individual ownership of land, it is becoming generally recognised now that to allow landowners complete freedom to manage their land as they wish would be to abdicate from our responsibility to future generations. Restrictions on building, mining, quarrying and tree felling are already accepted, whilst considerable influence over farming and other activities is achieved through fiscal measures, such as grant aid or tax incentives. Some people have argued that agriculture and forestry should be

PLATE 40 An encouraging sign photographed west of Blairgowrie in the borders of the Scottish Highlands

brought within the Town and Country Planning system[14], but others doubt the competence of planners to deal with the complex issues involved in the management of rural land. The present planning system is perceived in a negative way, as its emphasis is on development control rather than positive land use planning. This has led to a preoccupation with details such as the materials and design of individual buildings and a reluctance to get to grips with major issues of the overall appearance of the landscape or balance of land uses.

A more positive approach is needed, involving land use planning at the national level and embracing everything from nature conservation and farming to building development. The ideas already applied to National Parks of a multi-purpose countryside, with farming, recreation and conservation as joint aims, should be extended to the wider countryside. It is no longer acceptable for vast areas of plantations to be dedicated solely to timber production or for large expanses of moorland to be managed purely as a sporting resource for the wealthy few. Neither is it desirable

that the character of upland grasslands should be determined by the changing fortunes of hill sheep farming or that the pursuit of profits for commercial entrepreneurs
should be allowed to impose inappropriate tourist developments on fragile mountain
top habitats.

In the struggle to achieve an acceptable balance of land uses, compromises
will have to be made and shared management of the land accepted. However, the
nature of the compromise must vary from area to area, if we are to preserve diversity
and key features of interest. The present trend towards the formulation of indicative
strategies for particular land uses, as illustrated by the indicative strategy for forestry
in the Flow Country (chapter 7), may offer a way forward[15]. For each major land use,
the indicative strategy would identify preferred, possible, undesirable or unsuitable
areas. The boundaries of these zones would vary between land uses and could be
designated on a national, regional or local scale, as appropriate. The suitability of all
areas of the countryside would thus be indicated for all potential land uses, and
landowners would have to take indicative strategies into account when managing
their land. Different interest groups within the community would be forced to work
together to achieve an integrated land use policy which took account of the area's
potential for all uses, not just the one which provided the greatest economic return.
Landowners would retain the right to manage their own land but would have to
recognise the interests of the community at large. Where disputes arose involving the
development of land of high conservation interest, the onus would be on the
developer to prove a case for abandoning the indicative strategy, rather than on the
conservationists to defend the status quo. To date, much of the time, energy and
resources of conservationists have been consumed in defending sites of proven ecological value, and many others have been damaged or lost as a result[16]. Scientific
expertise could be used more effectively in identifying new sites and carrying out
research into the management of wildlife, if designated sites were protected with the
full force of planning laws and not just under the wildlife legislation.

Conclusion

The British uplands have been intensively used by people for practically the whole of
the Post-glacial period, and much of their interest stems from this long history of
exploitation. Current land use practices, such as grazing, burning and woodland
management, have their roots in prehistory. Now that we have unravelled the story
of the past, we can begin to understand the present landscape and plan for its future
conservation. The last few years have seen a remarkable awakening of public interest
in nature conservation and a fundamental change in the way we view farming and
forestry. Increasing leisure time and mobility have brought more and more people
into direct contact with the landscape and wildlife of the uplands, and we are now
poised for major changes in the way we manage them.

The mountain tops, moorlands, woods, grasslands and wetlands represent a
unique and priceless heritage, which is the result of a combination of natural forces

and human impact over many millennia. In order to conserve them for future generations to enjoy, it is essential that we should continue to use them and interact with their plant and animal life. This will inevitably mean that they will change through time, and, as a result, some cherished landscapes will disappear whilst others will acquire new interest and attraction. The aim of conservation is not to fossilise the present landscape but to manage future changes to maintain the variety of habitats and the genetic richness of the plants and animals. In this way, we shall keep our options open for the future.

We are privileged to be stewards of a rich and productive upland landscape, showing amazing variety in its animal and plant life. The responsibility to manage it wisely is an onerous and challenging one but brings its own rewards. Anyone who has watched the sun setting over Snowdon, smelled the heather in full bloom on a Yorkshire moor or heard the call of the curlew echoing over the bogs of the Flow Country, will know that the challenge is well worth meeting.

References

1 Allen, D E, *The naturalist in Britain*. Penguin, London, 1976.
2 Ratcliffe, D A, *A nature conservation review*. Cambridge University Press, Cambridge, 1977.
3 Usher, M B (ed), *Wildlife conservation evaluation*. Chapman and Hall, London, 1989.
4 Nature Conservancy Council, *Guidelines for selection of biological SSSIs*. Nature Conservancy Council, Peterborough, 1989.
5 Moore, N W, *The bird of time*. Cambridge University Press, Cambridge, 1987.
6 Allaby, M, *The Woodland Trust book of British woodlands*. David and Charles, Newton Abbot, Devon, 1986.
7 National Parks Review Panel, *Fit for the future*. Countryside Commission, Cheltenham, 1990.
8 Eadie, J, Trends in agricultural land use: The hills and uplands. In Jenkins, D (ed), *Agriculture and the environment*, pp 13–20. Institute of Terrestrial Ecology, Cambridge, 1984.
9 Evans, S and Felton, M, Hill livestock compensatory allowances and upland management. In Bell, M and Bunce, R G H (eds), *Agriculture and conservation in the hills and uplands*, pp 66–72. Institute of Terrestrial Ecology, Grange-over-Sands, 1987.
10 Ball, D F et al, *Vegetation change in upland landscapes*. Institute of Terrestrial Ecology, Cambridge, 1982.
11 Orme, E, *Environmentally Sensitive Areas: assessment and recommendations*. Friends of the Earth, London, 1992.
12 Bell, M and Bunce, R G H (eds), *Agriculture and conservation in the hills and uplands*, 1987.
13 Stephenson, T, *Forbidden land*. Manchester University Press, Manchester, 1989.
14 Shoard, M, *This land is our land*. Paladin, London, 1987.
15 Nature Conservancy Council, 17th report. Nature Conservancy Council, Peterborough, 1991.
16 Mowle, A, Nature conservation and rural development. In Bell, M and Bunce, R G H (eds) *Agriculture and conservation in the hills and uplands*, pp 120–3.

GLOSSARY OF PLANT AND ANIMAL NAMES

Flowering plants, ferns and mosses

Adder's-tongue *Ophioglossum vulgatum*
Alder *Alnus glutinosa*
Alder buckthorn *Frangula alnus*
Alexanders *Smyrnium olusatrum*
Almond willow *Salix triandra*
Alpine bistort *Polygonum vivipara*
Alpine penny-cress *Thlaspi caerulescens*
American willowherb *Epilobium ciliatum*
Amphibious bistort *Polygonum amphibia*
Annual wall-rocket *Diplotaxis muralis*
Arctic sandwort *Arenaria norvegica* subsp *norvegica*
Ash *Fraxinus excelsior*
Aspen *Populus tremula*
Aubretia *Aubrieta deltoidea*
Baneberry *Actaea spicata*
Barley *Hordeum vulgare* subsp *distichum*
Barren strawberry *Potentilla sterilis*
Bay willow *Salix pentandra*
Bearberry *Arctostaphylos uva-ursi*
Beech *Fagus sylvatica*
Beech fern *Phegopteris connectilis*
Bell heather *Erica cinerea*
Betony *Stachys officinalis*
Bilberry *Vaccinium myrtillus*
Birches *Betula* spp
Bird cherry *Prunus padus*
Bird's-eye primrose *Primula farinosa*
Biting stonecrop *Sedum acre*
Black bog-rush *Schoenus nigricans*
Black mustard *Brassica nigra*
Blackthorn *Prunus spinosa*
Bladderworts *Utricularia* spp
Bloody crane's-bill *Geranium sanguineum*
Bluebell *Hyacinthoides non-scripta*
Blue moor-grass *Sesleria caerulea*
Bog asphodel *Narthecium ossifragum*
Bogbean *Menyanthes trifoliata*
Bog-myrtle *Myrica gale*
Bog orchid *Hammarbya paludosa*
Bog-rosemary *Andromeda polifolia*
Bottle sedge *Carex rostrata*
Box *Buxus sempervirens*
Bracken *Pteridium aquilinum*
Bramble *Rubus fruticosus* agg
Brittle bladder-fern *Cystopteris fragilis*
Broad-leaved helleborine *Epipactis helleborine*
Brooklime *Veronica beccabunga*

Broom *Cytisus scoparius*
Buckthorn *Rhamnus cathartica*
Bugle *Ajuga reptans*
Bulbous rush *Juncus bulbosus*
Burnt orchid *Orchis ustulata*
Butterbur *Petasites hybridus*
Buttercups *Ranunculus* spp
Butterfly-bush *Buddleia* spp
Butterworts *Pinguicula* spp
Canadian waterweed *Elodea canadensis*
Cat's-ear *Hypochaeris radicata*
Charlock *Sinapis arvensis*
Chickweed wintergreen *Trientalis europaea*
Cloudberry *Rubus chamaemorus*
Club-mosses *Lycopodium* spp
Clustered bellflower *Campanula glomerata*
Cock's-foot *Dactylis glomerata*
Common bent *Agrostis capillaris*
Common bird's-foot-trefoil *Lotus corniculatus*
Common centaury *Centaurium erythraea*
Common cow-wheat *Melampyrum pratense*
Common juniper *Juniperus communis*
Common knapweed *Centaurea nigra*
Common nettle *Urtica dioica*
Common poppy *Papaver rhoeas*
Common reed *Phragmites australis*
Common rock-rose *Helianthemum nummularium*
Common sorrel *Rumex acetosa*
Common spike-rush *Eleocharis palustris*
Common spotted-orchid *Dactylorhiza fuchsii*
Common toadflax *Linaria vulgaris*
Common valerian *Valeriana officinalis*
Common whitebeam *Sorbus aria* agg
Copper beech *Fagus sylvatica* var *purpurea*
Coralroot orchid *Corallorrhiza trifida*
Cornflower *Centaurea cyanus*
Corsican pine *Pinus nigra* var *laricia*
Cotoneasters *Cotoneaster* spp
Cottongrasses *Eriophorum* spp
Cowberry *Vaccinium vitis-idaea*
Cow parsley *Anthriscus sylvestris*
Cowslip *Primula veris*
Crab apple *Malus sylvestris*
Crack-willow *Salix fragilis*
Cranberry *Vaccinium oxycoccus*
Creeping buttercup *Ranunculus repens*
Creeping lady's-tresses *Goodyera repens*
Creeping willow *Salix repens*

Crested dog's-tail *Cynosurus cristatus*
Cross-leaved heath *Erica tetralix*
Crowberry *Empetrum nigrum*
Crowfoots *Ranunculus* spp
Daisy *Bellis perennis*
Dame's-violet *Hesperis matronalis*
Dark-leaved willow *Salix myrsinifolia*
Dark-red helleborine *Epipactis atrorubens*
Deergrass *Tricophorum cespitosum*
Diapensia *Diapensia lapponica*
Dog's mercury *Mercurialis perennis*
Dogwood *Cornus sanguinea*
Douglas fir *Pseudotsuga menziesii*
Downy birch *Betula pubescens*
Downy willow *Salix lapponum*
Duckweeds *Lemna* spp
Duke of Argyll's teaplant *Lycium barbarum*
Dwarf birch *Betula nana*
Dwarf cherry *Prunus cerasus*
Dwarf cornel *Cornus suecica*
Dwarf juniper *Juniperus communis* subsp *alpina*
Dwarf milkwort *Polygala amarella*
Dwarf willow *Salix herbacea*
Eared willow *Salix aurita*
Early-purple orchid *Orchis mascula*
Elder *Sambucus nigra*
Elms *Ulmus* spp
Emmer wheat *Triticum dicoccum*
Enchanter's-nightshade *Circaea lutetiana*
English stonecrop *Sedum anglicum*
European larch *Larix decidua*
European silver-fir *Abies alba*
Fairy flax *Linum catharticum*
False oat-grass *Arrhenatherum elatius*
Field bindweed *Convolvulus arvensis*
Field gentian *Gentianella campestris*
Field maple *Acer campestre*
Filmy-ferns *Hymenophyllum* spp
Floating sweet-grass *Glyceria fluitans*
Fox-and-cubs *Pilosella aurantiacum*
Foxglove *Digitalis purpurea*
Fragrant orchid *Gymnadenia conopsea*
Frog orchid *Coeloglossum viride*
Globeflower *Trollius europaeus*
Goat willow *Salix caprea*
Gorse *Ulex europaeus*
Grass-of-parnassus *Parnassia palustris*
Great sundew *Drosera longifolia*
Great wood-rush *Luzula sylvatica*
Greater butterfly-orchid *Platanthera chlorantha*
Greater plantain *Plantago major*
Greater stitchwort *Stellaria holostea*
Green alkanet *Pentaglottis sempervirens*
Green-ribbed sedge *Carex binervis*
Green spleenwort *Asplenium trichomanes-ramosum*

Green-winged orchid *Orchis morio*
Grey willow *Salix cinerea*
Guelder-rose *Viburnum opulus*
Hair-mosses *Polytrichum* spp
Hard-fern *Blechnum spicant*
Hart's-tongue *Phyllitis scolopendrium*
Hawkweeds *Hieracium* spp
Hawthorn *Crataegus monogyna*
Hazel *Corylus avellana*
Heath bedstraw *Galium saxatile*
Heather *Calluna vulgaris*
Heath milkwort *Polygala serpyllifolia*
Heath rush *Juncus squarrosus*
Heath spotted-orchid *Dactylorhiza maculata*
Hedge woundwort *Stachys sylvatica*
Herb Paris *Paris quadrifolia*
Hoary rock-rose *Helianthemum canum*
Hogweed *Heracleum sphondylium*
Holly *Ilex aquifolium*
Holly-fern *Polystichum lonchitis*
Honeysuckle *Lonicera periclymenum*
Hornbeam *Carpinus betulus*
Horse-radish *Armoracia rusticana*
Hutchinsia *Hornungia petraea*
Hybrid lime *Tilia × europaea*
Iceland-purslane *Koenigia islandica*
Indian balsam *Impatiens glandulifera*
Ivy *Hedera helix*
Ivy-leaved toadflax *Cymbalaria muralis*
Jacob's-ladder *Polemonium caeruleum*
Japanese knotweed *Fallopia japonica*
Juniper *Juniperus* spp
Knotgrass *Polygonum aviculare*
Lady-fern *Athyrium filix-femina*
Lady's bedstraw *Galium verum*
Lady's-mantles *Alchemilla* spp
Lady's-slipper *Cypripedium calceolus*
Larch *Larix* spp
Large-leaved lime *Tilia platyphyllos*
Least water-lily *Nuphar pumila*
Lesser butterfly-orchid *Platanthera bifolia*
Lesser celandine *Ranunculus ficaria*
Lesser spearwort *Ranunculus flammula*
Lesser swine-cress *Coronopus didymus*
Lilac *Syringa vulgaris*
Lily-of-the-valley *Convallaria majalis*
Limes *Tilia* spp
Lodgepole pine *Pinus contorta*
Londonpride *Saxifraga × urbium*
Lords-and-ladies *Arum maculatum*
Lupins *Lupinus* spp
Maidenhair spleenwort *Asplenium trichomanes*
Male-fern *Dryopteris filix-mas*
Marsh-marigold *Caltha palustris*
Mat-grass *Nardus stricta*
Meadow crane's-bill *Geranium pratense*

Meadow foxtail *Alopecurus pratensis*
Meadow-grasses *Poa* spp
Meadow oat-grass *Helictotrichon pratense*
Meadow saffron *Colchicum autumnale*
Meadowsweet *Filipendula ulmaria*
Melancholy thistle *Cirsium heterophyllum*
Monkeyflowers *Mimulus* spp
Moonwort *Botrychium lunaria*
Moss campion *Silene acaulis*
Mossy saxifrage *Saxifraga hypnoides*
Mountain avens *Dryas octopetala*
Mountain bearberry *Arctostaphylos alpinus*
Mountain everlasting *Antennaria dioica*
Mountain sorrel *Oxyria digyna*
Mountain willow *Salix arbuscula*
Mouse-ear-hawkweeds *Hieracium* spp
Navelwort *Umbilicus rupestris*
Net-leaved willow *Salix reticulata*
Northern bedstraw *Galium boreale*
Northern marsh-orchid *Dactylorhiza purpurella*
Northern rock-cress *Arabis petraea*
Norway spruce *Picea abies*
Oak fern *Gymnocarpium dryopteris*
Oaks *Quercus* spp
One-flowered wintergreen *Moneses uniflora*
Opium poppy *Papaver somniferum*
Osier *Salix viminalis*
Oxeye daisy *Leucanthemum vulgare*
Oxford ragwort *Senecio squalidus*
Parsley fern *Cryptogramma crispa*
Parsley water-dropwort *Oenanthe lachenalii*
Pedunculate oak *Quercus robur*
Perennial rye-grass *Lolium perenne*
Pillwort *Pilularia globulifera*
Pineappleweed *Matricaria discoidea*
Pines *Pinus* spp
Plantains *Plantago* spp
Polypody *Polypodium vulgare*
Pondweeds *Potamogeton* spp
Primrose *Primula vulgaris*
Privet (garden) *Ligustrum ovalifolium*
Purple moor-grass *Molinia caerulea*
Purple saxifrage *Saxifraga oppositifolia*
Purple toadflax *Linaria purpurea*
Purple willow *Salix purpurea*
Pyramidal orchid *Anacamptis pyramidalis*
Quaking-grass *Briza media*
Quillwort *Isoetes lacustris*
Ragged-robin *Lychnis flos-cuculi*
Ramsons *Allium ursinum*
Rare spring-sedge *Carex ericetorum*
Red bartsia *Odontites vernus*
Red campion *Silene dioica*
Reed sweet-grass *Glyceria maxima*
Reflexed saltmarsh-grass *Puccinellia distans*
Reflexed stonecrop *Sedum rupestre*

Rhododendron *Rhododendron ponticum*
Ribwort plantain *Plantago lanceolata*
Rock-rose *Helianthemum nummularium*
Rock whitebeam *Sorbus rupicola*
Rosebay willowherb *Chamerion angustifolium*
Roseroot *Sedum rosea*
Round-leaved sundew *Drosera rotundifolia*
Rowan *Sorbus aucuparia*
Royal fern *Osmunda regalis*
Rushes *Juncus* spp
Salad burnet *Sanguisorba minor* subsp *minor*
Sanicle *Sanicula europaea*
Saw-wort *Serratula tinctoria*
Saxifrages *Saxifraga* spp
Scots pine *Pinus sylvatica*
Scottish asphodel *Tofieldia pusilla*
Scottish primrose *Primula scotica*
Sea arrowgrass *Triglochin maritimum*
Sea campion *Silene uniflora*
Sea plantain *Plantago maritima*
Sedges *Carex* spp
Sessile oak *Quercus petraea*
Sheep's-fescue *Festuca ovina*
Shoreweed *Littorella uniflora*
Shrubby cinquefoil *Potentilla fruticosa*
Silver birch *Betula pendula*
Sitka spruce *Picea sitchensis*
Small-leaved elm *Ulmus minor* subsp *minor*
Small-leaved lime *Tilia cordata*
Small toadflax *Chaenorhinum minus*
Snapdragon *Antirrhinum majus*
Snowberry *Symphoricarpos* spp
Snow-in-summer *Cerastium tomentosum*
Speedwells *Veronica* spp
Spindle *Euonymus europaeus*
Spring gentian *Gentiana verna*
Spring sandwort *Minuartia verna*
Spruces *Picea* spp
Starry saxifrage *Saxifraga stellaris*
Sticky groundsel *Senecio viscosus*
Stiff sedge *Carex bigelowii*
Stonecrops *Sedum* spp
Stoneworts *Chara* spp *and Nitella* spp
Sundews *Drosera* spp
Sweet chestnut *Castanea sativa*
Sweet vernal-grass *Anthoxanthum odoratum*
Sycamore *Acer pseudoplatanus*
Tea-leaved willow *Salix phylicifolia*
Teesdale sandwort *Minuartia stricta*
Teesdale violet *Viola rupestris*
Three-leaved rush *Juncus trifidus*
Thrift *Armeria maritima*
Timothy *Phleum pratense*
Toothwort *Lathraea squamaria*
Tormentil *Potentilla erecta*
Tufted hair-grass *Deschampsia cespitosa*

Twinflower *Linnaea borealis*
Upright hedge-parsley *Torilis japonica*
Velvet bent *Agrostis canina*
Violets *Viola* spp
Viviparous sheep's-fescue *Festuca vivipara*
Wall lettuce *Mycelis muralis*
Wall-rue *Asplenium ruta-muraria*
Water avens *Geum rivale*
Water-cress *Rorippa nasturtium-aquaticum*
Water lobelia *Lobelia dortmanna*
Water-milfoils *Myriophyllum* spp
Water mint *Mentha aquatica*
Water-starworts *Callitriche* spp
Wavy hair-grass *Deschampsia flexuosa*
Weld *Reseda luteola*
Wellingtonia *Sequoiadendron giganteum*
Welsh poppy *Meconopsis cambrica*
Western gorse *Ulex gallii*
Western hemlock-spruce *Tsuga heterophylla*
White beak-sedge *Rhynchospora alba*
White water-lily *Nymphaea alba*
White willow *Salix alba*
Whortle-leaved willow *Salix myrsinites*
Wild angelica *Angelica sylvestris*
Wild carrot *Daucus carota* subsp *carota*
Wild cherry *Prunus avium*
Wild mignonette *Reseda lutea*

Wild privet *Ligustrum vulgare*
Wild service-tree *Sorbus torminalis*
Wild strawberry *Fragaria vesca*
Wild thyme *Thymus polytrichus*
Willows *Salix* spp
Winter aconite *Eranthis hyemalis*
Wood anemone *Anemone nemoralis*
Wood avens *Geum urbanum*
Wood crane's-bill *Geranium sylvaticum*
Wood-sorrel *Oxalis acetosella*
Woolly fringe-moss *Racomitrium lanuginosum*
Woolly willow *Salix lanata*
Wych elm *Ulmus glabra*
Yarrow *Achillea millefolium*
Yellow corydalis *Pseudofumaria lutea*
Yellow iris *Iris pseudacorus*
Yellow pimpernel *Lysimachia nemorum*
Yellow water-lily *Nuphar lutea*
Yew *Taxus baccata*
Yorkshire-fog *Holcus lanatus*

Sources:
Stace, C, *New flora of the British Isles.* Cambridge
    University Press, Cambridge, 1991.
Smith, A J E, *The moss flora of Britain and Ireland.*
    Cambridge University Press, Cambridge,
    1978.

Fungi

Blusher *Amanita rubescens*
Conifer heartrot *Heterobasidion annosum*
Club foot *Clitocybe clavipes*
Deceiver *Laccaria laccata*
Dryad's saddle *Polyporus squamosus*
False chanterelle *Hygrophoropsis aurantiaca*
Fly agaric *Amanita muscaria*
Inkcap *Coprinus atramentarius*
Jew's ear *Hirneola auricula-judae*
King Alfred's cakes *Daldinia concentrica*
Red milk cap *Lactarius rufus*

Saffron milk cap *Lactarius deterrimus*
Sickener *Russula emetica*
Wood woolly-foot *Collybia peronata*

Sources:
Bramley, W G, *A fungus flora of Yorkshire.*
    Yorkshire Naturalists' Union, Leeds, 1985.
Kibby, G, *Mushrooms and toadstools: A field guide.*
    Oxford University Press, Oxford, 1979.
Phillips, R, *Mushrooms and other fungi of Great
    Britain and Europe.* Pan Books, London, 1981.

Mammals, amphibians and reptiles

Adder *Vipera berus*
Badger *Meles meles*
Bank vole *Clethrionomys glareolus*
Beaver *Castor fiber*
Bison *Bison bonasus*
Brown bear *Ursus arctos*
Brown hare *Lepus capensis*
Common frog *Rana temporaria*
Common lizard *Lacerta vivipara*

Common long-eared bat *Plecotus auritus*
Common shrew *Sorex araneus*
Common toad *Bufo bufo*
Daubenton's bat *Myotis daubentoni*
Elk *Alces alces*
European lynx *Lynx sp*
Fallow deer *Dama dama*
Ferret *Mustela furo*
Field vole *Microtus agrestis*

Fox *Vulpes vulpes*
Goat *Capra (domestic)*
Grey squirrel *Sciurus carolinensis*
Harvest mouse *Micromys minutus*
Hedgehog *Erinaceus europaeus*
Lesser horseshoe bat *Rhinolophus hipposideros*
Mole *Talpa europaea*
Mountain hare *Lepus timidus*
Muntjac deer *Muntiacus reevesi*
Natterer's bat *Myotis nattereri*
Newts *Triturus* spp
Noctule bat *Nyctalus noctula*
North American mink *Mustela vison*
Otter *Lutra lutra*
Pine marten *Martes martes*
Pipistrelle bat *Pipistrellus pipistrellus*
Polecat *Mustela putorius*
Pygmy shrew *Sorex minutus*
Rabbit *Oryctolagus cuniculus*
Red deer *Cervus elephas*
Red squirrel *Sciurus vulgaris*

Reindeer *Rangifer tarandus*
Roe deer *Capreolus capreolus*
Sheep *Ovis (domestic)*
Sika deer *Cervus nippon*
Slow-worm *Anguis fragilis*
Stoat *Mustela erminea*
Water shrew *Neomys fodiens*
Water vole *Arvicola terrestris*
Weasel *Mustela nivalis*
Wild boar *Sus scrofa*
Wild cat *Felix silvestris*
Wild cattle *Bos* spp
Wild horse *Equus* spp
Wild ox *Bos primigenius*
Wolf *Canis lupus*
Wood mouse *Apodemus sylvaticus*

Source
Corbet, G B and Southern, H N (eds), *Handbook of British Mammals (second edition)*. Blackwell, Oxford, 1977.

Fishes

Arctic char *Salvelinus alpinus*
Bullhead *Cottus gobio*
Common eel *Anguilla anguilla*
Fresh-water herring *Clupea harengus*
Grayling *Thymallus thymallus*
Gudgeon *Gobio gobio*
Minnow *Phoxinus phoxinus*
Perch *Perca fluviatilis*

Pike *Esox lucius*
Roach *Rutilus rutilus*
Salmon *Salmo salar*
Three-spined stickleback *Gasterosteus aculeatus*
Trout *Salmo trutta*

Source
Bagenal, T B, *Identification of British fishes*. Hulton Educational Publications, Amersham, Bucks, 1973.

Birds

Arctic skua *Stercorarius parasiticus*
Barn owl *Tyto alba*
Blackbird *Turdus merula*
Blackcap *Sylvia atricapilla*
Black grouse *Tetrao tetrix*
Black-headed gull *Larus ridibundus*
Black-throated diver *Gavia arctica*
Blue tit *Parus caeruleus*
Canada goose *Branta canadensis*
Capercaillie *Tetrao urogallus*
Carrion crow *Corvus corone corone*
Chaffinch *Fringilla coelebs*
Chiffchaff *Phylloscopus collybita*
Coal tit *Parus ater*
Common buzzard *Buteo buteo*
Common crossbill *Loxia curvirostra*
Common redstart *Phoenicurus phoenicurus*
Common scoter *Melanitta nigra*

Common whitethroat *Sylvia communis*
Coot *Fulica atra*
Crested tit *Parus cristatus*
Curlew *Numenius arquata*
Dabchick *Tachybaptus ruficollis*
Dipper *Cinclus cinclus*
Dotterel *Eudromias morinellus*
Dunlin *Calidris alpina*
Dunnock *Prunella modularis*
Garden warbler *Sylvia borin*
Goldcrest *Regulus regulus*
Golden eagle *Aquila chrysaetos*
Golden plover *Pluvialis apricaria*
Goldeneye *Bucephala clangula*
Goosander *Mergus merganser*
Goshawk *Accipiter gentilis*
Grasshopper warbler *Locustella naevia*
Great black-backed gull *Larus marinus*

Great spotted woodpecker *Dendrocopos major*
Greenshank *Tringa nebularia*
Green woodpecker *Picus viridis*
Grey heron *Ardea cinerea*
Greylag goose *Anser anser*
Grey wagtail *Motacilla cinerea*
Hen harrier *Circus cyaneus*
Hooded crow *Corvus corone cornix*
Kestrel *falco tinnunculus*
Kingfisher *Alcedo atthis*
Lapwing *Vanellus vanellus*
Lesser black-backed gull *Larus fuscus*
Magpie *Pica pica*
Mallard *Anas platyrhynchos*
Meadow pipit *Anthus pratensis*
Merlin *Falco columbarius*
Mute swan *Cygnus olor*
Nightjar *Caprimulgus europaeus*
Nuthatch *Sitta europaea*
Osprey *Pandion haliaetus*
Oyster-catcher *Haematopus ostralegus*
Peregrine falcon *Falco peregrinus*
Pied flycatcher *Ficedula hypoleuca*
Pochard *Aythya ferina*
Ptarmigan *Lagopus mutus*
Raven *Corvus corax*
Red-breasted merganser *Mergus serrator*
Red grouse *Lagopus scoticus scoticus*
Red kite *Milvus milvus*
Red-necked phalarope *Phalaropus lobatus*
Redpoll *Acanthis flammea*
Red-throated diver *Gavia stellata*
Reed bunting *Emberiza schoeniclus*
Reed warbler *Acrocephalus scirpaceus*
Ring ouzel *Turdus torquatus*
Robin *Erithacus rubecula*

Ruff *Philmachus pugnax*
Sand martin *Riparia riparia*
Scottish crossbill *Loxia scotica*
Sedge warbler *Acrocephalus schoenobaenus*
Short-eared owl *Asio flammeus*
Siskin *Carduelis spinus*
Skylark *Alauda arvensis*
Snipe *Gallinago gallinago*
Snow bunting *Plectrophenax nivalis*
Snowy owl *Nyctea scandiaca*
Song thrush *Turdus philmelos*
Sparrowhawk *Accipiter nisus*
Spotted flycatcher *Muscicapa striata*
Stonechat *Saxicola torquata*
Tawny owl *Strix aluco*
Teal *Anas crecca*
Temminck's stint *Calidris temminckii*
Treecreeper *Certhia familiaris*
Tree pipit *Anthus trivialis*
Tufted duck *Aythya fuligula*
Wheatear *Oenanthe oenanthe*
Whinchat *Saxicola rubetra*
White-fronted goose *Anser albifrons*
Whooper swan *Cygnus cygnus*
Willow warbler *Phylloscopus trochilus*
Woodcock *Scolopax rusticola*
Wood pigeon *Columba palumbus*
Wood sandpiper *Tringa glareola*
Wren *Troglodytes troglodytes*
Yellowhammer *Emberiza citrinella*

Source
Harrison, C, *An atlas of the birds of the Western Palaearctic*. Collins, London, 1982.

Invertebrates

Ants *Formica* spp
Aphids *Aphididae*
Bees Hymenoptera
Beetles Coleoptera
Blue hawker dragonfly *Aeshna caerulea*
Bordered white *Bupalus piniaria*
Brown argus *Aricia aethiops*
Buff-tip *Phalera bucephala*
Bugs Hemiptera
Burnet moths *Zygaena* spp
Butterflies and moths Lepidoptera
Caddis flies Trichoptera
China-mark moths Nymphulinae
Clegs *Haematopota* spp
Cloud-bordered brindle *Apamea crenata*

Comma butterfly *Polygonia c-album*
Common blue *Polyommatus icarus*
Common rustic *Hoplodrina blanda*
Damselflies Zygoptera
Dark arches *Apamea monoglypha*
Dark green fritillary *Argynnis aglais*
Dingy skipper *Erynnis tages*
Dragonflies Odonata
Duke of Burgundy *Hamearis lucina*
Elm bark beetle *Scolytus scolytus*
Emperor moth *Saturnia pavonia*
Flies Diptera
Fox moth *Macrothylacia rubi*
Fresh-water crayfish *Austropotamobius pallipes*
Fresh-water mussel *Unio* spp

Fresh-water pearl mussel *Margaritifera margaritifera*
Fresh-water shrimp *Gammarus pulex*
Gall wasps Cynipidae
Gatekeeper *Pyronia tithonus*
Grasshoppers Orthoptera
Great spruce bark beetle *Dendroctonus micans*
Green hairstreak *Callophrys rubi*
Ground beetles Carabidae
Heather beetle *Lochmaea suturalis*
Horse-flies Tabanidae
Hover-flies Syrphidae
Kentish glory *Endromis versicolora*
Lacewings Neuroptera
Ladybirds Coccinellidae
Large heath *Coenonympha tullia*
Large white butterfly *Pieris brassicae*
Leaf hoppers Cicadellidae
Longhorn beetles Cerambycidae
Marble gall *Andricus kollari*
Marsh snail *Lymnaea palustris*
Mayflies Ephemeroptera
Meadow ant *Lasius flavus*
Meadow brown *Maniola jurtina*
Midges Chironomidae
Millipedes Diplopoda
Mining bees *Andrena* spp
Mining wasps Specidae
Mites Acarina
Mosquito *Aedes aegyptii*
Mother Shipton *Callistege mi*
Mountain ringlet *Erebia epiphron*
Netted mountain moth *Semiothisa carbonaria*
Northern eggar *Lasiocampa quercus* var. *callunae*
Peacock *Inachis io*
Pine beauty *Panolis flammea*
Pine sawfly *Diprion pini*
Pine shoot moth *Rhyacionia buoliana*
Pine weevil *Hylobius abietis*
Pond skaters *Gerris* spp
Purple hairstreak *Quercusia quercus*

Red admiral *Vanessa atalanta*
Ringlet *Aphantopus hyperantus*
Robin's pincushion *Diplolepis rosae*
Sap-sucking bugs and hoppers Homoptera
Sawflies Hymenoptera
Scotch argus *Erebia aethiops*
Sheep tick *Ixodes ricinus*
Small heath *Coenonympha pamphilus*
Small copper *Lycaena phlaeas*
Small pearl-bordered fritillary *Boloria selene*
Small tortoiseshell *Aglais urticae*
Spangle gall *Neuroterus quercusbaccarum*
Speckled wood *Pararge aegeria*
Spiders Arachnida
Spruce budworm *Choristoneura tumiferana*
Stoneflies Plecoptera
True lover's knot *Lycophotia porphyrea*
Wall butterfly *Lasiommata megera*
Wasps Hymenoptera
Water boatman *Notonecta glauca*
Water crickets *Velia* spp
Water flea *Daphnia pulex*
Water spider *Argyroneta aquatica*
Whirligig beetle *Gyrinus natator*
White ermine moth *Spilsoma lubricipeda*
Winter moth *Opesophtera brumata*
Woodlice Diplopoda
Wood tiger *Parasemia plantaginis*

Sources
Carter, D, *Butterflies and moths in Britain and Europe*. Pan Books, London, 1982.
Chinery, M, *A field guide to the insects of Britain and Northern Europe*. (second edition). Collins, London, 1976.
Stubbs, F B (ed), *Provisional keys to British plant galls*. British Plant Gall Society, Hawes, N. Yorkshire, 1986.
Sutton, S L and Beaumont, H E (eds), *Butterflies and moths of Yorkshire*. Yorkshire Naturalists' Union, Doncaster, 1989.

INDEX